(23) 4-

D1236626

Figures of Division

Figures of Division

WILLIAM FAULKNER'S MAJOR NOVELS

JAMES A. SNEAD

Methuen · New York and London

First published in 1986 by
Methuen, Inc.
29 West 35th Street,
New York, NY 10001

Published in Great Britain by
Methuen & Co. Ltd
11 New Fetter Lane,
London EC4P 4EE

© 1986 James A. Snead

Typeset by Hope Services,
Abingdon, Oxfordshire
Printed in Great Britain at the
University Press, Cambridge

All rights reserved. No part of this
book may be reprinted or reproduced
or utilized in any form or by any
electronic, mechanical or other
means, now known or hereafter
invented, including photocopying
and recording, or in any information
storage or retrieval system, without
permission in writing from the
publishers.

*Library of Congress Cataloging in
Publication Data*
Snead, James A., 1953–
Figures of Division.
Bibliography: p.
Includes index.
1. Faulkner, William, 1897–1962 –
Criticism and interpretation. 2.
Faulkner, William, 1897–1962 –
Political and social views. 3. Polarity in
literature.
I. Title.
PS3511.A86Z9726   1986   813'.52
86–8440

ISBN 0 416 01261 2

*British Library Cataloguing
in Publication Data*
Snead, James A.
Figures of Division: William Faulkner's
major novels.
1. Faulkner, William – Criticism and
interpretation
I. Title
813'.52   PS3511.A86Z

ISBN 0 416 01261 2

For James T. Snead
and
Helen W. Snead –
finis origine pendet

Contents

Preface

To what extent does Faulkner work in terms of polarities, oppositions, paradoxes, inversions of roles! How much does he employ a line of concealed (or open) dialectic progression as a principle for his fiction! The study of these questions may lead to the discovery of principles of organization in his work not yet defined by criticism.[1]

(Robert Penn Warren)

William Faulkner's major novels, written between 1929 and 1942, explored, earlier than most critics did, the systematic paradoxes within the fabric of literary discourse, and exposed, earlier than many Americans, related paradoxes in the institution of American racial segregation, whose statutory divisions began slowly to be dismantled just before Faulkner's death in 1962. In this study, I take up Warren's forty-year-old observation that Faulkner's words scrutinize apparent social polarities, an enterprise that shows conventional oppositions to be a kind of willful linguistic and social error. In Faulkner's novels, "polarity" means racial division, racial segregation, and the mythologies surrounding it, which collectively try to outlaw interracial contiguity, cohabitation, and consanguinity. Faulkner's characters, black and white, live under a body of racial barriers and prohibitions that structure the self-understanding of Yoknapatawpha County. The futility of applying strictly binary categories to human affairs is the main lesson of Faulkner's novels, which dramatize the problematics of division through sensitive white characters such as Quentin Compson,

Darl and Addie, and Ike McCaslin. By accident, intelligence, or pure stubbornness, these Faulknerian protagonists reject division, discovering instead those social and psychological margins where merging, opposition's opposite, may exist unassailed. Faulkner's narratives utter a truth of merging across social boundaries that his contemporaries found unspeakable. Faulkner himself set this truth in an elusive, complex discourse of indirection, a literary disfigurement of divisive social figures.

The human casualties of divisions may be sensitive to what their fellow citizens ignore, but racial oppositions overwhelm even those who recognize and seek to change them. In a radically segregationist society, polar thinking supports a thoroughly destructive economic system. In *Absalom, Absalom!*, Thomas Sutpen encounters "a land divided neatly up," yet division "had never once been mentioned by name." One Mississippi woman speaks of " 'race talk' . . . euphemisms and pretense under certain circumstances," whereby racial ideologies are covered up.[2] The central concerns of Faulkner scholarship up to now – "the Negro," "endurance," "the human heart" – overlook, much in the manner of Southern "race talk," the oppressive social rhetorics that have produced the need to "endure." The novels I treat here, as much as any others in modern fiction, self-consciously analyze the linguistic supports of an immoral social system, examining those buried rhetorical ploys underlying the "natural" division of the races. Faulkner's novels illustrate how the separating process in Yoknapatawpha County employs rhetorical strategies that facilitate racial segregation – figures of division that show their flaws best in written form.

Racism in general might be considered a normative recipe for domination created by speakers using rhetorical tactics. The characteristic figures of racial division repeat on the level of phoneme, sentence, and story: (1) the fear of *merging*, or loss of identity through syneristic union with the other, leads to the wish to use racial purification as a separating strategy against difference; (2) *marking*, or supplying physically significant (usually visual) characteristics with internal value equivalents, sharpening by visual antithesis their conceptual utility; (3) *spatial and conceptual separation*, often facilitated through unequal verbal substitutions that tend to omit and distance a subordinate class from realms of value and esteem; (4) *repetition*, or pleonastic reinforcement of these antitheses in writing, storytelling, or hearsay; (5) *invective* and threat, exemplified in random and unpredictable violence to punish real or imagined crimes; (6) *omission* and concealment of the process by a sort of paralepsis that claims discrimination to be self-evidently valid and natural.

Faulkner counters these social figures with literary devices of his own. Gérard Genette describes the practice as follows:

> one of the newest and most fruitful directions that are now opening up for literary research ought to be the structural study of the "large unities" of discourse, beyond the framework – which linguistics in the strict sense cannot cross – of the sentence. . . . There would then be a linguistics of discourse that was a *translinguistics*, since the facts of language would be handled by it in great bulk, and often at one remove – to put it simply, a rhetoric, perhaps that "new rhetoric" which Francis Ponge once called for, and which we still lack.[3]

I would extend these meditations to apply to the author who would both describe and write against large-scale ideological concepts encoded in the form of rhetorical narratives. "Translinguistics" would then address figures of *social* as well as *narrative* discourse. Faulkner's challenge to reigning figures of division emerges in a style that mixes and connects entities as much as their social function tends to divide and distinguish them, and in a sequencing of plot that unravels rather than fastens conceptual threads and customary endings. Faulkner's discourse of connection employs a variety of effects, including chiasmus, an A : B : : B : A figure that conjugates and reverses plot elements (what Robert Penn Warren calls Faulkner's "inversions of roles"); anticipations of plot that effectively reverse causal sequence (prolepsis and *hysteron proteron*); plot and character mergings (syneresis); and emphatic repetitions of new conjugations in successive clauses and plot sequences (anaphora).[4]

While frequently useful as a general anatomical practice, acts of classification become especially insidious when connected with notions of hierarchy and authority. Although Carl Linnaeus's taxonomy of race in *Systema Naturae* (1758) never implied hierarchy or ranking, it came to be elided with the metaphysical concept of the Great Chain of Being. By accident of timing, in the eighteenth century (within the context of European exploration and colonization of Africa), blacks appeared in the Chain of Being somewhere between man and ape; hierarchies of oppression received the ostensible assent of anatomy and nature.[5] Faulkner's major novels must be seen as exercises in explicating a certain reality from this tangle. They enjoy the advantage of their locale, a region whose segregationist thinking furnishes us with an extreme case of social classification. Yoknapatawpha's major classifications – "white/black," "poor/rich," "male/female" – depend on polar thinking.[6] The reality of the human beings thus classified remains absent. Faulkner's narratives mainly concern the effects of these classifications on human sensibilities, white and black, rich and poor, male and female: how can we ever know each other, if our society works through a forced organization into distinct groupings? As Faulkner repeatedly said in interviews, "the white man has forced the Negro to be always a Negro rather than another human being . . . the white man can never really know the Negro."[7] In accepting markings such as skin color, sexual difference, dress, and dialect as significant indices of social value, the trusting reader must initially repeat and reinforce the figures whereby blacks, poor whites, and women have been classified, separated, and dominated. Later, through adopting (at least temporarily) the town's racist perspectives, the reader may discern that the plot of societal division – with every trace of prior preparation and rehearsal removed – suddenly becomes credible and soon seems an indispensable attitude towards reality.

Figures of division fail on two counts: they are binary and as such require an opposite term in order to signify anything; moreover, absolute segregation, in trying to enforce an unreal polarity, only further agitates the psychic desire to exceed its artificial boundaries. The system of Southern apartheid wishes to freeze polar pairs into dominant/subordinate, master/slave terms, yet, as Robert Penn Warren implies, there is a "concealed . . . dialectic progression" in Faulkner whereby the dominant term seems – in the manner of Hegel's master–slave relationship – to depend upon and often to merge with its polar opposite:[8]

Psychologically and logically, all association implies dissociation, and conversely: the same form which unites various elements into the well-organized whole dissociates them. ... The two techniques are complementary and always at work at the same time; but the argumentation through which a datum is modified can stress the association or the dissociation which it is promoting without making explicit the complementary aspect which will result from the desired transformation.

Rhetorical figures of division, particularly when relied upon to underpin a shaky social ideology, prove untrue, contradicting themselves even as they attempt to state truth. The mutuality of separation and merging throws an unexpected shadow, a black one, on the white screen of social normality. *"To divide . . . in order to unite. . . .* Is this not the formula of language itself?"[9]

Since figures of division are at the same time social and linguistic, Faulkner's novels, as literary texts, can examine their invention and demise on both thematic and stylistic levels of analysis. Particularly germane to Faulkner's novels as an instance of actual and stylistic merging is the issue of *miscegenation.* The system of racial division elicits the desire for racial mixing or miscegenation, the South's feared, forbidden, denied, yet pervasive release from societal division. Notions such as "white racial purity," aimed at underpinning the economic order, underlie figures of division. Southern society typically and publicly abhorred racial mergings by integration, cohabitation, and miscegenation. Yet Faulkner's narratives repeatedly present a world in which blacks and whites eat, live, and often sleep together, despite written Jim Crow laws and spoken categories of racial differentiation. Faulkner's narratives dismember figures of division at their weakest joint, the "purity" notion that seems the requirement for white supremacist logic. White skin could never be the certain signifier of the absence of "black" blood (white racial purity), because white skin, as Faulkner amply demonstrates, can also signify "mixed" blood.

Faulkner's most compelling protagonists do not seek division, but rather its often non-conventional remedies: miscegenation, incest, Edenic refuge in the Big Woods, or schizoid mental mergings. Absolutisms, facing the test of experience, break down under the pressure of the unsystematic real. Faulkner's major novels, *The Sound and the Fury, As I Lay Dying, Light in August, Absalom, Absalom!, The Hamlet*, and *Go Down, Moses*, primarily concern the white mind and its struggles with the systems of division it has created. The stylistic strangeness of Faulkner's novels is not purely post-Joycean experimentalism, as often suggested, nor even a residue of his infatuation with Romanticism and French symbolism. Instead, Faulkner's narratives are accurate reconstructions and dismantlings of linguistic and social classifications, proving that some extraordinary human beings struggle, against overwhelming odds, to reverse a separation that rhetoric has tried to make into a permanent reality.

Notes

1 Robert Penn Warren, "William Faulkner" (1946), reprinted in Frederick J. Hoffman and Olga W. Vickery, *William Faulkner: Two Decades of Criticism* (East Lansing: Michigan State College Press, 1951), p. 100.
2 Robert Coles, *Children of Crisis: A Study of Courage and Fear* (Boston: Little, Brown, 1964), p. 251.
3 Gérard Genette, *Figures of Literary Discourse*, trans. Alan Sheridan, intro. Marie-Rose Logan (New York: Columbia, 1982), p. 10; French title: *Figures I, II, III* (Paris: Seuil, 1966–1972). Elsewhere, in the chapter called "Order," in *Narrative Discourse*, trans. Jane E. Lewin (Ithaca: Cornell University Press, 1980), pp. 33–85, Genette translates this enthusiasm for large-scale rhetorical analysis of narrative into specific rhetorical terms, such as *prolepsis, analepsis*, and *metalepsis*. I share his enthusiasm but not his terminology, preferring terms customized to Faulkner's rhetorical enterprise.
4 Roland Barthes pioneered the notion of using a linguistic model of syntax to discuss large plot units, without pointing to conceivable political ramifications of discursive reversals and overturnings. See his "Introduction to the Structural Analysis of Narratives," in *Image/Music/Text*, trans. Stephen Heath (London: Fontana, 1977), pp. 79–124; Terence Hawkes, *Structuralism and Semiotics* (London: Methuen, 1977): "Greimas and Structural Semantics," in Jonathan Culler, *Structuralist Poetics: Structuralism, Linguistics, and the Study of Literature* (Ithaca: Cornell University Press, 1975), pp. 74–95.

5 Winthrop Jordan has written the definitive account of how
the slave system and Western colonialism justified themselves
by falsely applying Darwinism and misappropriating notions of
evolutionary anatomy in the second, *marking* phase of racial
division. See *White over Black: American Attitudes Toward the
Negro, 1550–1812* (New York: Norton, 1968), p. 510. See especially
chapters 6, "The Bodies of Men," and 13, "The Negro Bound by the
Chain of Being."
6 Classical philosophy, and our own, might be said to have been
founded on the antagonism between "polarity" and "analogy" that
underlies racial perception and sociological organization generally.
See G. E. R. Lloyd, *Polarity and Analogy* (Cambridge: Cambridge
University Press, 1966).
7 William Faulkner, *Faulkner in the University: Class Conferences
at the University of Virginia, 1957–1958*, ed. Frederick L. Gwynn
and Joseph Blotner (Charlottesville: University of Virginia Press,
1959), p. 211.
8 G. W. F. Hegel, *Phenomenology of Spirit*, section B, IV A,
"Independence and Dependence of Self-Consciousness: Lordship
and Bondage." Also Chaim Perelman and L. Olbrechts-Tyteca,
The New Rhetoric: A Treatise on Argumentation (Notre Dame:
University of Notre Dame Press, 1969), p. 190; French title: *La
Nouvelle Rhétorique: traité de l'argumentation* (Paris: Presses
Universitaires de France, 1958).
9 Genette, op. cit., p. xii.

Acknowledgments

It is a pleasure to acknowledge here my indebtedness to many friends and colleagues. An earlier and somewhat different form of this study was completed at Cambridge University under the generous support of the Keasbey Memorial Foundation. At Cambridge, Colin MacCabe was the first to suggest that I give Faulkner a new look and, along with Tony Tanner, helped sustain the work's early stages. At Yale, the A. Whitney Griswold Fund provided financial support, while a community of readers nurtured the thinking and writing. Foremost of these was the late Paul de Man, a scholar whom I knew far too briefly, who generously shared his time with me when it was most precious to him. Indispensable encouragement and advice came from J. Hillis Miller, Geoffrey Hartman, Richard Brodhead, Alan Trachtenberg, James Winn, Robert Brumbaugh, Stanley Leavy, Thomas Gould, and Heinrich von Stadten. I have benefited greatly from the advice and camaraderie of Michael Seidel, Charles Berger, Kitty Mrosovsky, and Charles Martin. Hugo Walter provided invaluable assistance in preparing the manuscript. Finally, I wish to thank the students in my

Faulkner courses between 1982 and 1985 – especially Peter Platt, Ben Watson, Leslie Brody, Esther Kaplan, and Laura Kellogg – for keeping Faulkner always new for me and keeping me always alive to Faulkner. In dedicating the book to my parents, I acknowledge their ingenious triumphs over society's figures of division and my debt to the spirit and humor that have kept them unvanquished.

1

Introduction

[My style is] the compulsion to say everything in one sentence ... [the attempt] to crowd and cram everything, all experience, into each paragraph ... something like the man who will write a book on the back of a postage stamp or a prayer on the head of a pin, to get it all said in one compact bundle before he quits ... trying to put the whole history of the human heart on the head of a pin.[1]

(William Faulkner)

Rhetoric and reality

Faulkner often commented publicly on the relationship between style and reality, and especially on how a writer reduces a real terrain. Yoknapatawpha County, "my postage stamp of native soil," imitates and reduces a particular Southern "country," but its conceptual and social operations have much more general pertinence. To avoid dividing a whole for analysis, Faulkner shrinks it to postage-stamp size. Reduction, not division, defines Faulkner's freedom – "complete liberty to use whatever talent I might have to the absolute top."[2] The challenges of Faulknerian prose result from his wish to utter the socially ineffable, because society restricts its own freedom of utterance. "That's why it's clumsy and hard to read."[3] He clarifies the difference between his style and "dead" rhetoric as follows: "Style if it's – like anything else, to be alive it must be in motion too. If it becomes fixed, then it's dead, it's just rhetoric."[4] Faulkner's style explores the difference between fluid style and "dead" rhetoric. The difference explains how he would put into motion "fixed" social relations that seem dead, frozen into a moribund *rigor figurae*.

Yet can a "stamp" – printed and printer – read itself? The difficulty of Faulkner's writing for early critics and many later ones is the challenge of miniaturization: will society be able to discern its own image from Faulkner's small-scale model, one that sets social fixities into motion? The "complete liberty" of, say, *The Sound and the Fury* or *As I Lay Dying* disrupts linguistic and social certainty. Faulkner's disfiguration of Yoknapatawpha, for instance, challenges us to uncover a century of usurpation during which white settlers separated the Indians from their own soil and land while appropriating their place-names as a rhetorical screen for the outrage. But the challenge, initiated by stylistic difficulty in the first instance, requires more than the merely stylistic analysis that it usually receives.

For Faulkner's texts describe an entire unhappy foundation of habit, custom, and law that divides certain races – particularly those defined as "Negro" and "white" – using skin color as the prime signifier of difference. All other social relations refer directly or indirectly to this basic color-coding.[5] Racism justifies blacks' lowly economic status through a self-validating picture of reality which produces ostensibly objective evidence to corroborate the segregationist view.[6] Moreover, such a picture is not just one "rationale" among many in a "marketplace of ideas," but a dominant narrative produced by a community of speakers – a fictional recovery of origins that never were, memorized and transmitted under threat of physical pain, justifying a system that itself requires the threat of violence. Such a narrative, like the primary account of choosing certain marks of difference, refers back for its legitimacy to a notion of "nature" and "the natural."

It appears that divisive social rhetorics became pathological in the South around the end of the nineteenth century, not as a reflection of true separation, but as a fearful reaction against what Frederick Law Olmstead calls in *Journey in the Seaboard Slave States* (1853–4) "the close cohabitation and association of black and white. . . . Negro women are carrying black and white babies together in their arms; black and white children are playing together . . . [there is] a familiarity and closeness of intimacy that would have been noticed with astonishment, if not with manifest displeasure, in almost any chance company in the North."[7] The Southern revisionist historians, foremost among them C. Vann Woodward, suggest that the system of segregation created a fictional bulwark against perceived merging. Whereas there was a "large degree of physical contact and association" under slavery, after emancipation the old order had to change:

> To the dominant whites it began to appear that the new order required a certain amount of *compulsory separation* of the races. ... The temporary anarchy that followed the collapse of the old discipline produced a state of mind bordering on hysteria among Southern white people. ... The very appearance of *segregation* ... *was a reaction to an opposite condition of racial mixing.*[8]

In his essay "Nobody Knows My Name" (1959) James Baldwin quotes a black man from Alabama as saying "Integration ... has always worked very well in the South, after the sun goes down."[9] Olmstead does not mention, but certainly would have seen, children neither black nor white, almost exclusively the product of white fathers, who gained the peculiar title of "mulatto" (literally, "young mule" – a usually sterile hybrid offspring). Racial *amalgamation* (mixing) became the pejorative *miscegenation* (*sexual* mixing), as Eric Sundquist shows, only when these practices had already become widespread, and by a peculiar reversal the term miscegenation applied not primarily to white males' actions with black servant women, but to fantasies of black males' intentions towards white women.

The casual interracial contacts of "Was" or *Absalom, Absalom!* would be outlawed under a strict reading of the Jim Crow laws of the 1890s. Yet these written prescriptions were alternately followed and disobeyed, introducing the linguistic and psychological disjunctions that Faulkner's narratives trace. "We've lived so *close* for so long" was a common sentiment, but the same speaker might say "we're brought up to expect niggers to be in one place and ourselves in another."[10] As we see in "The Fire and the Hearth," blacks and whites were allowed to intermingle as children, but less openly in schools or at dances, and only clandestinely as adults. Faulkner and the codification of racial division in legal texts (Jim Crow) were born in the same decade (1890–1900). Jim Crow provided a

solution to a problem that was constantly (yet imprecisely)
called the "Negro's" – namely, what to do with the proximity
and threat of unskilled former slaves whose presence and labor
were becoming increasingly superfluous to the white main-
stream. As a "free" agent, the black was threatening to the
white mind as never before. The belated system of separation
adopted and augmented narrated myths about black inferiority
and incapacity, confirming in an oral register the written
statutes of Jim Crow. A violent revision occurred, a denial of
much Southern history and the invention of an Old South
mythology. Secured by such a powerful mythopoesis of the
South, segregation and racial division, inconsistently practiced
before 1890, became the practice of an ideology during this
century's early decades. Segregation provided a system of control
appropriate to the needs of an already discriminating society;
its language was a prime example of what Marxists call
"mystification." The South indeed lived out a world of pure
legend.[11]

The white woman, rather than sharing the white male's
dominance over society's black oppressed, herself falls victim
to certain figures of division. Faulkner's women characters are
desperate. One rarely thinks of them without noticing a sense
of deprivation and resentment – Addie Bundren, Dewey Dell,
Eula Varner, Mrs Armstid (all of them), Mrs Compson, Ellen
Coldfield, Miss Rosa, Emily Grierson, Mrs Hightower, and
Minnie Cooper would head but by no means exhaust the list.
Extant criticism on Faulkner's women characters almost
exclusively overlooks their discontent and its causes, seeing
them instead as largely negative types to be arrayed within
some usually impertinent scheme. Even women critics tend
to consider women in Faulkner's fiction from a dominant
ideology, submitting women characters to categories of "psyche"
and "myth" or "nature" and "natural reproductive processes,"
the very man-made categories that have facilitated and perpetuated women's oppression.[12]

The Sound and the Fury's Mrs Compson provides an
interesting case-study, both of the social coercions faced by
women and of how most critics blame the women concerned
for their malaise. The mother of Quentin, Jason, Benjy, and
Caddy is a virtual magnet of abuse from Faulkner scholars, and
even the more sympathetic critics call her compulsively self-

absorbed, infatuated with appearance, selfish, paranoid, and retrospective. Many would approve of Cleanth Brooks's statement that Mrs Compson is a "cold and self-centered mother" who is "the basic cause of the breakup of the Compson family . . . let the more general cultural causes be what they may." However, if Mrs Compson is truly "the basic cause" of the family's problems, then "more general cultural causes" are exonerated.[13] Society all along has expected her and Caddy to fulfill a false standard of perfection. Might not the role of Southern white woman, whose honor "must be defended whether it was or not," also separate women from each other and from political authority, creating such pathology as we see here? For many Southern white women, exaltation is merely another kind of division, a state in which, as Lillian Smith so aptly states, "protection" is tantamount to "enslavement." A southern white woman slightly younger than Faulkner puts it this way: "My mother and I were supposed to mind the house, the garden, and ourselves."[14] Foremost, but hardly unique in Faulkner's novels, Mrs Compson and Addie Bundren in *As I Lay Dying* are victims of what the latter calls "*aloneness.*" Both find themselves outside of a system into which they are supposed to be fully integrated.

The black male and the white woman, paradoxically similar, inhabit mutually remote corners. They experience similar mistreatment, because the distance between them is what, on the deepest level, segregation aims to perpetuate. As McLendon says to the white men of Jefferson in Faulkner's short story "Dry September" (1931), "are you going to sit there and let a black son rape a white woman on the streets of Jefferson?" In a section entitled "Dismemberment, Physiology, and Sexual Perceptions" Winthrop Jordan notes that the punishment of castration seemed more appealing to Southern whites than to any other practitioners of New World slavery. Castration was "reserved for Negroes and occasionally Indians. . . . In some colonies, moreover, the specifically sexual aspect of castration was so obvious as to underline how much of the white man's insecurity vis-à-vis the Negro was fundamentally sexual."[15] This particular ritual of "division" repeats in an especially grisly fashion the overall societal effort to separate blacks from all creative or procreative access, and says more about the psychosexual deviances of the lynch mob than about their victims.

Division occurs in such castration "parties," as in more subtle quotidian instances, by a determined and even violent effort, but one made to seem natural to future practitioners of that initial separating act. The concept of strict *separation* (*apartheid*, in Afrikaans) seems to typify post-bellum Southern social organization. Yet because of the arbitrariness of marks such as skin colour, strict separations threaten to break down. Any quality signifies only by referring to its opposite: the very notion of "white" needs a category of "non-white" to support it. The dilemma for white supremacists is extreme, for their own desires have led them into a peculiar predicament. The designation "white" is doubly vulnerable – physically, to future mixings, which could eliminate in one generation any reliable criterion for "whiteness"; conceptually, to the progeny of prior racial mixings, which have made the relationship of white skin to white blood unclear.

Yet the central paradox of Southern society is that the threat of chaos through racial mixing comes almost exclusively from white males. The invention of the "oversexed" black reverses and hides the white male's desire. In the same mythology, however, the projection of an ideal purity onto the white woman puts her blood in perpetual danger of dilution by the black male. Hence the white male has ample cause to confine the actions of both parties. But the basis for division, Faulkner makes clear, is not only psychosexual but economic. As *The Hamlet* demonstrates, agrarian capitalism requires classifications and separations even between various groups of white laborers. So, although Faulkner's plots refer to the effects of miscegenation, their subplots describe how fraudulent mythologies are created to maintain more generally inequitable economic relations. In a 1956 article published in *Harper's* called "On Fear: The South in Labor," Faulkner writes:

It is our Southern white man's shame that in our present economy the Negro must not have economic equality; our double shame that we fear that giving him more social equality will jeopardize his present economic status; our triple shame that even then, to justify our stand, we must becloud the issue with the bugaboo of miscegenation.[16]

Faulkner's linguistic mergings and "inversions" (Warren's

term) relate directly to a clandestine yet visible heritage of racial mixing. Division in Yoknapatawpha leads not to segregation into homogeneous enclaves, but only to further versions of merging.

Chaos and separation

Aber Lebendige machen
alle den Fehler, daß sie zu stark unterscheiden.
("But the living all err: they distinguish too strictly.")
(Rainer Maria Rilke)

The total character of the world . . . is into eternity chaos. . . . Not in the sense of a lack of necessity, but lack of classification. (Friedrich Nietzsche)[17]

Chaos has a long history – indeed, perhaps even the longest history. It seems that the mind uses various figures of division to defend itself against chaos—figures which, however, seem only to reintroduce it. Faulkner's genealogical obsession resembles, yet ultimately contradicts, Southern segregationist logic which seeks racially pure pedigrees in the past. Faulkner's genealogical research discovers not purity but rather merging and chaos, states against which the traditions of social classification and division vainly struggle. Indeed, Southern racism would prevent any other (woman, black, Indian, foreigner) from being a definitive specimen of the human, since each seems somehow anomalous and inferior compared to the white male. Genealogy is the typical mode of Faulkner's novels, in the Nietzschean sense of a search for the origins of value as well as the more usual sense of exploring familial lineage. Such heroes as Ike McCaslin pose the following questions: How did the present state of things come to be? What was the first cause of things? Who were the first "forebears," the "ancestors," the "nameless progenitors"? What "old tongue" did they speak? Where were the "primal woods," the "primal uterus," the "original quarry, abyss itself"? Separation is one of the founding paradigms of Western thought, and is discernible in the earliest myths of origin. Southern segregation is only one among many offshoots of this seemingly aboriginal obsession. Yet, although the quest for pure separations may be primal, it soon becomes clear that purity itself, whether of the races or of any other category – according to the same early myths – is not.

In the West's chief myths of origin, we seem to find chaos and mixture at every beginning. Chaos is the original state in which the Judaeo-Christian version says "the earth was without form, and void." Even if we look at psychological origins, what might be called "chaos" would be the state of psychic merging in which an infant would not be able to distinguish itself from the mother. One of the first steps in the child's separation from the mother, according to Freud's "The Infantile Genital Organization" (1923), is the awareness of sexual difference in the castration complex. Indeed, any separation – from the womb; from the breast; from the parent as ego ideal – entails both the birth of identity and the death of a prior narcissistic merging.[18] Order and its various guises – thought, character, culture – hence arise not as naturally prior states, but in opposition to a hitherto undefined and unclassifiable reality. For thought and speech come after separation; chaos dismantles all dialectic. The pre-Socratic philosophers, such as Anaxagoras, think of chaos as an earlier state out of which mind (*nous*) orders the world:

> Mind [nous] is unlimited, autonomous, and unmixed with anything, standing entirely by itself. . . . Mind, because of its exceptional fineness and purity, has knowledge of all that is, and therein it has the greatest power. . . . When Mind first set things in motion, there began a process of separation in the moving mass.[19]

Genesis describes a similar separation of darkness from light, distinction from chaos. A pagan account of origins occurs in Ovid's *Metamorphoses*.

> Before there was any earth or sea. . . . Nature presented the same aspect the world over, that to which men have given the name of Chaos [*quem dixere chaos*]. This was a shapeless uncoordinated mass [*rudis indigestaque moles*] nothing but a weight of lifeless matter, whose ill-assorted elements were indiscriminately heaped together in one place. . . . Nothing had any lasting shape [*nulli sua forma manebat*], but everything got in the way of everything else;

for, within that one body, cold warred with hot, moist with dry, soft with hard, and light with heavy. (5–9; 17–20)[20]

In view of the South's use of lynching and other forms of violence against blacks (and whites, when necessary) to enforce segregation, Ovid's description of how first "chaos" was eliminated by "separation" is revealing:

The strife was finally resolved by a god, a natural force of a higher kind, who separated the earth from heaven, and the waters from the earth. . . . When he had freed these elements, sorting them out from the heap where they had lain, indistinguishable from one another, he bound them fast, each in its separate place, forming a harmonious union.[21]

In this version, classifications emerge from chaos by the force of "a god" who remains unnamed (a rare omission in Ovid's poem): "a natural force of a higher kind." Yet gods in the *Metamorphoses* are rarely natural forces but more often quite distinguishable manipulators. Indeed, the poem concerns transformation, yet the agent of its first transformation is anonymous. Ovid's coyness about the name of the ordering "god" is curious: "In this way the god, whichever of the gods it was, set the chaotic mass in order, and, after dividing it up, arranged it in its constituent parts." Violent division, the tale implies, is anonymous, natural, in the general good, creating a "harmonious union." Freud offers a similar argument about how culture anonymously perpetuates violent acts in the service of general "harmony." In order to fend off the somewhat Nietzschean scenario in which "social relationships" would be "subject to the arbitrary will of the individual," society takes a decisive step: "the replacement of the power of the individual by the power of community."[22] The "nameless force" shields the responsible agents, and liability is general.

Plato's myths of origin also posit separation as a prerequisite for, among other things, logical thought. In *Phaedrus*, Socrates prescribes what good orators should know about "division" (*dielomenos*), including his advice that the good rhetorician should dwell on prominent distinctions, ones obvious to even the most superficial glance:

the would-be exponent of the art of rhetoric ought, before all else, to make a regular division [*diheresthai*], and discover a

characteristic mark [*charaktera*] of each class. ... The
second principle is that of division into species according
to the natural formation. ... I am myself a great lover of
these processes of division and separation [*dihaireseon kai
synagogon*]; they help me to speak and think. (sec. 266b)[23]

Proper persuasion, Socrates argues, will find the strongest
marks to facilitate division. The language of taxonomy is hard
to miss here: "division into species according to the natural
formation" reduces living things into concepts that are all but
natural.

In Plato's *Cratylus*, Hermogenes wonders whether the
names by means of which separations function are themselves
really "natural." Hermogenes concludes: "I have often talked
over this matter, both with Cratylus and others, and cannot
convince myself that there is any principle of correctness in
names other than convention and agreement" (sec. 384d). The
fallacy of division is to believe that the "mark" of a thing is
also its "character," rather than a conventional designation.
Black skin is a mark, a stamp, but character is normally
understood as coming from within. The mark is assigned –
indeed, Socrates claims that "the process of speech is one of
assigning names . . . a name is an instrument of teaching and of
distinguishing natures, as the shuttle is of distinguishing the
threads of the web" (sec. 388c). Naming must be done by
someone who can separate: "the work of the legislator is to
give names, and the dialectician must be his director if the
names are to be rightly given" (sec. 390d).

"Convention and agreement" lend power to the name.
Nomos is both "name" and "law"; description becomes
prescription. Naming is law-giving by the few for the many, a
law-giving that separates. Shelley completes Plato's notion:
"poets are the unacknowledged legislators of the world." For
Shelley, "poets, in the most universal sense of the word," ratify
the arbitrary, if imaginative, exercise of "naming." The poet
sees the "unapprehended relations of things," and puts them
into words which "become, through time, signs for portions or
classes of thoughts. . . . Poets, according to the circumstances
of the age and nation in which they appeared, were called, in
the earlier epochs of the world, legislators, or prophets."
Nietzsche says: "It is the powerful who make the names of

things into law," not nature. The poet-legislator is more effective than the rest of mankind because of his or her *activeness* (*poiein*, "to do"). The active name-coiners create for others' passive consumption, but Faulkner speaks to active, not passive, readers.[24] Indeed, the fiction-maker has *brought about* the present, by anterior "foresight."

Yet the name is also a false marking, an imprimatur reducing human beings to symbolic entities; a "nigger," once marked by the signifier of black skin, is no longer a person but a social reference point, a concept denoting abasement and exclusion. Markings, like brand-names, scorch onto human flesh the rules whereby people will be owned or exchanged. For example, in Joe Christmas's case, one racial epithet makes his guilt seem suddenly plausible: " 'A nigger,' the marshall said. 'I always thought there was something funny about that fellow.' "

Already in *Cratylus* Socrates sees that names, far from describing character, tend to solidify error:

Socrates: Why clearly he who first gave names gave them according to his conception of the things which they signified – did he not?

Cratylus: True.

Socrates: And if his conception was erroneous, and he gave names according to his conception, in what position shall we who are his followers find ourselves? Shall we not be deceived by him?

Culture – in Freud's language, "a kind of repetition compulsion which, when a regulation has been laid down once and for all, decides when, where, and how a thing shall be done" – risks conserving and perpetuating error. In society as in the unconscious, "fundamentally things remain as they were in the beginning."[25] Mystifications, conspiring with immediate economic needs, are reified. Nietzsche sees oppositional and antithetical categories – albeit necessary for the smooth functioning of society – as valid only in provisional terms:

For one may doubt, first, whether there are any opposites at all, and secondly whether these popular valuations and opposite values on which the metaphysicians put their seal, are not perhaps merely foreground estimates, only provisional perspectives. . . . It might even be possible that what constitutes the value of these good and revered things is precisely that they are insidiously related, tied to, and involved with these wicked, seemingly opposite things – *maybe even one with them in essence.*[26]

Nietzsche reveals our drive to classify as a futile compensation for the threat of chaos. Returning for a moment to the Southern context, it would seem that the peculiarly racist appropriation of comparative anatomy and the "Chain of Being" idea "was bound to elaborate differences between the races . . . the Chain of Being was only one (unusually specific) projection of a profound sense of and yearning for hierarchical arrangement."[27] In this way, the past is reinvented by a myth that justifies and falsifies an act of original violence. Harmful figures of division, never valid as deliverance from chaos, and erroneous from a standpoint of here and now, may remain active and virulent.

Socrates admires the "separation" that allows one "to speak and think," yet if we read him closely we will find a telling irony: he has promised an impossible – or at best gross – merging. He says that, on finding a master "dialectician" to teach him division, he would "walk in his footsteps as if he were a god." The dialectician/god/teacher would be male by grammar and by custom. Socrates quotes Book V of Homer's *Odyssey* (possibly for the benefit of Phaedrus, who misses the allusion). Here (line 193) the actual wording is "So saying, the beautiful goddess led the way quickly, and he followed in the footsteps of the god*dess*," not of a "god."[28] So even Socrates does not divide the sexes properly; if he were to "walk in the footsteps" of this "master dialectician," he would be following a woman. By custom, a woman would not be a "dialectician," and hence the "dialectician" would not be the "goddess" of his allusion. The confusion is heightened because the Homeric passage Socrates cites comes when Odysseus has just decided to *separate* himself from the "goddess" Calypso ("the engulfer") and to sail from her island Ogygia ("the navel of the sea"). Indeed, Odysseus mistrusts Calypso. Why, if he is about to desert her, does he walk "in the footsteps of the goddess"? He does this for the very same reason – a simple one – why Southern white males in great numbers found it impossible to obey their own separationist decrees:

[Odysseus] followed in the footsteps of the goddess. And they came to the hollow cave, the goddess and the mortal, and he sat down upon the chair from which Hermes had arisen . . . and the sun set and darkness came on. And the two went into the innermost recess of the hollow cave, and took their joy of love, abiding each by the other's side. (V, 193–6; 225–7)

If Odysseus will follow a goddess despite rejection and suspicion, then it seems that there are things – such as *eros* – that overcome the sharpest disjunctions and lead to conjunction. Odysseus sits in the chair of Hermes, the god of communication. Having entered the goddess's "cave," then, Odysseus takes "the chair from which Hermes had arisen," literally "presiding" over the art (and, soon afterwards, the act) of verbal and sexual communication: "the two went into the innermost recess of the hollow cave, and took their joy of love."

The myth would seem to show the primary falsity of the notion of absolute differentiation. Conjunction and disjunction are inseparable; Socrates praises a "division" presided over by a "master" who has no definite gender. Socrates has in fact *condensed*, rather than *divided*, the sexes, even in an example meant to praise separation. His figure of the "master dialectician" cunningly merges opposites, and one gradually understands that the "dialectician's" separating faculty is only a temporary and cosmetic front against real chaos. Socrates affirms separations, but hopes to change male–female intercourse into an all-male zone of reasoning. He creates order by forced division, but cites a text where union is achieved through the conjunctions of *eros*.

Nous and chaos in Faulkner's novels

Faulkner's novels describe the results of the anxious struggle between *nous* and chaos, with the temporary elimination of chaos, and the overthrow of *nous* in its long-term battle against *eros*. In American racial relations, even now, whites' statutory and linguistic monopoly on the identification and definition of reality is a major factor in separation:

Good and evil, morality, social position, worth are not

substantial, but belong rather to the order of the signifier. [Hence we find] the creation of possession and differentiation where previously there had been none. The difference is symbolized by that between black and white, though this is but the most immediate and visible realization of a larger problem.[29]

The "larger problem" is the power of *nous* as conceived in Western epistemology: the power to legislate separations using blatant differences.

The length of Faulkner's sentences, the Old Testament sonorities of his prose, the overblown speech of his characters – these formal elements tend to be treated piecemeal by Faulkner criticism. All too often, style as a subject has been construed in its most naïve sense as a set of narrative fingerprints peculiar to a given writer. A few critics, such as Warren Beck and Walter Slatoff, have questioned how style and rhetoric relate to wider concerns, yet even they privatize Faulkner's stylistic configurations, in terms of either his "genius" or his "eccentric" mind. Neither explanation is sufficient.

Nous requires the wish to separate, order, and convince, while effacing these procedures under the name of "reason." Certain societies, under economic and other kinds of duress, take this function to a pathological limit. Faulkner's style is not solely under the influence of Southern oral narrative and cadence, though this influence is strong. Rather, it also replicates and then tries to counteract linguistically a narrated noetic of separation. A community of speakers and listeners solidifies its own corporate identity and "natural authority" by repeating a series of highly figured stories that approximate a sense of the real, even if, as in *Light in August* and *Absalom, Absalom!*, that "real" narrative actually depends upon rampant misinformation or multiple omissions.

Faulkner traces the mind's tragic irresolution between the organizing polarities of society and the integrative needs of the self. The emphasis throughout Faulkner's language on the moment of "merging" suggests a radical attempt to reintegrate, at least in linguistic terms, what society has sundered. In demonstrating the difficulty of permanently fixing hierarchies, Faulkner's works raise the possibility that societal markings might be susceptible to revision. However, a no less insistent message in Faulkner's major novels is that the escape from division can take dangerous forms: madness (Darl Bundren, Quentin Compson), social exclusion (Joanna Burden, Caddy Compson), or even death (Addie Bundren, Joe Christmas).

Faulkner's major novels, in a rather uncanny manner, follow the reaction of *nous* to the threat of social chaos: (1) anxiety; (2) classification; (3) ranking the classifications; (4) dissemination by written and oral repetition; (5) enforcement by threatened or real violence; (6) effacement of the process. Faulkner's life-work develops along the lines of such a defense against chaos, discovering particular pitfalls at each stage. The early works, *The Sound and the Fury* and *As I Lay Dying*, concern minor revolts against the discriminations of the anxious *nous*: Quentin's and Benjy's syntax, the novel's typography, and the general lack of sequence in thought processes; Quentin's incestuous wish to merge with his sister, and, finally, his desire to escape individuation entirely by means of madness or suicide. *Light in August* and *Absalom, Absalom!* portray the inability to distinguish racial identity by inherited marks of distinction. They reveal the forms of repetition that condition consensus and erect false versions of reality. As we learn in *Light in August*, "when anything gets to be a habit, it also manages to get a right good distance away from truth and fact." *The Hamlet* and *Go Down, Moses* illustrate how division victimizes all-white realms. In sharing a common currency of hearsay and (usually deceitful) financial exchanges, the whites of Frenchman's Bend and Jefferson seem to think themselves in a state of equality among themselves – and in a state of superiority with respect to blacks everywhere. In fact, they only share the same forms of impoverishment. Their "common sense" does not observe the blatant inequalities of their own economic and social exchanges. The alternatives to economic and sociopolitical corruption are imaginary versions of purity – in Eula Varner's case, the "purity" of the white woman. In Ike McCaslin's case, purity seems accessible in aboriginal domains of natural splendor, such as the Big Woods. Yet even here we find the vitiating effects of Ovid's dividing "natural force."

Finally, Faulkner seems to displace the yearning for a harmonized society onto the actual interchange between text and audience that reading entails. My concluding chapter shows that he succeeds where he exploits the diverse linguistic possibilities arising from ambiguities in social and racial classifications. He fails in later novels, however, where – contrary to earlier practice – he seems content to repeat fixed gestures of style, and rely upon a habituated reader, even as his county had perpetuated its divisive mythologies through an unquestioning, habituated citizenry.

Notes

1 William Faulkner, *Faulkner at Nagano*, ed. Robert A. Jelliffe (Tokyo: Kenkyusha, 1956), pp. 94, 137, 153, and *Faulkner in the University*, ed. Frederick L. Gwynn and Joseph Blotner (Charlottesville: University of Virginia Press, 1959), p. 84.

2 *Writers at Work: The* Paris Review *Interviews*, ed. and intro. Malcolm Cowley (New York: Viking, 1959), p. 127.

3 *Faulkner at Nagano*, p. 37.

4 *Faulkner in the University*, p. 279.

5 See Eric J. Sundquist, *Faulkner: The House Divided* (Baltimore: Johns Hopkins University Press, 1983), pp. 63–130. Sundquist's splendid study treats the "division" theme in Faulkner largely in terms of contemporary historical and political theory.

6 James A. Kushner, *Apartheid in America: A Historical and Legal Analysis of Contemporary Racial Segregation in the United States* (Frederick, Md: University Publications of America, 1980), p. 137. Also see I. A. Newby (ed.), *The Development of Segregationist Thought* (Homewood, Ill.: Dorsey Press, 1968), p. 19.

7 Quoted in Malcolm Cowley, "William Faulkner's Legend of the South" (1945), in John Bassett (ed.), *William Faulkner: The Critical Heritage* (Boston: Routledge & Kegan Paul, 1975), p. 307.

8 C. Vann Woodward, *The Strange Career of Jim Crow*, 2nd rev. edn (New York: Oxford University Press, 1966), pp. 22–3, 14; my italics.

9 James Baldwin, *The Price of the Ticket: Collected Nonfiction 1948–1985* (New York: St Martin's, 1985), p. 192.

10 Robert Coles, *Children of Crisis* (Boston: Little, Brown, 1964), pp. 14, 362.

11 Frederick J. Hoffman and Olga W. Vickery, *William Faulkner* (East Lansing: Michigan State College Press, 1951), p. 190, and John W. Cell, *The Highest State of White Supremacy: The Origins of Segregation in South Africa and the American South* (Cambridge: Cambridge University Press, 1982), pp. 142–3, 119.

12 See, for instance, Dolores E. Brien's "William Faulkner and the Myth of Woman," *Research Studies*, 35 (1967), pp. 132–40, a study that anticipates David Williams's Jungian reading, *Faulkner's Women: The Myth and the Muse* (Montreal: McGill/Queen's University Press, 1977). A more harmful reading of the subject comes from Sally R. Page, in *Faulkner's Women: Characterization and Meaning* (DeLand, Fla: Everett/Edwards, 1972). Male critics' demonization of Faulkner's female characters begins as early as Maxwell Geismar's unfortunate "William Faulkner: the Negro and the Female," in *Writers in Crisis* (Boston: Houghton Mifflin, 1942), pp. 143–83, and has continued with little relief through more recent readings – such as Leslie Fiedler's sentiment in *Love and Death in the American Novel* (New York: Stein & Day, 1966), pp. 320–2: "Unlike the natural women of Hemingway, Faulkner's dewiest dells turn out to be destroyers rather than redeemers, quicksands disguised as sacred groves." Critics who point to more relevant issues include Olga Vickery, *The Novels of William Faulkner: A Critical Introduction* (Baton Rouge: Louisiana State University Press, 1959; rev. edn 1964), Melvin Bradford, "Addie Bundren and the Design of *As I Lay Dying*," *Southern Review*, 6 NS (Autumn 1970), pp. 1093–9, and Elisabeth S. Muhlenfeld, "Shadows with Substance Exhumed: The Women in *Absalom, Absalom!*," *Mississippi Quarterly*, 25, 3 (Summer 1972), pp. 289–304.

13 Cleanth Brooks, *William Faulkner: The Yoknapatawpha Country* (New Haven: Yale University Press, 1963), p. 334. See also May Cameron Brown, "The Language of Chaos: Quentin Compson in *The Sound and the Fury*," *American Literature*, 51, 4 (January 1980), who speaks of "Mrs Compson's self-pity and hypochondria," p. 544.

14 Coles, op. cit., p. 255.

15 Winthrop Jordan, *White over Black* (New York: Norton, 1968), pp. 155–6.

16 Quoted in Charles D. Peavy, *Go Slow Now: Faulkner and the Race Question* (Eugene, Oreg.: University of Oregon, 1971), p. 80.

17 Rainer Maria Rilke, *Duineser Elegien*, "Die Erste Elegie," and Friedrich Nietzsche, *The Gay Science*, trans. Walter Kaufmann (New York: Vintage, 1974), sec. 109.

18 See Freud's articles "Die infantile Genitalorganisation (eine Einschaltung in die Sexualtheorie)" (1923), *Studienausgabe* vol. V, pp. 239–40, and "Der Untergang des Oedipuskomplexes" (1924), *Studienausgabe*, vol. V, p. 247; "The Infantile Genital Organization," *The Standard Edition of the Complete Psychological Works of Sigmund Freud*, ed. James Strachey (London: Hogarth

Press, 1953–74), vol. 19, pp. 144–5, and "The Dissolution of the Oedipus Complex," *Standard Edition*, vol. 19, p. 175.

19 See fragments 15, 19, 20, in Philip Wheelwright (ed.), *The Presocratics* (Indianapolis: Bobbs-Merrill, 1960), pp. 162–3. Plato, in *Phaedo*, cites Anaxagoras' doctrine: "Or if all things were mixed together and never separated [synkrinoito men panta diakrinoito], the saying of Anaxagoras, 'all things are chaos,' would soon come true" (72c); *Plato in Twelve Volumes*, vol. 1, trans. H. N. Fowler (1914; Cambridge, Mass.: Harvard University Press, 1977), p. 251.

20 *The Metamorphoses of Ovid*, trans. Mary M. Innes (1955; Harmondsworth: Penguin, 1970), p. 29; Latin version: *Ovid in Six Volumes*, vol. III: *Metamorphoses*, with trans. by Frank J. Miller (1916; Cambridge, Mass.: Harvard University Press, 1971), p. 2.

21 Ovid, *Metamorphoses*, trans. Innes, p. 29.

22 Sigmund Freud, *Civilization and its Discontents* (1930), *Standard Edition*, vol. 21, p. 94; *Das Unbehagen in der Kultur, Studienausgabe*, vol. IX, p. 225.

23 Plato, op. cit., vol. 2, p. 218.

24 Conrad Aiken, in his 1939 essay "William Faulkner: The Novel as Form," says, "The reader must simply make up his mind to go to work, and in a sense to cooperate"; quoted in Hoffman and Vickery, op. cit., p. 138. For Arthur L. Scott, Faulkner's "novels demand of the reader an effort commensurate with the author's": see "The Myriad Perspectives of *Absalom, Absalom!*," *American Quarterly*, 6 (Fall 1954), p. 219. Peter Brooks, referring to *Absalom, Absalom!*, puts this insight into more formal language: "The distance between telling and listening, between writing and reading, has collapsed; the reader has been freed to speak in the text, towards the creation of the text": "Incredulous Narration: *Absalom, Absalom!*," *Comparative Literature*, 34, 3 (Summer 1982), p. 263.

25 Freud, *Civilization*, vol. 21, pp. 94, 126; *Studienausgabe*, vol. IX; pp. 224, 252.

26 Friedrich Nietzsche, *The Will to Power* (New York: Vintage, 1968), sec. 419; *The Gay Science*, sec. 109; *Beyond Good and Evil* (New York: Vintage, 1966), sec. 2, all translated by Walter Kaufmann; my italics.

27 Jordan, op. cit., pp. 509–10.

28 Homer, *The Odyssey in Two Volumes*, vol. I, trans. A. T. Murray (New York: G. P. Putnam, 1930), p. 185.

29 Peter Brooks, op. cit., p. 260.

2

The Sound and the Fury (1929)

Through the fence, between the curling flower spaces, I could see them hitting. They were coming toward where the flat was and I went along the fence.... They took the flag out and they were hitting. Then they put the flag back and they went to the table, and he hit and the other hit. Then they went on, and I went along the fence.

To understand Faulkner's early attempts to rewrite large-scale social rhetorics, we need go no further than the first page of *The Sound and the Fury*: " 'Listen at you, now,' " Luster said. " 'Aint you something, thirty-three years old, going on that way.' "[1] The real problem of the first page, which one reviewer calls an "implicit" key to the rest of the novel, cannot be expressed by any narrow definition of plot or style.[2] The question of who speaks where is not unimportant. Benjy's subordinate standing, and not his syntax, represents chaos for the typical reader. Even though Luster acts as caretaker for Benjy, he also exercises a great amount of control and dominance over the "master's son." Benjy is further compromised because he, like Jake Barnes in Hemingway's *The Sun Also Rises*, is "impotent." Benjy's condition undercuts and opposes all linguistic and, even more, political expectation. Faulkner's "race talk" is a subtle indictment: we must appreciate Faulkner's "remarkable indirection" about the real nature of racial and sexual politics. Therefore the first page tricks us into the point of view of a castrated white whom a younger black serves yet completely dominates. Against all precedent, the reader must adopt the chaotic "I" of someone under the control of a black and reverse the normative polarities of slave/master, black/white.

The novel deviates in many ways from standard fictional treatments of the white, and also of the black, for the main narrative conflict is not any putative "negro" problem. The problem in fact, is white; we here inquire into the deleterious effects of racial division upon the *nous*, the "white mind." The white Compsons' perceptions are askew, each in its own way. A narrative of Negro suffering, ignorance, or endurance is not forthcoming. Whether by its unusual syntax or by its skewed social relations, *The Sound and the Fury* features a discourse that puts its readers *somewhere else*. One problem concerns the peculiarity that, in the same turn as Benjy has lost his customary ascendancy in the social hierarchy, readers have also lost their ability to understand the novel. Many readers have confused their own displacement with a suspicion that the author was unskilled or fuzzy in his aesthetic aims: "I tried to finish the first section [of *The Sound and the Fury*], and each time either fell asleep or started gnawing at the wallpaper after ten pages"; "If Mr Faulkner were asked to tell a straight tale and tell it straight, I presume he would be physically unable to." *The Sound and the Fury*'s mergings indeed begin, within ten pages, to seem a kind of chaos.[3]

Benjy's chaos

Chaos appears in the first words of *The Sound and the Fury* (see chapter opening). The language seems pure realism, yet we seem to lack a metalanguage governing our interpretation of these words. Something is deeply awry here, with the sorry repetitions ("and", "they were hitting") and the ambiguous pronouns "he" and "they". The text fails the task of realism "to grant direct access to a final reality." Possibly, "Faulkner refrains ... from the rhetorical bombardments that mar a number of his other books." Yet readers, once annoyed by the weight of Southern rhetorical cadences in Faulkner, now puzzle over the seeming absence of rhetoric: "Rarely has a novel appeared so completely disordered and unconnected and accidental in its concreteness."[4] Benjy's prose gives a disjointed impression because it does not assemble events in a causal fashion or manipulate large-scale analytic propositions any more complex than the simple connective "and." His discourse signifies by non-linear association rather than syntactical and causal linearity. His prose, then, is the kind of chaos "whose ill-assorted elements [are] indiscriminately heaped together in one place," to quote Ovid. "Mind" has given way to metaphor, with its unpredictable, seemingly random connections:

Mrs Patterson came to the door and opened it and stood there.

Mr Patterson was chopping in the green flowers. He stopped chopping and looked at me. Mrs Patterson came across the garden, running. (14)

"Stay on your side now," Dilsey said. "Luster little, and you don't want to hurt him."

You can't go yet, T.P. said. Wait. (38)

In the first example, Benjy connects Mrs Patterson in the present with an incident in which, while taking his Uncle Maury's adulterous messages to Mrs Patterson, he was caught by her jealous husband. In the second example, Benjy connects two examples of physical separation. Such abstract notions as "separation" or "absence" remain the crucial abstractions in Benjy's consciousness, since he constantly wonders whether he is about to lose or regain a beloved object.[5] Faulkner has created in Benjy a highly unusual and even risky exception to Jefferson, Mississippi's rule of division: since Benjy cannot "order" chaos, he represents Faulkner's first experiment in creating a character who has no capacity to discriminate racially. Benjy knows fire and darkness, presence and absence, but not hierarchy. *Nous* has given way, and Benjy sees color as color, not as an index of power and privilege. Indeed, Benjy, as we shall see, enjoys one privilege denied any other white man: he travels to the church service in "Nigger Hollow."

In·*Beyond the Pleasure Principle*, Freud reports the *"fort/da"* ("gone/here") game wherein his grandson gets pleasure from making a toy vanish and reappear. Similarly, Luster toys with the childlike Benjy's automatic reactions to presence and absence:

A long piece of wire came across my shoulder. It went to the door, and then *the fire went away*. I began to cry.

"What you howling for now," Luster said. "Look there."
The fire was there. I hushed. (70; my italics)

"Whyn't you hush?" Luster said, "You want me to give you
somethin' to sho nough moan about? Sposin I does dis." He
knelt and swept the bottle suddenly up and behind him. Ben
ceased moaning. He squatted, looking at *the small depression
where the bottle had sat,* then as he drew his lungs full
Luster brought the bottle back into view. "Hush!" he hissed,
"Dont you dast to beller! Dont you. Dar hit is. See?" (392;
my italics)

Benjy reacts to absence by crying; white Southern customs
react to the absence or presence of white skin by classifying.
Perhaps now the novel's underlying irony becomes clear, and
the "initial obscurity" as well.

Benjy's odd syntax manifests his underlying inability to
handle extended figures of racial designation. As Ferdinand
de Saussure says in discussing the basic nature of linguistic
signification, so-called "metonymic" relations concern how
any message is spoken or written in a linear connecting
chain. "Metaphoric" relations, in their turn, are virtual, not
combinational, and concern the pool from which a particular
message's elements are selected. Applied to social groups,
racial hierarchies would employ the rule of metonymy.
Metaphor, for its part, would determine the "natural" marks of
generic similarity by which these groups would be identified
and discriminated against.[6] Benjy seems to have the metaphoric
but not the metonymic capacity. Benjy cannot despise blacks,
being fully unaware of their metonymic positions in the social
array. He might associate their skins with night or soil, but
never with enslavement or debasement. Roman Jakobson
invented a term that seems quite apt for Benjy's utterances –
"contiguity disorder," wherein "word order becomes chaotic;
the ties of grammatical coordination and subordination, whether
concord or government, are dissolved."[7] For their part, readers
are not immediately aware of Luster's color exactly because
the narrative is in the first place from Benjy's point of view.
Through the manipulations of style early on, the reader's sense
of familiarity with racial categories is fundamentally questioned.
Benjy's section engages our talent, or rather our dire necessity,
to *classify,* precisely because he cannot. "The Benjy section

forces the reader to participate in the novel, to become, as it were, a surreptitious narrator; otherwise he cannot read it at all."[8] But the reader must be extremely careful to mark what type of narrator he or she becomes, and with what types of prejudices.

The Compson family, particularly Mrs Compson, has had to face the trauma of not knowing whether their youngest son was one of *us* ("Maury") or one or *them* ("Benjy"). But Benjy's chaotic otherness only continues the larger collapse of definition that the Confederate Army's losses began, given that the Civil War was largely fought over definitions: who is a "free man" and who a "slave"? What does "white" mean in terms of civil and social rights? The disarray of Lee's fighting machine was a "chaos" which ended the privilege of the Southern male to define social relations: master/slave, husband/wife, and so on. Jim Crow legislation, written to curb heretical whites as much as uppity blacks, sought a definitional consensus, but the unwritten history of racial mixing, inscribed into the skin of the mixed-race progeny, gave it the lie.

The tensions within the Compson family only underscore public tensions. Yet the notion that the substance of racial politics in America is not primarily a "Negro problem" but rather a problem of white psychic, economic, and family structure would not have gone down terribly well in 1929. In effect, the complexity of the novel's first page and its jumbled "chaos" repeats and reverses the South's distorted legacy of white racial superiority, exposing the manner of both its construction and its eventual self-destruction.

Plots of exchange: Benjy, Quentin, Jason

Traces of unequal relations occur and recur in the speech of the main narrators of *The Sound and the Fury* (Benjy, Quentin, and Jason), mitigated by a countervailing prose that, often against the speaker's wishes, dissolves these relations. Such dissolution even extends to the unexpected and often uncanny relationships between the three brothers' narratives. Links between Benjy's and Quentin's sections abound: Benjy ends his chapter by falling asleep, and Quentin wakes up to begin his. Benjy "is filled with a kind of primitive poetry"; Quentin's poetry is "essentially decadent."[9] Benjy is castrated, and Quentin wishes to be castrated. But physical castration is only part of the story. Quentin perhaps wishes to destroy not merely his own sexual organs but all other evidence of separations as well. But, even here, the matter is not so clear-cut. Consider for a moment Quentin's seeming hatred of time. First he hides the watch face, then he twists off its hands. He does not destroy the watch; he merely defaces it. It seems, then, that Quentin wants to reject conventional measures of time, but not time itself, which relies on the less arbitrary measure of planetary movement. Indeed, Quentin spends much of the day telling time by the length of his sun-cast shadow. To tear off watch hands removes only the signifiers of real time. Such a separation, generalized, between thing and signifier would kill language, but would also allow Quentin an ideal realm in which the tabooed "other" would no longer be other. Quentin tears off the watch hands because he wants to "castrate" conventional division, render separation impotent by means of separation – an impossible, because contradictory, goal. Failing in this attempt, he stages his own final separation in search of oneness, a separation from life itself.

One figure that pervades the speech and experience of Jason and Quentin involves actual or rhetorical acts of exchange and substitution. Normally, exchange and substitution separate groups (replacing black presence and/or resistance with signs of black absence and/or servility) or encourage an illusory belief in the equalizing properties of the exchange channel. In a manner similar to the operation of the poetic metaphor, substitutions conjure up a wished-for reality as if by magic. Quentin and Jason delight in exchanges both real and imaginary, yet neither can tell one from the other. Quentin is a speculator, but, unlike Jason, not on the cotton exchange. He speculates against *nous*, coining impossible grammars, thinking: *"Non fui. Sum. Fui. Nom sum"* (216). If the *"Nom sum"* means what it says ("I am a name", if *"Nom"* is a form of *nomen*), then the crippling connection Quentin makes between his "I am" and his "name" becomes clear: he is a name – Quentin Compson. If *"Nom"* refes to "non", the point remains: Quentin sees himself as the toy of grammar. He tries to alter his psyche by altering syntax: "thinking I was I was not who was not was not who" (211). In a flashback to his childish sex play with Natalie,

Quentin uses a chiasmus to figure an imagined interchange of sexual position:

> *I used to hold like this you thought I wasnt strong enough didnt you*
>> *Oh Oh Oh Oh*
>
> *I hold to use like this I mean did you hear what I said I said*
>> *oh oh oh oh* (168)

Other exchanges inform the shape of Quentin's day. He overhears two boys fishing and talking about a large trout that people have been trying to catch "for twenty-five years." A Boston store has offered a "twenty-five dollar fishing rod" for catching it. One boy says he would exchange the rod for the twenty-five dollars. "Then they talked about what they would do with twenty-five dollars . . making of unreality a possibility, then a probability, then an incontrovertible fact, as people will when their desires become words" (145). By the end, the fish has become "a horse and wagon." Quentin leaves one of the boys "looking down at the trout which he had already spent" (146). He gives a quarter to the Italian girl as if to substitute it for another quarter, the one that Jason elsewhere withholds from Luster, who needs it to see a show. In another example, Quentin gives a cigar to one bootblack and a quarter to the other, noticing how "The one with the cigar was trying to sell it to the other for the nickel" (102). Finally, only the exchange of the Compsons' pasture for money, a pasture that for Benjy has to substitute for Caddy, has enabled Quentin to be at Harvard at all.

Although he is subject to various exchanges, Quentin none the less bemoans his entrapment within fixed categories. Quentin has a primal and ineluctable question: "Why couldn't it have been me and not her who is unvirgin?" (96). The negative prefix to "unvirgin" denotes the overall impossibility of an exchange between Quentin and his sister ("me and not her"). Quentin repeatedly finds himself on the wrong side of division. In fact, he should be the one who has had sex before marriage; he should be able to "protect" his sister from that experience – but this time roles, though fixed, have reversed: Caddy is more like a man than he is. Quentin tries to reverse in so many words the unhappy exchanges of his life. But exchange does not lead to change. Quentin is, like the fishing boys, only "making of unreality a possibility, then a probability, then an incontrovertible fact, as people will when their desires become words" (145).

Neither Quentin nor Benjy can be defined according to convention. The division Quentin insists upon seems to bring about a racial and sexual mixing he both desires and fears. Whether Quentin likes it or not, people consider him at times "black" and at times a "woman." The New Englanders he meets are not particularly helpful, saying "he talks like a coloured man" (148), or that his hand is feminine, as if "just out of convent" (135–6). He confronts Dalton Ames, but cannot defend his sister, and "just passe[s] out like a girl" (201). Spoade repeatedly taunts him by saying that Shreve is Quentin's "husband" (213). Caddy names a daughter after him, so that not even his name, "Quentin," is unequivocally male. If Quentin identifies himself with his name (*"Nom[en] sum"*), then the terms of his identity are collapsing all around him.

Yet Quentin at times wishes to unite with his antithetical counterparts. He tries to reverse separation to re-create an original wholeness. If language represents "unreality," then one must take this shortcoming into account, "for desire depends entirely on difference; on the establishment of an object that can be desired insofar as it does not appertain to the subject, insofar as it is radically other."[10] In *Beyond the Pleasure Principle*, Freud shows desire ending temporarily by coupling with the "other," reinstating for a time what Plato describes in *The Symposium* as an originally merged state of two sexes separated later: "After the division had been made, 'the two parts of man, each desiring his other half, came together, and threw their arms about one another eager to grow into one.'"[11] The compulsion to merge, reducing distance and difference, seems only human, but so is its opposite compulsion, to separate and divide, as facilitated by analytical thought. Quentin has settled upon an almost unimaginably difficult ambition. Whereas the plot of *The Sound and the Fury* consists of its characters' errors, its greatest challenge is to ask whether alternatives to error are possible. Such alternatives would have to overcome formidable conflicts between desire and large-scale barriers.

Time and space are also a kind of barrier. The phrase

"Tomorrow and tomorrow" begins the *Macbeth* soliloquy that suggested *The Sound and the Fury* as a title. Separations brought about by time and space are the chief causes of desire. "Tomorrow" postpones satisfaction, for "today" is never the end of the line – there is always an other, a *différance*.[12] Quentin intuitively knows he is fighting a losing battle, against, above all, time. His suicide letter says "Not good until tomorrow" (122). Thoughts need articulation and dissemination – they are not "good" until they become "later." But articulation makes language, distanced from the point of conception, only a "bad" secondary version of things. Quentin will not be "good" until "tomorrow" – when he will no longer be torn between antagonisms, because he will be dead. Indeed, in this novel, the unfulfilled state of being constantly *before*, the state of the *not yet*, intrigues Faulkner. There seems to be a "day before" pattern throughout this novel, in which crucial plot events occur one day before a religious or historical, usually Confederate, commemoration. Historical myths, no less than literary plots, seem to require varieties of temporal separation – usually delay, retrospection, or anticipation – in order to function at all.[13] Quentin's suicide letter is also the literal letter, for a written narrative really comes into its own when separated by space or time from its producer – indeed, as Barthes reminds us, with the death of the author comes the birth of the book.[14]

Barriers of society and time often appear in the form of spatial barriers in *The Sound and the Fury*. For instance, in the seminal image of the novel, Caddy disobediently peers at her grandmother's corpse through a window. Her daughter Quentin later escapes by climbing through a window and down a pear tree (or rainpipe, as in the "Appendix"). Her brother, also a Quentin, tries to shoot her and Herbert Head's voices "through the floor." The theme of "barriers" comes up most tellingly in the opening words: "Through the fence, between the curling flower spaces, I could see them hitting." Fences separate ("crossing the fence" is a standard term for black–white miscegenation) and enclose a normative space – the ironic reader of the novel might actually question which side of the Compson fence constitutes normality. Benjy keeps peering through the fence at a plot of earth once his, now sold. Were Benjy to go "through the fence," he would violate the contract that exchanged his precious land for money, but he does not know this, and breaks through the barrier. The first time he tries actually to cross the fence, he also tries to speak – "I opened the gate and then stopped, turning. I was trying to say and I caught her, and she screamed and I was trying to say and trying" (64). Benjy has spotted a girl who presumably resembles Caddy. He really wants Caddy, as signified by the girl. If he could speak, he would probably tell the girl "My name is Benjy" or say "Hello." But he cannot say "Hello" because he is congenitally mute, and, even were he not, he could not know his real name ("Maury") because his family has exchanged it for a substitute ("Benjy"). The family at first names Benjy after his alcoholic uncle Maury. But once Benjy's condition manifests itself they change his name. Versh tells Benjy: "Your mamma too proud for you" (86). Quentin, appropriately, invents the new name: "rechristened Benjamin by his brother Quentin (Benjamin, our lastborn sold into Egypt)" (211); "Benjamin the child of mine old age held hostage into Egypt" (423); "Benjamin came out of the bible, Caddy said. It's a better name for him than Maury was" (71). Then the family makes the name fixed: challenged to say why Benjy is a "better name," Caddy simply replies, "Mother says it is" (71). Benjy, then, succumbs to a form of division by the exchange of names (only Dilsey protests at the substitution – she has seen its like before), a separation perpetuated by family custom. Benjy cannot speak a name that, even if he could speak, he would not actually know. By "trying to say" a lost name without actually uttering it, he loses his testicles, whose pale replicas he later seeks "through the fence" in the first lines of the novel.

Benjy's frustration with words, his "trying to say," resembles a more general insufficiency. In accosting the girls, he cannot speak, he cannot attain his desire. Even were he to speak, he would be giving out a false name, "a better name for him." He tries to speak and is castrated for it. After the operation, he sees lost golf balls "through the fence, between the curling flower spaces." These events have already occurred before we peer with him "through the fence spaces." So the opening of the novel reveals an already irremediable loss, and further loss follows any attempt to recapture what was lost. In this way, *The Sound and the Fury* forces the reader to participate in the novel not merely as a white under the dominance of chaotic language and a canny black, but also as an already castrated viewer. We assume Benjy's point of view here; language has already undone our efforts to stave off its amputative effects. Human language cannot echo God's performance in Genesis. Names, voice, and mastery are already lost; one cannot even utter replacements. From the first word we are unable to "say," and "trying to say" only worsens things. Interestingly, Quentin equates sexlessness with a linguistic exclusion: "But that's not it. It's not not having had them [genitals]. It's never to have had them then I could say O That That's Chinese I dont know Chinese" (143).[15] Benjy gazes into "spaces" that "signify nothing." Yet, unlike Benjy, the "sane" mind does not react to verbal impotence with silence and tears but rather with *nous*, which manipulates language to simulate facts, and constructs "reality" from the simulations. By this process, "basically and from time immemorial we are – *accustomed to lying*," in Nietzsche's words.[16] Society and language become "rhetorical"; they are the chief ways in which *nous* tries to fend off chaos and hide all consequent deprivations.

As we have seen, the fifth figure of division describes a procedure of *threat* and violence, the brutal supports given to the reductions of *nous*. Signification may be a form of conceptual violence, but the Yoknapatawpha enforcers of specious division often have recourse to actual, less indirect, forms of coercion. Quentin's cerebral bent does not keep him from sharing his brother Jason's tendency towards violence; he provokes at least two fights during the course of the day. Public tensions, created by the need to rank diverse entities, are now Quentin's "private" agonies. Illicit attempts at sexual coupling, failure, and guilt over trying now comprise a palpable shadow that hovers about Quentin. Quentin perhaps never grasps what his father means when he says that "it was men invented virginity not women" (96): the very concept of "virginity," like the idea of "nigger," is a mask covering the urge to violate these categories. Neither term has much to do with what it presumably describes. Black skin only signifies for the white eye: "there was a nigger on a mule ... like a sign put there saying You are home again" (106). The black face is a *sign* to Quentin, not a personality, and the "shadow" that tracks him all day long is a certain ideational impurity he cannot countenance. The sign of the "nigger on a mule" must be taken together with Benjy's carriage ride at the end of the novel, when Benjy sees "post and tree, window and doorway, and signboard, each in its ordered place." Quentin wants to kill a black sign of his own mental chaos, even as Benjy wants to cling to his white "signboard" of order. Quentin would kill the black other in himself, the shadow that must be separated from his "I," either by violence or by the threat thereof.

Quentin's futile violence comes to designate a kind of *Spaltung* or "splitting" in his psyche, a struggle by the "master's son" (*nous*, the white mind, purity, virginity) against "the master's black" (chaos, mud, black people, sexual intruders). Quentin, who wants Caddy's body to be as pure as his mind, does not realize that his mind can be no purer than Caddy's body. He tries to defend his conceptual purity against reality, even as he tries to defend his sister's purity against her various suitors. Only a convincing display of violence, of which he is not capable, would actually separate "virgin" from "unvirgin," "white" from "nigger," in the way Quentin desires. His futile violence falls far short of what would be required to "legislate" truth — witness his bungled fight with Dalton Ames. Quentin resists every male suitor who threatens his and Caddy's hermetic and incestuous "blue flame." His vigor can only recall the diligence with which the ideal of "white womanhood" traditionally guarded against any interlopers, black or white. Yet Caddy, whom Quentin wants to be pure, has "muddy drawers."

Benjy's "contiguity disorder" – an inability to form complex linear propositions from smaller units – prevents him from having any investment in racist hierarchies. Yet even Benjy, as we have seen, needs to rely on borrowed perceptual codes, including his *idiotaxis* of Jefferson signboards, a form of organization that he cannot control in the end. *Nous* takes chaos and structures it into "common sense" and "experience"; the writer stamps the chaos of reality with Nietzsche's "lie" and calls it "art." In both cases, taxonomies appeal to the inactive mind. The constructs of man-made reality aid and are aided by conservatism in reading, so readers are also implicated in Benjy's failed security. Audiences expect realism to yield a certain order, sequence, and content. From Plato's insistence on a poetry of "the good" to Artistotle's "unities"; from Hume's "relations of *resemblance, contiguity,* and *causation*" to Dr Johnson's "just representations of a general nature"; and implicit in Shelley's and Nietzsche's Platonic reading of the "poet" as "legislator", we discern a bias in favor of well-ordered narratives.[17]

Yet seeing through the social order of things is perhaps as difficult as trying to change the direction of reading from "left to right" to "right to left."[18] In the last line of the novel, we see Benjy misinterpreting the signboards he has clung to for order. The commercial façades of Jefferson seem to pass him, although he is moving: "his eyes were empty and blue and serene again as cornice and façade flowed smoothly once more from left to right; post and tree, window and doorway, and signboard, each in its ordered place" (401). Benjy literally "reads" the façades, but he mistakes their stasis for motion and his own activity for passivity. In the first chapter as in the last, we attain a new perspective, but at a price: Benjy's habitual, yet lazy and erroneous "perspective" resembles our various misreadings, including our understanding of skin color. The semiotics that make color into a socially meaningful "sign" clearly mirror the somewhat idiotic requirement that the same order be maintained indefinitely without alteration. Benjy, reading "left to right," hopes through this order to repair a brokenness represented by the failed phallic signifier, the "broken flower" that "drooped over Ben's fist" (401) – but the prospects are not good. In the first line of the novel, we already gaze at a loss through interliteral spaces: Benjy sees lost white golf balls through the fence and remembers his castration; black letters, for the reader, futilely address the silence of white paper.

Skin color is a biological characteristic that can separate for a probing, classifying eye. One reduces the visual sign of color as under a microscope's objective. Yet, unlike a dead specimen, race examines the examiner; it is a relational dieresis: "a nigger is not a person so much as a form of behaviour; a sort of obverse reflection of the white people he lives among" (106). The semiotic black exists in order to redress a prior white loss of meaning and authority: "They [blacks] come into white people's lives like that in sudden sharp black trickles that isolate white facts for an instant in unarguable truth like under a microscope" (211). Even if isolation and objectification distort both viewer and object, Quentin needs these defenses against what he considers to be chaos. He yearns for separating, dieristic figures; his prose is discrete, fragmentary, lacking any synthesis.[19] He spends most of his day trying to prove to himself that he is white and not black, male and not female. For instance, his black/white and female/male confusion comes up in a memory shortly after he confesses his incestuous urges to Caddy. He suggests that they perform a *Liebestod* so that Caddy will never love another man. She rejects his advances. In the end, they stand, "their shadows one shadow her head . . . her shadow high against his shadow one shadow" (192).

Quentin is the gnomon of a sundial that is himself. As in *Absalom, Absalom!*, his shadow conveys a sense of antithesis dying. Quentin walks both inside and outside his shadow. He wishes both to integrate himself with the black and to punish the color that stands for his tabooed wishes, particularly the wish to sleep with his sister: "I stood in the belly of my shadow. . . . I went back to the post office, treading my shadow into the pavement" (124).[20] The empty signifier of black skin can support Quentin's paradoxical handling, and can be for others a "sign" for "white facts," an "obverse reflection of . . . white people." Shadows, as we have seen, represent Quentin's frustrated wish to merge with what the law says he must be separate from. Merging takes place, but under penalty of law: Quentin carries out the sentence upon himself – he jumps.[21] Through one monumental action, Quentin ends separation from blackness exactly where he had hoped to assert his white uniqueness: he jumps into "my shadow, leaning flat on the water."

Jason's ploys of exchange are less psychological in nature than Quentin's. Jason, unlike his brothers, is a pragmatist who tries to cope with the "real" world. None the less, his exchange transactions also go awry. Jason's section seems accessible, delivered in first-person, conversational style, recalling *Catcher in the Rye* or *Babbit*. His colloquial tone presents a discourse whose main topic seems to be *exchange*, and whose basic tonalities view life as equitable or disequitable exchange. Jason, more than either his older or his younger brother, seems to know how society sets its values.[22] Indeed, Jason's "sanity" is all too close to our own obsession with economic value. Perhaps for this reason more than any other, Jason's motives seem less complex than those of his brothers. Yet, ironically,

Jason cannot control any of the exchange systems to which he belongs. The first-person "I" in which he speaks is the most unfixed pronoun of all; in the "I," anyone and everyone finds their identity. His world rests on the valorized "I," but there is nothing behind the "I." In any case no one will see his "I" as being as privileged as he does. Jason's life in the community effectively separates him from it. Jason has little to say to Earl or the cotton traders. One feels that, even in a third-person narration, Jason would always wish to be the first.

Jason encounters a series of ambiguous exchanges: he seeks redemption through a "cotton exchange," but its true activity and power is absent, and Jason has a substitute, the "telegraph wire" that gives him deferred reports of the market events. He pays ten dollars a month for a broker's advice, yet ends up losing 200 dollars in one day. He has exchanged his mother's thousand dollars for a car, but he cannot drive the car because he is allergic to its gasoline fumes. His sister Caddy's husband-to-be promises him a bank job in exchange for his consent to their marriage, but soon he reneges on his promises. Jason takes revenge, stealing the money that Caddy sends her illegitimate daughter Quentin. He does it by exchanging a false check for the real one that Caddy sends every month, and banking the sum while their mother burns the substitute check. He deposits his salary under his mother's name as a bogus gesture of faith, but withdraws Caddy's money and spends it. His niece Quentin ultimately steals from him the money he has stolen from her. All these exchanges are symbolic acts that paradoxically act against their agent:

> Of his niece he did not think at all, nor of the arbitrary valuation of the money. Neither of them had had entity or individuality for him for ten years; together they merely symbolized the job in the bank of which he had been deprived before he ever got it. (382)

Jason's "similarity disorder" complements Benjy's "contiguity disorder"; people are interchangeable for him, valuable only as adjacent steps towards forever deferred ends.

Mrs Compson calls Jason "the only one who had any business sense," but Jason cannot keep his dominant position in the marketplace, in the town, or in the family, because exchange, by definition, both encourages and disallows fixed positions. Even though markets require traders to "take positions," these positions are in constant flux. Jason does not acknowledge the reciprocity that rules economic (and ultimately social) interaction: his loss of 200 dollars is someone else's (he suspects a "damn New York jew"; 329) gain. Even millionaires face monetary limitations, as Jason realizes in trying to calculate how much it would cost to poison the pigeons in the town square, saving the "forty-five dollars to clean it." Not even a millionaire could "afford to shoot them at five cents a shot" (309).

Exchange in the cotton markets is similar to the exchanges of metaphor which "will never make a profit."[23] Money, like paper, is just another kind of writing, symbolizing only what others desire. Jason can only make temporary "paper profits." In joining his aims with the ends of money-making, Jason is exchanged by the exchange, and trades advantage for adversity. Rhetorical merging, like a financial exchange market, may feature rapid, antithetical reversals.

Jason was a small-scale tattletale and bully as a child, as we recall from the short story "That Evening Sun." Now he has graduated to more widely sanctioned forms of brutality. Jason, whom the "Appendix" calls the most "sane" Compson, is also the most violent. For violence of every sort, from the whip to the KKK lynch mob, underpins the so-called "sanity" of Faulkner's Yoknapatawpha. In the "Appendix" we learn of Jason's violent wish to catch his niece Quentin "without warning, springing on her out of the dark, before she had spent all the money, and murder her before she had time to open her mouth" (426). In the novel's last scene, Jason, beating Luster for a minor infraction, apes other symbolic acts of violence against blacks, trying, in a forceful symmetry, to restore in the end, at Luster's expense, the "order" of white authority that was lost to Luster in the beginning on account of Benjy's "chaos": "Then he struck Luster over the head with his fist."

Jason's section continues the novel's inquiry into rhetoric. The novel's various narrators journey "from the sensory to the interpretive"; the "progression from Benjy's section through Quentin's to Jason's is accompanied by an increasing sense of reality," a "progression from murkiness to increasing enlightenment." Indeed, more than half of the interest in the novel comes from its style and not its narrative development. So critics' elaborate plot summaries and charts of time levels (as in Stewart and Backus or Volpe), while helpful, cannot properly illustrate the aims of the novel.[24]

The hollow heart

The Sound and the Fury's most remarkable section, "April 8, 1928," contrasts Jason with Dilsey, the one divisive and irascible, the other conciliatory and level-headed. Jason ranges over a thirty-mile radius in his mad car-chase after his niece Quentin, who has stolen his money. He journeys the most widely, but the least successfully; Dilsey simply walks to church and back. We are less in the dark than ever before – the narrative is comprehensible, taking up a single day, not thirty years, as in Benjy's section. There are few flashbacks; events are linear. One expects a conclusion, a moral, a statement of some kind, for there is no "tomorrow and tomorrow and tomorrow"; April 8, 1928 is the final day.

More so than the ludic narrators of previous chapters, the lucid one of the fourth seems fully reliable. Yet the narrator is still questionable; critical opinion has not yet decided whose voice informs the final chapter. Millgate says that Dilsey is the "immensely positive figure" who centers the last section; Kinney agrees that we see Dilsey "directly" here for the first time; Waggoner claims that the last section is "effectively hers [Dilsey's] even though told from the narrative point of view of [an] omniscient author." Others differ about the degree of "omniscience." Matthews, hedging his bets, calls the last section "Faulkner's"; Reed claims that "Faulkner turns to the third person to finish the novel" with "absolute objectivity"; Slatoff agrees that the last section is "narrated from an omniscient and objective point of view."[25] Whether the section is "Faulkner's" (As Faulkner himself once claimed) or "Dilsey's" (by analogy with the other three sections) is important, since one might read its events differently in either case. If Dilsey, as important as she is to the plot and to the household, cannot narrate her own section, then the novel contains a peculiar imbalance: why should Dilsey, the most sympathetic character, be denied a privilege granted to Jason, the least sympathetic? If Dilsey is not the narrator, then this chapter deviates from the novel's typical practice, not just by being relatively readable and coherent, but by separating Dilsey from the narrative's habitual mode of expressing consciousness.

The chapter's highpoint comes in a scene that is almost theatrical in its location and impact. "Highpoint" perhaps misnames the actual location – a deep hollow, "the section known as Nigger Hollow" (377).[26] This black world is a "scene like a painted backdrop . . . the whole scene was as flat and without perspective as a painted cardboard set upon the ultimate edge of the flat earth" (364). Dilsey's and Benjy's spiritual migration takes them to the most separate place possible. They travel (in an unmistakable reference to Odysseus' journey to the Underworld in Book XI of *The Odyssey*) to "the ultimate edge of the flat earth." What could be more remote than "the ultimate edge of the flat earth"? They find what they must know only after tracing a depression or hollow in the ground to attract the shades and spirits of the supernatural.

The trip to Nigger Hollow takes the reader through a fence that is both linguistic and racial. Benjy, a white separated from whites, is well qualified to be the white reader's *psychopomp* through the Underworld. *The Sound and the Fury* from the first to last is Benjy's book: "Benjy's fusion of life and death correlates to what seeing the first and last means to Dilsey, and, finally, to us."[27] He is the only white in Nigger Hollow. He may never speak, castrated in the first place as a result of his wish to speak. He therefore perceives the otherworldly events with inarticulate and "slackjawed" wonder, but the price of his ticket to Nigger Hollow is that he cannot reveal a black language that Faulkner calls "ejaculant" – a language sexually potent, delivering meaning. Benjy is privileged above the whites who have excluded him, privileged exactly by that exclusion. Not incidentally, his censored actual name, "Maury," comes from the Latin *Maurus*, "a Moor." This "white Moor," then, hears black language using the password of his suppressed name, a name that, like the vibrant black tongue itself, is to be neither known nor uttered within the conventional discourse of white society. Yet Benjy is not the only white who "crosses the fence" of race and language, because, miraculously, the white reader has also come along.

The first three sections of the novel have shown the failures of white society and its discourses. By the end of *The Sound and the Fury*, the choice seems to be either to admit that language is a castrated compromise (to be content with passive left-to-right orderings) or to annihilate the self in a final suicidal revenge against the letter. Neither of these choices seems really satisfactory. The fourth section tests whether non-whites can negate such a white language with a non-denotative language of otherness. In the last chapter we seek answers in that place most marginal to white society – Nigger Hollow. The novel's Easter Sunday project is to descend into Nigger Hollow, yet still ascend to tell the tale to a thirsting white world. The narrator wants to "cross the fence" of language and race, possibly taking the reader there too. To write differently, to write in "black language," might be to read and to experience differently. Only a person who straddles both worlds can eavesdrop on the language of blacks speaking *for themselves*. Benjy witnesses it, but cannot speak of it. Dilsey witnesses it, but she is not the narrator. So who narrates? One would not necessarily need to be black in order to know. Here, the consistent point of view, such as it is, is neither Dilsey's nor Faulkner's, but both: an integrated audience, and an integrated narrative voice.

In "*The Sound and the Fury* and *As I Lay Dying* everything is subordinated to the voices of the characters – the voices are the characters."[28] Hearts speak: "the voice consumed him, until he was nothing and they were nothing and there was not even a voice" (367). The voice engulfs both source and listener, seeming the sort of language that black worshippers share. Within this voice, identities melt into the chaos of unity, like a suicide note that would self-destruct with its author in a pure blue flame, or even like *The Sound and the Fury* itself, a novel that consumes us and our reading.[29] Black words are hardly language at all. Benjy's speech, like blacks' language, seem "just sound" (400), and both transcend words "like an alto horn, sinking into their hearts and speaking there . . . beyond the need for words" (367).

Aside from the black congregation and the one white, Benjy, we have the preacher himself, the heart at the heart of the voice, Reverend Shegog. But not only Shegog. His description gives us the major clues:

> The visitor was undersized, in a shabby alpaca coat. He had a
> wizened black face like a small, aged monkey. . . . When the
> visitor rose to speak he sounded like a white man. . . . They
> did not mark just when his intonation, his pronunciation,
> became negroid, they just sat swaying a little in their seats as
> the voice took them into itself. (365–8)

He is, as André Bleikasten was the first to point out, an
analogue of the novelist himself, reaching the point of inspired
dispossession where his individuality gives way to the "voice."[30]
And the mystical vision granted to the preacher may likewise
be said to metaphorize the poetic vision sought after by the
writer. Note Faulkner's self-portrait as a black–white composite,
a voice "crossing the fence" of race and language, transcending
opposition in its imaginary journey to "Nigger Hollow." The
white narrator places himself here into that lost black language
"for itself" that he had only conjectured about before, and into
the communality of voice that enwraps the congregation with
invisible bonds.

The Easter Sunday scene is refreshing in contrast to earlier
scenes. Bleikasten captures its tone of hopeful ending, but also
indirectly names its greatest failure:

> The orderly discourse of cold reason . . . has given way to the
> spontaneous language of the heart, which alone can break
> down the barriers of individual isolation . . . all that "white"
> rhetoric could achieve was "a collective dream"; what is
> accomplished now is a truly collective experience, a welding
> of many into one. For the first time in the novel, separation
> and fragmentation are at least temporarily transcended. . . .
> Another language is heard, unprecedented in the novel,
> signaled at once by the cultural-ethnic shift from "white" to
> "black," the emotional shift from rational coldness to
> spiritual fervor, and lastly by the stylistic shift from the
> mechanical cadences of shallow rhetoric to the entrancing
> rhythms of inspired speech.[31]

Shegog's emancipatory speech seems to satisfy the novel's
overall hope of ending "separation and fragmentation." Bleikasten seems to have followed Faulkner down this path of
hope. But on second view this path seems too "ordered" to be
entirely trustworthy.[32]

Reverend Shegog gives us a way out of language, and perhaps of racial politics, but does so on the "edge of the flat earth". The black ecstatic concord might be "collective," but it is figuratively posthumous.[33] Let us not forget that, for Homer, Hades – the land of the dead – was at the "edge of the flat earth"; to be resurrected, you first need to have been crucified. The Shegog unification is *non-temporal*. Without time, there is no separation and frustration, but also no articulation; "the language of the heart" can alter nothing – particularly not Southern apartheid. The ahistorical timelessness in which Dilsey and Benjy – to name only two – exist has for far too long received the title "redemptive."[34] If the oppressed tolerate outrages past and present, and the threat of future outrages, then they have no choice but to "endure" into eternity. Their "redemption," by this measure, is eternal damnation. The sermon by Reverend Shegog may be a structural and even ethical highpoint in the novel, but its futility becomes clear as soon as Dilsey leaves the all-black church for the Compson household.[35] Shegog has, in the standard manner of the Afro-American gospel sermon, allowed blacks to speak freely *for themselves*, in the jazz-like counterpoint of call-and-response repetition.[36] He may even be aware of the ultimately futile exercise of liberty involved here, but wants to lift his listeners for the moment beyond order and class. A black Mississippi congregation in 1928 would certainly be in the "hollows" of death, the "pit" of social value, but Easter is the day of resurrection, a lifting up out of suffering. Shegog promises his flock that they will ultimately be lifted from the dead. In his self-portrait as Shegog, Faulkner forges the most delicately poised ambiguity of his literary career, precisely illustrating both the promise and peril of a racial fence-crossing that would have been a legal, if not a literary, misdemeanor in 1929. Later, he would canonize in his Nobel Prize acceptance speech "the old verities and truths of the heart." As if we also needed our hands on his heart too, he would exalt the writer's "privilege to help man endure by lifting his heart." But *The Sound and the Fury* delivers a different sermon – perhaps Faulkner had forgotten it twenty years later – even on Easter Sunday, the most angelic blacks have no choice but to walk from the church.

Notes

1 William Faulkner, *The Sound and the Fury* (New York: Vintage, 1954), p. 1. All subsequent quotations from this edition will be cited by page numbers in parentheses in the text.

2 James Burnham, "Trying to Say," *Symposium*, 51–9, in John Bassett (ed.), *William Faulkner: The Critical Heritage* (Boston: Routledge & Kegan Paul, 1975), p. 104.

3 Dudley Fitts, "Two Aspects of Telemachus," *Hound and Horn*, 3 (April–June 1930), pp.445–7, and Gerald Gould's review of September 29, 1935, in the *Observer*, both quoted in Bassett (ed.), op. cit., pp. 88 and 97, respectively. Michael Groden relates the syntax of Quentin's section to Molly Bloom's soliloquy in *Ulysses*, which "Faulkner seems to have read . . . as a representation of chaos," adding that Faulkner "often employs the 'Penelope' technique to indicate the loss of control": "*Ulysses* and *The Sound and the Fury*," *Twentieth Century Literature*, 21 (1975), pp. 267–8.

4 Colin MacCabe, *James Joyce and the Revolution of the Word* (London: Macmillan, 1978), p. 12; Irving Howe, *William Faulkner* (1951), 3rd edn (Chicago: University of Chicago Press, 1975), p. 162; and Cleanth Brooks, *William Faulkner: The Yoknapatawpha Country* (New Haven: Yale University Press, 1963), p. 331.

5 John T. Matthews, *The Play of Faulkner's Language* (Ithaca: Cornell University Press, 1982), especially the chapter entitled "The Discovery of Loss in *The Sound and the Fury*," and Gail L. Mortimer, *Faulkner's Rhetoric of Loss* (Austin: University of Texas Press, 1983), "Introduction," both expand upon Faulkner's theme of "loss" and absence, both of which his central characters refuse to acknowledge.

6 See Ferdinand de Saussure, *Course in General Linguistics*, trans. Wade Baskin (New York: McGraw-Hill, 1966), pp. 111–34.

7 See Roman Jakobson, "Two Aspects of Language and Two Types of Aphasic Disturbances," in *Selected Writings*, vol. II: *Word and Language* (The Hague: Mouton, 1971), p. 251.

8 Howe, op. cit., p. 160.

9 Brooks, op. cit., p. 326.

10 MacCabe, op. cit., p. 28.

11 Sigmund Freud, *Beyond the Pleasure Principle, Standard Edition*, vol. 18, p. 57; *Jenseits des Lustprinzips, Studienausgabe*, vol. III, p. 266.

12 "The law of différance is that any law is constituted by postponement and self-difference": Jacques Derrida, *On Grammatology*, trans. Gayatri Spivak (Baltimore: Johns Hopkins University Press,

1974), "Translator's Preface," p. lvii; French title: *De la gramma-tologie* (Paris: Minuit, 1967).

13 Arthur Geffen notes that the day after Quentin's suicide, June 3, is Jefferson Davis's birthday and a Confederate holiday. The day after the last section of the novel, April 9, is also the anniversary of the surrender at Appomattox. See "Profane Time, Sacred Time, and Confederate Time in *The Sound and the Fury*," *Studies in American Fiction*, 2, pp. 175–97.

14 See particularly in this regard Maurice Blanchot, "Literature and the Right to Death," in *the Gaze of Orpheus and other Literary Essays*, preface by Geoffrey Hartman, trans. Lydia Davis (Barrytown, NY: Station Hill Press, 1981), pp.21–62. See also Roland Barthes, "The Death of the Author," in *Image/Music/Text*, trans. Stephen Heath (London: Fontana, 1977), pp. 142–8.

15 A critic of Joyce has described a similar effect in more Lacanian terms: "the subject, considered in these terms, is no longer a full entity, but a constant set of displacements inaugurated by a primal (but never original) exclusion (castration) from a world that was never full until it became empty; which emptiness we continually attempt to fill": MacCabe, op. cit., p. 58.

16 Friedrich Nietzsche, *Beyond Good and Evil*, trans. Walter Kaufmann (New York: Vintage, 1966), p. 192.

17 David Hume, *An Inquiry Concerning Human Understanding*, ed. with intro. by Charles W. Hendel (1748; Indianapolis: Bobbs-Merrill, 1955), p. 39, in section "Of the Association of Ideas"; Samuel Johnson, "Preface to Shakespeare", in *Selected Poetry and Prose*, ed. with intro. and notes by Frank Brady and W. K. Wimsatt (Berkeley: University of California Press, 1977), p. 301.

18 One Southern woman explains the paradoxical results of convention. Her friend admires and associates with a black man, but cannot treat him as a friend: "I was surprised at the man's ability to miss the logic of his own behavior. Ted wants a friend's company, but he has to call for his 'help.' That means Ted, despite all his money and influence in our community, *follows the rules rather than makes them*" (my italics): Robert Coles, *Children of Crisis* (Boston: Little, Brown, 1964), p. 252.

19 May Cameron Brown, "The Language of Chaos: Quentin Compson in *The Sound and the Fury*," *American Literature*, 51, 4 (January 1980), p. 544, notes this oscillation, citing "an unusual blend of order and chaos in Quentin's section."

20 Just as the white desires the tabooed black servant, the black servant may experience what Eugene D. Genovese calls a "longing for the master, understood as absolute other": *The World the Slaveholders Made: Two Essays in Interpretation* (New York: Pantheon/Random House, 1974/1976), pp. 7–8.

21 See John T. Irwin, *Doubling and Incest/Repetition and Revenge: A Speculative Reading of Faulkner* (Baltimore: Johns Hopkins University Press, 1975). Irwin's elegant and "speculative" argument reads Quentin's dilemma as a futile "revenge" against the past which would suppress all memory of time, desire, and difference, missing in large part the racial and gender implications of Quentin's behavior. According to Irwin, Quentin takes "revenge" against the repetitious self-enclosures and incestuous pairings within the current and ancestral family line by reproducing them in his own, hermetic terms. But thé taboo against such merging reintroduces the differentiations of society into Quentin's conception. Each object of Quentin's desire reacquaints him with loss and impurity, even as he had hoped to banish these hindrances. Irwin suggests that Southern racial and sexual politics work by exploiting without resolving these tensions between "purity/endogamy/incest" on the one hand and "miscegenation/exogamy/intermarriage" on the other.

22 Brooks thinks that "Jason feels victimized," but Howe is closer in noticing "the numerous references to money that wind through the Jason section": Brooks, op. cit., p. 326; Howe, op. cit., p. 171. But they have less to do with money itself than with an entire monetary approach that treats others as exchange objects.

23 Jacques Derrida, *Margins of Philosophy*, trans., with additional notes, by Alan Bass (Chicago: University of Chicago Press, 1982); French title: *Marges de la philosophie* (Paris: Minuit, 1972).

24 Hyatt H. Waggoner, *William Faulkner: From Jefferson to the World* (Kentucky: University of Kentucky Press, 1959), p. 58; Michael Millgate, *The Achievement of William Faulkner* (London: Constable, 1966), p. 99; Brooks, op. cit., p. 325. For standard plot reconstructions, see George R. Stewart and Joseph M. Backus, "Each in its Ordered Place: Structure and Narrative in 'Benjy's Section' of *The Sound and the Fury*," *American Literature*, 29 (January 1958), pp. 440–56, and Edmund Volpe, *A Reader's Guide to William Faulkner* (New York: Farrar, Straus and Giroux, 1964), pp. 353–77.

25 Millgate, op. cit., p. 101; Arthur F. Kinney, *Faulkner's Narrative Poetics: Style as Vision* (Amherst: University of Massachusetts Press, 1978), p. 154; Waggoner, op. cit., p. 55; Joseph W. Reed, *Faulkner's Narrative* (New Haven: Yale University Press, 1973), p. 82; Matthews, op. cit., p. 106; and Walter J. Slatoff, *Quest for Failure: A Study of William Faulkner* (1960; Westport, Conn.: Greenwood Press, 1972), p. 155.

26 *As I Lay Dying*, as we shall see, repeats this originally Homeric interrelationship between the *bothros*, or "hollow," and black "otherness," "death," but also transcendence.

27 Kinney, op. cit., p. xv.

28 Howe, op. cit., p. 214.

29 Faulkner wrote to Malcolm Cowley: "It is my ambition to be, as a private individual, abolished and voided from history, leaving it markless, no refuse save the printed books": letter dated 11 February 1949, in William Faulkner, *Selected Letters of William Faulkner*, ed. Joseph Blotner (New York: Random House, 1977), p. 285. In his next novel, Faulkner will conceive of the narrative voice as Blanchot's "neuter."

30 André Bleikasten, *The Most Splendid Failure: Faulkner's* The Sound and the Fury (Bloomington: Indiana University Press, 1976), p. 205.

31 Ibid., pp. 205, 197, 199.

32 Richard Forrer, in "*Absalom, Absalom!*: Story-telling as a Mode of Transcendence," *The Southern Literary Journal*, 9, 1 (1976), voices the same hopes as Bleikasten, but, more plausibly, in a scene of conflict: the "collision" in *Absalom, Absalom!* between Henry and Charles. Here, "All distinctions between the present and the past virtually disappear, all barriers of culture, race, and class are temporarily suspended – or hurdled – while they imaginatively act out the inevitable collision between two unyielding wills" (p. 42).

33 Myra Jehlen is one of the few Faulkner critics who notices the paticularly *un*satisfactory "salvation" of the Dilsey section, which "is really no more redemptive than any other section." For her, *The Sound and the Fury* also implies that "there is no way out of history and time but in death": Myra Jehlen, *Class and Character in Faulkner's South* (New York: Columbia University Press, 1976), p. 44.

34 To one critic, Benjy, for instance, seems "an essentially timeless mind which contains thirty years of time": Richard P. Adams, *Faulkner: Myth and Motion* (Princeton: Princeton University Press, 1968), p. 239. For another, Benjy's "moment *is* eternal, always present, forever recallable": Waggoner, op. cit., p. 57. Benjy seems superior to others on the basis of this quality, and this critical mishandling has been applied to black characters as well. For many, Shegog's "rhetoric . . . succeeds partly because it . . . enables him to telescope time": Adams, op. cit., p. 227. Incredibly – but typically – one even encounters the sentiment that "to Dilsey, neither the past nor the future nor the present is oppressive, because to her they are all aspects of eternity, and her ultimate commitment is to eternity": Brooks, op. cit., p. 330. More blatantly, Douglas Messerli says, "Dilsey transcends time while Quentin seeks time's extinction. . . . Nowhere in the later novels, except perhaps in *A Fable*, does a character transcend time and space in the way in which Dilsey does": "The Problem of

Time in *The Sound and the Fury*: A Critical Reassessment and Reinterpretation," *The Southern Literary Journal*, 6, 2 (1974), pp. 23, 34.

35 Kinney (op. cit., p. 158) suggests that "the power of Shegog's Word – in a novel so concerned with the power of words – does not finally convert anyone previously unconverted. Everyone and everything return to what they were before." Millgate is equally unmoved: "the sense of human communion rapidly dissolves as [the blacks] move into the world of 'white folks' " (op. cit., p. 102).

36 Helen Swink has speculated on the possible influences of black oral narratives upon Faulkner's general written style in "William Faulkner: The Novelist as Oral Narrator," *The Georgia Review*, 26 (1971), p. 188.

3

As I Lay Dying (1930)

As I Lay Dying can be called a "test case" of narrative form, defying literary conventions of space, time, and narrative voice. There are fifteen narrators, each marked out by first names. Eight come from "the town" (Jefferson) or "the hamlet" (Frenchman's Bend); seven are members of the Bundren family, including one who is dead. The narration divides into fifty-nine segments told by the fifteen narrators, who seem at first not to be unified by any overarching voice. A description of what happens might be that we watch eight members of the town watching a rather bizarre family, even as we watch that family watching itself through the eyes of its seven members as they execute the last wish of the mother to be buried among her kinfolk in a family burial site forty miles away. It is literally a "family plot."

Commentators on *As I Lay Dying* who confine themselves to discussing the psyches of characters obey the silent command of a society that wants to efface its own violence. The thrust of criticism of this novel has been psychological, and has neglected the possible effects of society's demands upon any given "internal drama." Critical concentration upon "personality" in *The Sound and the Fury* and *As I Lay Dying* conceives a set of pre-existing types.[1] Quentin is "intellectual," "sensitive," "verbal"; Benjy is "sensual," "childlike," "innocent"; Jason is "egocentric," "sadistic." Darl is "the artist as visionary," "a poet of contemplation," "a lunatic ... who is thoroughly 'sane'"; Cash is "the artist as craftsman," "methodical," "dull"; Jewel is "Dionysiac," "impetuous," "suspicious," ".a poet of action"; Vardaman is "disturbed mentally," "sensitive," and so on. Yet, even if one takes these categories seriously, are they "innate"? Hardly: the "I" that is dying in the title is the "I" that is trying to liberate itself from various systematic wrongs.

Faulkner once said of *As I Lay Dying*: "If there is a villain in that story it's the convention in which people have to live."[2] Faulkner's fifth novel generates uncanny responses because it disguises its critique of convention within a harmless family yarn. *As I Lay Dying* continues Faulkner's inquiry into the interaction of language, society, and the family, whose tensions give the novel its pull. Figures of speech, sayings, and expressions hold people together in this text. But these figures also may pull people apart, barely managing to cover over the direst tensions of an economic, sexual, and racial sort. Supported by force, sayings create realities that persist, and what people say often becomes what people expect to hear.

Family plots and social classes

The Odyssey, Faulkner claims, was the source of his ambiguous title *As I Lay Dying*. The title comes from a Homeric scene rich with meditations on the exclusionary properties of discourse, even that of the dead. In Book XI, Odysseus heads for "the limits of the world" beyond the River Oceanus in order to contact the dead. For the dead, dying has only exacerbated the ancient male/female antinomy of Greek myth. Odysseus must expel the female spirits before listening to the males. The women's voices gone, the plaintive males can be heard. Foremost among them is Agamemnon, who speaks, dead, to the living wanderer. His wife Clytemnestra has murdered him, but has also neglected to do the fitting thing. The 1925 William

Marris Oxford translation, Faulkner's likely direct source,[3] reads:

> But in mine ears
> Most piteous rang the cry of Priam's daughter,
> Cassandra, whom the treacherous Clytemnestra
> Slew at my side, while I, *as I lay dying*
> Upon the sword, raised up my hands to smite her;
> And shamelessly *she turned away, and scorned*
> *To draw my eyelids down or close my mouth,*
> Though I was on the road to Hades' house.
>
> (XI, 421–6; my italics)

Clytemnestra has "scorned" to complete or to finish her husband. Agamemnon, in short, is bitter because he has no control over his own death and burial. It seems a clear answer that Faulkner's Addie gives, because she achieves after death a completion and control denied in her lifetime – she gives the family explicit orders for the burial of her corpse. Her posthumous narrative reaches backwards to control the historical account that contains it.

Unlike Theseus, Hercules, and Aeneas, Odysseus does not "descend" to the Underworld. Rather, Circe has told Odysseus to slaughter a "lamb and ewe" and to let "their black blood stream" into a pit. Odysseus first learns his destiny by emptying out blood into a shallow pit. The word for "shallow pit" here is *bothros*, meaning "a hole or pit dug in the ground," and the same word is used for the "hollow" by the river where Nausicaa washes her clothes in Book VI. So the Homeric space of the *bothros* affirms the merging of so-called opposites: emptiness/fullness; cleanliness/being soiled; death/life. One empties blood to attract bloodless ghosts; one washes garments so that they might become clean.[4] Immediately after Odysseus empties out blood into the *bothros*, a crowd of ghostly women approach: the dead come to *him* and, in the first instance, the dead are women. Odysseus must repel all women, including his mother, in order to converse with male heroes. In confronting death and female otherness, Odysseus sees here for the first time the opposite of "fullness" and "completion." The *bothros* tempers heroic bravado. Agamemnon's complaints about not being in total control seem ridiculous, given the futility of his dying defense against Clytemnestra: "I, as I lay dying upon the sword, raised up my hands to smite her."

Emptying and filling are crucial actions for Darl and Addie, as well. Faulkner's version differs from Homer's in that the Homeric dead speak by filling themselves with blood, whereas Darl, Addie, and Dewey Dell empty themselves, not of blood, but of words. Darl says:

> And when you are emptied for sleep, you are not. And when you are filled with sleep, you never were. I dont know what I am. I don't know if I am or not . . . sleep is is-not. . . . Addie Bundren will not be . . . if I am not emptied yet, I am *is*.[5]

Darl wants to be "emptied" of the "I am"; he seeks the viewpoint of an other, or even of all others. Addie, on the other hand, wants to find a place where she is neither "other" nor "mother": she wants to empty out her conventional behaviors. If Dewey Dell describes pregnancy in terms of "filling" (she decides to have sex with Lafe only after he has "filled her sack" with his cotton), Addie describes freedom of consciousness in terms of "emptying out."

Both Addie and Darl exemplify lost selfhood. They find freedom in places that designate loss, places outside conventional language, and even outside life. One may read Darl's puzzling statement about "emptying" in several ways: perhaps it manifests Darl's "neurosis", given that only mental illness could lead to such an unstable identity; perhaps it is a literary game wherein Faulkner experiments with syntax; possibly, given that in the excerpt Darl uses both the first and second person as a form of address, Darl means that the generalized "you" of society (as in "you never were") is quite different from the way people address themselves – "I" (as in "I dont know what I am"). The latter interpretation is the most likely. Darl's "neurosis" results from a split between what everyone else thinks "Darl" or "you" signifies and what Darl feels himself to be as "I." Vardaman also senses a severe disparity between what others call him (second and third person) and how he experiences himself (first person): "I am not anything. Dewey Dell comes to the hill and calls me. Vardaman. I am not anything. I am quiet. You, Vardaman" (55). Both young men seem vexed at a certain false self-understanding signified by the pronouns, names, and titles that they must bear. What seems difficult in reading the prose of the novel is the major characters' problem of self-definition. Darl and Vardaman, neither "lunatic" nor "mentally disturbed," cannot be glibly dismissed.

When the language of the self breaks down, then language in general might be inadequate. The reigning expectation for the relationship between language and society would commonly resemble Hobbes's seventeenth-century conception:

> But the most noble and profitable invention of all other, was that of *speech*, consisting of *names* or *appellations*, and their connection whereby men register their thoughts, recall them when they are past, and also declare them one to another for mutual utility and conversation; without which there had been amongst men neither commonwealth, nor society, nor contract, nor peace, no more than amongst lions, bears, and wolves.[6]

Yet, to the reader of *As I Lay Dying*, the act of speaking disconnects; to its characters, speech creates and ensures distance. The Bundrens are a family, but they are not relatives; they are a family not speaking the same tongue. The children neither expect nor receive badly needed advice from their parents. Jewel earns money for his horse by secret work; Dewey Dell is pregnant, but incompetently arranges for a clandestine abortion. Vardaman's obsessively repeated phrase "my mother is a fish," strange as it is, goes virtually unnoticed by his family. Language, memory, and other common carriers of tradition prove defective. The wife Addie dies in the beginning with two of her children miles away. In the end her husband Anse replaces his dead wife without so much as consulting the children on his choice. In *As I Lay Dying*, Hobbes's "mutual utility and conversation" seem fully out of the question. The myth of family unity breaks up: "the whole family is isolated from society by its mad journey, and individuals within the family are isolated from others in the family."[7]

The loss of communication it seems, has something to do with the family's exclusion from the community that surrounds them. In *As I Lay Dying* the failures of shared language appear as distortions in normal narrative relations and, most spectacularly, in the example of the corpse that speaks. Their "mad journey" does not unify, but rather makes a prior isolation explicit. The Bundrens' excommunication from the town is clear: residents of Mottstown and Jefferson stare at their poor clothes (despite Dewey Dell's attempts to look presentable) and the shoddy wagon; they are poor whites and country folk, dead to the town; their payload of death smells. The two things that separate the Bundrens and the town are, first, economic class; and, second, the thing that embodies division all too aptly: a stinking corpse. When sharable discourse no longer exists, things fall apart. Hobbes would say that without shared language we become animals, having "neither commonwealth, nor society, nor contract, nor peace." Yet commonwealth, in America, is not common wealth. The quasi-equality of a language that all share only covers over the lack of community. The idea of "community" appeals to the dream of "connections," yet community, as an ideal unit of purity, requires separations.[8] The "villain" here is "convention." Society, left to itself, critiques itself best. The fact that the upper classes have traditionally taken themselves as synecdoche for all classes in society as well as the proper conditions of their relations may derive from their control over the institutions which fund and formulate the coinage of linguistic authority. And here we have named the hidden villain of the family plot.

The *Oxford English Dictionary* defines "social" tautologically, as "living in companies, gregarious, not fitted for or not practising solitary life, interdependent, co-operative, practising division of labour. . . . Concerned with the mutual relations of men or classes of men." "Society" is a "social mode of life"; its secondary meanings are "the customs and organization of a civilized nation. . . . Any social community. . . . The upper classes of a community . . . fashionable and well-to-do and well-connected people . . . companionship, company." Society, because the infant is in the first instance outside of it, necessitates "socialization." The passage from child to adult entails, among other things, a journey from non-verbal to verbal forms of communication, aided by the child's first "society," the family. Along this journey, the child, through what the family teaches, learns society's main distinctions: language; gender; class; race.

Thus, birth itself becomes the implicit swearing of a series of oaths, of a series of group affiliations. . . . The baptism of newborn children (rather than of consenting adults) may serve as the symbol of this process which allows the newborn to join the larger group unities at once, to preserve the continuity of social institutions, to avoid the suspension of a "state of nature."[9]

These classifications tend to subsume uniqueness under competing, always generalized, orders of difference. Discovering which differences are important and which are not, the child becomes an adult after an inexorable pedagogy about exchange values. Yet the newborn cannot speak until adults pour on their categories of division, ones that remain in effect for the rest of the child's life. Only beyond the limits of language – a limit defined by death, in Addie's case – can the "pouring out" of truth begin; beyond the edge of the flat earth, Odysseus empties out sacrificial blood into the *bothros*, and only then do the dead begin to speak the truth.

Value arises in society through exchange and substitution. Addie and Anse master substitution, but, as would be expected, they are also its victims, although neither Anse nor Addie ever finds out. Anse never learns that Addie has emptied herself of his "sane" name.[10] She has replaced Anse's name with a white space, Reverend Whitfield ("white field"), the *tabula rasa* that has, amazingly, made her pregnant, and she has named the offspring of this blank coupling "Jewel." The "white field" – punning on the name of the usurping lover – is replaced on page 82 with the white space of Addie's coffin. Death, the "white field" of the diagrammed coffin, has replaced Whitfield (who had replaced Anse); here death has become (as Donne might suggest) the adulterer *par excellence*. Yet, as we shall see, substitutions also victimize Addie, for, even before her corpse has filled up its plot, an anonymous substitute woman fills up her wifely title of "Mrs", an irony Faulkner underscores by ending the novel with the empty title "Mrs Bundren." Society organizes its members mainly by placing them within figures and repeating the same alignments, hoping to flatten their uniqueness in the process.

Furthermore, repetition encourages this process by perpetuating an illusion of presence. The very concept of structure really means little more than repetition of typical configurations. Yet even a sense of change (increase or decrease) relies upon the contrast offered by exact repetition. Therefore, repetitions are much more frequent than language's seeming novelty or society's apparent alteration would indicate. Especially in the closely knit, oral tradition of Yoknapatawpha, "tales" are largely accumulations of agreed-upon verbal conventions. In the North and the South, the conventional sense of the real comes primarily not from reading law or scripture, but from a web of repeated verbal hearsay, gossip, anecdotes, jokes, and maxims – so-called "common" sense. The *raconteur*, and not the poet, may be the true "legislator" of mankind. Societal values are rarely explicit but more commonly result from repeated omissions – the withdrawal of value or attention from certain groups – or repeated juxtapositions: valuelessness by association.

Composing society: figures of repetition and exchange

There are at least three kinds of repetition in *As I Lay Dying*: exact repetition; ring structure; and incremental repetition. In each case, connotation has less import than reiterative rhythm. The only purpose is to repeat clichéd phrases so as to create an illusion of plausibility and universality. In them one almost hears society's command to omit *what should go without saying* and repeat *what everybody knows*. Here, language may be playing with itself, but society is also toying with the "free" will of the individual. These clichéd repetitions issue from and return to a pool of apparently static phrases without giving any sense whatsoever of conscious intervention in their utterance.

As I Lay Dying refuses to hide oral repetitions; the text foregrounds them and underlines the estrangement of speakers from their speech. Communication and community seem absent when the meaningless repetitions of common parlance are seen for what they are. Through repetitions, conventional discourse inside and outside the Bundren family weakens the very notions that it, by repetition, tries to reaffirm:

"If there was ever such an unfortunate man," pa says. . . .
". . . if there was ere a man in the living world suffered the trials and floutings I have suffered," . . . "God knows, if there

were ere a man," he says ... "I won't be beholden ..."
(Anse; 180–1)

You could do so much for me if you just would. If you just
knew ... you could do so much for me if you just would. ...
he could do so much for me if he just would. ... And he
could do so much for me. ... He could do everything for me.
... He could do everything for me if he just knowed it.
(Dewey Dell; 50, 56, 58, 61)

Darl is my brother ... I am. Darl is my brother. ... *Darl he*
went to Jackson is my brother Darl is my brother. ... *Darl is*
my brother. My brother is going to Jackson. ... My brother
... Darl is my brother. ... Darl he went to Jackson my
brother Darl. ... He went to Jackson. ... My brother is Darl.
He went to Jackson on the train ... Darl. Darl is my brother.
Darl. Darl. (Vardaman; 95, 239–42)

"She ought to taken them cakes anyway," Kate says. ...
"She ought to taken them," Kate says. ... "She ought to
taken those cakes," Kate says. (7, 9)

"I am bounding toward my God and my reward. ... I'm
bounding toward my God and my reward," Cora sung. (86–7)

"You aint going to take my mule into that water," I say. ...
"my mule aint going into that water," I say. ... "My mule
aint going into that water," I say. (Tull; 120)

"The Lord giveth," he says. ... "The Lord giveth," I say. ...
"The Lord giveth," we say. ... "The Lord giveth." (the
assembled men; 29, 81)

Do these repetitions reflect personal obsession or the playful-
ness of language, with words chasing words in an infinite loop
of false reference? Possibly not: much more can be glimpsed in
these examples of dispersed repetition. In the last example, we
see a group of men disseminating a saying. The stock phrase
becomes the "joint stock" of the company. The sequence here
retraces the way the child is "socialized," or learns to use
words like an adult: the young "I" hears what "he says,"
repeats it is "I say," until at last society is sharing what "we
say," but that sharing, and not the content of the utterance,
is the true point. Although repetitions strengthen group

consensus, they call into question the referentiality of their message.

The last example documents how repetition of absence creates not absence but a "present" omission. The change from the biblical "the Lord giveth and the Lord taketh away" to "the Lord giveth" shows how the repeating and reducing of figures aims to replace a balanced maxim with a onesided précis. Here, the omission, not the utterance, is performative.[11] The shortened version pretends there is no "taketh away" and no "death." The omission can be known only by the initiate, who has no interest in restoring the absent phrase, since the paralepsis exactly defines his membership in the group. The complete phrase becomes, through repeated censorship, the partial phrase that leaves no evidence that it has been cropped. Death does not exist unless one already knows the complete phrase. The truncated maxim recirculates a static oratory by perpetuating its willed omissions. Future speakers will take "the Lord giveth" as a queer phrase to use of death, but will use it anyway, despite the seemingly total absence of the death that provoked its utterance.

In ring composition, something seems to speak *through* a person. Ring structures balance the first term equally with the recapitulation. One might see ring composition as an elliptical figure that deviates and returns:

> *Jewel, I say.* Overhead the day drives level and gray. ... Jewel, I say. ... Jewel, I say, she is dead, Jewel, Addie Bundren is dead. "It's not your horse that's dead, Jewel," I say. ... "But it's not your horse that's dead." (Darl; 48, 51, 88)

> Addie: And so I took Anse.
> Anse: "That's what I come to see you about."
> Anse: "That's what I come to see you about."
> Addie: So I took Anse. (162–3)

In the last example, Anse's repetitions are confined within Addie's entrapment ("So I took Anse"). The figuration of the utterance actually does linguistically what it denotes physically. Instead of an engagement symbolized by the bond of the wedding ring, we have a binding ring structure, Addie trapping Anse with her repetitive prose even as Anse thinks he has trapped her with his. Ring composition illustrates that words do not add up to profit for the Bundrens and their society. Language alone will not bring about the end of social division and lead to better communication, where arrangement is more important than reference.[12]

"Faulkner's vision of the world can be compared to that of a man sitting in a convertible looking back" reads Sartre's famous formulation.[13] This rearward view entails a kind of retrograde movement that brings about a text marked by frequent instances of repetition and reversal:

> Motionless, the tall buzzards hang in soaring circles, the clouds giving them an illusion of retrograde. . . . He lifts his head and looks at the sky. High against it they hang in narrowing circles, like the smoke, with an outward semblance of form and purpose, but with no inference of motion, progress or retrograde.(89, 216).

The twin concepts of profit and progress die fittingly here, supervised by the circlings of hungry buzzards. Even their numerical increase connotes only their greater hope for human decay:

> Now there are seven of them, in little tall black circles. . . .
> Now there are nine of them, tall in little black circles. . . .
> Now there are ten of them, tall in little tall black circles in the sky. . . . Now there are five of them, tall in little tall black circles . . . (185–7, 200)

> the fan still moving like it has for ten days . . . the fan in one hand still beating with expiring breath into the quilt . . . the clutched fan now motionless on the fading quilt . . . (47–9)

The buzzards, smelling death but seeing no carrion, depart. As Dewey Dell's fan in the last example expires, Addie is dying. Repetition is not an aid to better understanding, but merely formulates society's decadent communal figures. Apparent increases become decay and death in this tropic world.[14]

Repetition also positions human beings as items in large-scale figures of exchange: "If the exchange form is the standard social structure, its rationality constitutes people; what they are for themselves, what they seem to be themselves, is secondary."[15] Exchange trades one entity for another, but one never receives the same thing. Even when one dollar bill is exchanged for another one, the second bill will be different in some way – crumpled, dirty, tattered – but the exchange value set by convention remains the same. In exchanging, say, German marks for dollars, one goes to a market where conventions of their exchange are acknowledged. Conventional monetary exchanges occur along a sliding scale, which is set by what we call "market forces." Exchange is both equal and unequal in social and economic orders. Faulkner begins an investigation here which *The Hamlet* will perfect – an inquiry into exchange as a possibly levelling but nevertheless mandatory element of social, linguistic, and economic systems.

In *As I Lay Dying*, the "marketplace" becomes efficient through verbal currencies: Yoknapatawpha's conventions reveal the desire to set for once and for all a "gold standard" of human intercourse, a "fixed rate of exchange" which would flatten all the objects that it handles. Fiction is a perfect site for dissecting such exchange rubrics. The novel can nourish an "experimental culture," even in the sense of bacterial "culture"; for the novel is a kind of beaker, retort, or petri dish where one can test and magnify those exchanges of value that remain largely latent or undiscovered by the less curious.

Community's coinages of market value change hands again and again in the novel. Signifiers pass into swift and indiscriminate circulation. Fixed identities dissolve: the "Bundrens" repeatedly call themselves or are called "burdens"; the town "Mottson" may be called "Mottstown"; Dewey Dell's boyfriend is "Lafe," and her father's twin brother is "Rafe"; Vardaman's "mother" is a "fish," sharing with the fish an exchange of absence for presence: "then it [the fish] wasn't and she [the mother] was, and now it is and she wasn't" (63). Even as Vardaman replaces his dead mother Addie with a fish, Anse replaces her with a new wife. Jewel has already replaced her with a new horse. He has worked all night in order to buy the horse (Cash thinks Jewel is seeing a girl). Addie is not blind to her devaluation: "she cried hard"; she knows she has been exchanged. She gets revenge in the same currency after her death; the ten dollars Lafe gives Dewey Dell for an abortion is the very currency that Anse appropriates to procure his new wife; Jewel must sell his horse in order to buy the mules that will get Addie's body across the river – in other words, he loses the horse that replaced Addie's living love in order to bury her dead corpse. Darl grasps the substitution: "Jewel's mother is a horse."

Alive, Addie speaks on three separate occasions. In the first, she calls out "You, Cash" (45, 47). The "you" could be anyone; "Cash" tries to remove the confusion, but only renders more troubling the referent of "you." The two other cases both concern exchanges. In the first of these, Addie says to Cora that "he will save me from the water and from the fire. Even though I have laid down my life, he will save me" (160). Cora is astonished, as she should be, because she realizes that Addie's "he" is not "He." Cora realizes for the first time that even God can be exchanged. The capital "H" of "He" would have eliminated Addie's blasphemy. But capitalization remains a convention only of writing. Threatened censure eliminates that ambiguity in spoken language, but Addie is beyond these threats: "Then I realised that she did not mean God. . . . She had closed her heart to God and set that selfish mortal boy in His place." Jewel actually does save Addie's body "from the water and from the fire" after she has "laid down" her life (in the barn-burning scene). Cora cannot know this meaning. Addie's words simply shock her. Were she speaking to a man, Addie might have been physically rebuked for replacing God with her own son. Cora resorts to a less violent action: "I went down on my knees right there." Addie's deliction is punished not by words, but by the repetition of violence or some ritualistic act: "I begged her to kneel and open her heart and cast from it the devil. . . . Kneeling there, I prayed for her. I prayed for that poor blind woman as I had never prayed for me and mine." But Addie has been either improperly trained or trained too well; Cora's appeals do not reach her – "She just sat there."

Addie has replaced God with Jewel, but Jewel turns around to replace Addie with a horse. Her reaction to his exchange is the third instance of her "living" speech:

> "Jewel," ma said, "Jewel . . . Jewel," ma said. "Jewel . . . "
> Then she said: "You come right to the house and go to bed
> . . . Jewel," ma said, looking at him. "I'll give – I'll give . . .
> give . . ." Then she began to cry. (128)

Addie is still an "exchange" item, even where she wishes to be most herself. Jewel's impersonal handling may relieve her of some personal responsibility, but only at the cost of killing off her unique, irreplaceable "I." Seeing Addie's tears, Darl says, "And then I knew that I knew" (129). Darl knows from Addie's tears what no one yet suspects: Jewel is the progeny of her adultery with Whitfield. She cries all night. "I'll give – I'll give . . . give," she says. Yet she is no longer an "I" to Jewel; she is a "thing" whose "I" can no longer "give" anyone anything.

Darl and Addie explore the two crucial stress-points of any grammar: the pronoun "I" and the verb "to be." They most desperately seek value here at the "heart" of language, but instead find lacks. The verb "to be" can mean either "to exist, occur, live," or "to coincide in identity with, amount to, cost, signify." These by no means agree; indeed, they oppose: "to be" versus "to signify"; intrinsic versus social value. Faulkner seems bent on probing every possible meaning and tense of "to be" here (as in Charles Bon's letter in chapter 4 of *Absalom, Absalom!*, in the first words of chapter 6 of *Light in August*, and in various other passages in his works). In all these cases, Faulkner seems to question any casual use of this most ambiguous verb. "To be," according to one definition, means that Darl exists: "Darl is." Another asserts his social predication: "*Darl is my brother.*" "Is" poses the question whether a sentence imitates or distorts what it modifies. "Is" centers both possibilities in one word, yet ultimately it is impossible to determine which possibility pertains. The question is temporal and spatial: is "to be" prior to (temporal) or outside of (spatial) social predication? Can one escape, after the fact, the corrosive baptism of society?

Addie has a role, not a room, of her own. As a woman she seems a rare dissident from her friends' protection racket. One way of escaping might be an Odyssean emptying. Addie's father – and possibly other males – have bequeathed to her corrupt utterances such as "the reason for living is to get ready to stay dead for a long time" (161). In her husband's name, "Anse," Addie deposits all the deceitful voices she wants to forget:

I would think about his name until after a while I could see the word as a shape, a vessel, and I would watch him liquefy and flow into it like cold molasses flowing out of the darkness into the vessel, until the jar stood full and motionless: a significant shape profoundly without life like an empty door frame; and then I would find that I had forgotten the name of the jar. (165)

The name of the husband signifies no life; it is a fullness that kills the wife, whereas the empty *bothros* brings the truth of death to the husband, Odysseus. Addie's oppression by the "name of the husband" exquisitely illustrates Jacques Lacan's notion of the "Name of the Father," "the symbolic function which, from the dawn of history, has identified [the father's] person with the figure of the law."[16] For Addie, "emptying" means to hear her own name and not "sane-Anse" language.

Dewey Dell lies down for sleep in order to feel empty:

When I used to sleep with Vardaman I had a nightmare once I thought I was awake but I couldn't see and couldn't feel I couldn't feel the bed under me and I couldn't think what I was I couldn't think of my name I couldn't even think I am a girl I couldn't even think I nor even think I want to wake up nor remember what was opposite to awake. (115)

Dewey Dell's sleep frees her of *nous* in all its forms – gender ("I couldn't even think I am a girl"), titles ("I couldn't think of my name"), and classificatory logic itself ("nor remember what was opposite to awake").[17] One never finds any collectivity beyond the normative "I." The best Addie, Darl, or Dewey Dell can hope for is the "not-I," pictured here by acts of public madness or private death. Yet the gap that allows these characters to absent themselves from society is still not a completion of a whole or prior state; it is a suspension. They experience the pronoun "I" as restriction rather than redemption.

The conventional link between the pronoun "I" and the person who utters it is more problematic than grammar would imply. "I" belongs to the verbal category called the "shifter," which includes such pronouns as "I," "you," "he," "she," or "it" that seem fairly well defined in context. Shifters are precisely those words that "cannot be defined without reference to the message."[18] In a spoken context, a pointed index finger can usually identify a pronoun referent (although Darl and Addie might question this assertion). In written texts, however, an author must specify referents, or else shifters mean little or nothing.[19] Hence, if the pronoun "I" is uncertain without a speaker present, then it denotes nothing more certainly than any other word does. The faults of the social context then become the weakness of the word. We cannot know an "I" unless the speaker can be placed in a larger context, since a pronoun is "a word used instead of a (proper or other) noun to designate a person or thing already mentioned or known from context." Hence, there is no extra-contextual "I" except as a written self-designation. Darl and Addie realize sooner than most people that "I" serves a linguistic compulsion to reduce uniqueness to generality. Society constructs the "I": any selfhood beyond the verbal function exists, if at all, within non-linguistic, "empty" moments such as sleep and death. The title *As I Lay Dying* poses the question "Who is that 'I' that is dying?" There are at least fifteen candidates, but none that any context identifies for certain. Although Joyce's "Wandering Rocks" may have suggested the idea of Faulkner's sections, Joyce preserves third-person, omniscient control, whereas Faulkner's dispersed first-person monologues seem to lack all sense of linkage or overview. In this respect, the title already names the central theme of the novel: how identity relies on context alone, and how that context, in society or in the sentence, is highly questionable.

Darl: the multiple "I"

Under most definitions, Darl's wish to diffuse his lonely "I" into an omnisentient consciousness is "mad." If the strangely callous Bundren family is "sane," then perhaps Cleanth Brooks is correct to say that "Darl, the lunatic, is indeed the only one of the three older brothers who is thoroughly 'sane.'"[20] Whatever the case, Darl's dilemma recalls Quentin's desire for the dissolution of his "I" in death (recall that, just before committing suicide, Quentin says *"Non fui. Sum. Fui. Nom sum.* . . . I was. I am not. . . . I am . . . I am not"; 216). Darl's consciousness, which perceives all persons, makes him a sort of ideal narrator, and explains why his perspective dominates from the novel's first words:

> Jewel and I come up from the field, following the path in single file. Although I am fifteen feet ahead of him, anyone watching us from the cottonhouse can see Jewel's frayed and broken straw hat a full head above my own. . . . *Jewel, fifteen feet behind me, looking straight ahead*, steps in a single stride through the window. Still *staring straight ahead*, his pale eyes like wood set into his wooden face, he crosses the floor in four srides with the rigid gravity of a cigar store Indian dressed in patched overalls and endued with life from the hips down, and steps in a single stride through the opposite window and into the path again just as I come around the corner.
>
> In single file and five feet apart and *Jewel now in front*, we go on up the path. (3–4; my italics)

Remarkably, Darl can see Jewel "staring straight ahead," even though Jewel is *behind* him. The quick change of physical position from Jewel–Darl to Darl–Jewel configures the mental exchanges Darl seems to achieve.

In the end, Darl's family is able to imprison him because he does not intuit their scheme; he lacks the omniscience he has earlier possessed:

> So Darl set still and we went on, with Jewel squatting on the tail-gate, watching the back of Darl's head. . . . He set that way all the time we was in front of Mrs Bundren's house, hearing the music, *watching the back of Darl's head with them hard white eyes of hisn*. (225; my italics)

Now the Jewel–Darl configuration of the first scene repeats with a difference. Earlier Darl had sensed Jewel's "pale eyes like wood" behind his head, whereas this time Darl cannot see Jewel's angered eyes behind him, "them hard white eyes of hisn." Darl has lost his omniscient clairvoyance. Prior to this point, Darl has been able to keep his family perplexed while keeping us informed and himself forewarned. Darl should know of the plot against him, just as he should know that Anse intends to get a new wife. His failure of omniscient empathy signals his ruin. His ruin, more immediately, results from his mad act of arson. Perhaps it is fitting that the super-pragmatic

Cash takes over from the visionary Darl, as the family moves
from candor to common sense as its preferred narrational tone.
In Max Horkheimer's words, "Suspicion of madness is the
unperishable source of persecution. It originates from distrust
of one's own pragmatic reason."[21] The "pragmatist" Cash
seems to take on Darl's lost clairvoyance, and hence replaces
him as the family's spokesman. Cash witnesses the Jewel–Darl
configuration as quoted above. "He set that way all the time
we was in front of Mrs Bundren's house, hearing the music,
watching the back of Darl's head with them hard white eyes of
hisn." The startling crux of this passage – one that has hardly
been commented upon – is that Cash here calls it "Mrs
Bundren's house," even though neither family nor reader yet
knows that Anse is here interring the old "Mrs Bundren" with
a spade borrowed in this scene from the soon-to-be Mrs
Bundren. Anse has expressed a wish for "new teeth," but not
yet for a "new wife." So if Cash can think "Mrs Bundren's
house," then he enjoys a prescience that Darl has, for whatever
reason, lost.

The transfer of narrative privilege from Darl to Cash leads us
to search for a narrator. One must choose between Darl, Addie,
and Cash, but we never know which of the three is trustworthy.
Without Darl's voice the novel funnels out into an uncertain
ending – is it tragic or comic? Hence the confusion among
critics about whether the novel has a moral.[22] Cash's "last
word" reinters the problems of a personal and linguistic nature
that Darl has dug up. His final moral represents only a rather
glib endorsement of public opinion:

> Sometimes I think it aint none of us pure crazy and aint none
> of us pure sane until the balance of us talk him that-a-way.
> It's like it aint so much what a fellow does, but it's the way
> the majority of folks is looking at him when he does it. (223)

If Cash does represent the "moral or ethical center," then his
attainment of narrative authority is a backward leap from the
abyss, a pattern of artificial redemption not uncommon
elsewhere in Faulkner. We shall examine other such "happy"
endings: the humorous escape from the hell of *Light in August*,
Shreve's flip apocalpyse at the end of *Absalom, Absalom!* – we
have already noted the ephemeral soteriology of the ending of
The Sound and the Fury. There is both a self-protection and a

self-ironization in this reflex, and perhaps the goal is to undermine the viewpoint even of a narrator – Darl – hostile to unitary viewpoints, for at the end of the novel Darl's mistrust of the single viewpoint itself seems untrustworthy.

Darl, as a narrative amalgam of several viewpoints, performs a dangerous narrative experiment, and the final result is failure. Vernon Tull says of him (but also of the very work of omniscient narrators): "It's like he had got into the inside of you, someway. Like somehow you was looking at yourself and your doings outen his eyes" (119). Darl's consciousness at times transcends perceptual limitations of the "eye" or "I" trapped in time and space. If, as Faulkner often claimed, *As I Lay Dying* proves that viewpoints both collide and collude to create satisfactory narrative, then Darl's fate is particularly harsh and troubling. The omniscient voice here is not any centric "voice of society" who narrates; Darl's and Addie's centrality to the narration only underscores their marginality to society. Indeed, their fates call into question the value of their attempts, not to become part of a fragmented community, but to integrate communal words within their minds.

At the beginning of the novel, a succession of viewpoints rather than a single one allowed us to trust the logic of sequence alone. The transfer of narrative focus from Benjy to Quentin to Jason to an omniscient narrator in *The Sound and the Fury* serves a similar aim. The river-crossing scene, for example, is a virtual narrative relay race; the narration describes a river-crossing and visualizes the crossing from different "I"s, each of which imagines what it would look like to be seen by the others. The river-crossing scene gives a visual equivalent of the "voice" of narrative that speaks through several discrete points of view (Darl, Vardaman, Tull). This voice mixes three "I"s: the "I" of the reader; the implied "I" of the author; and the "I" of the narrated characters. In each case, the individual "I" feels itself to be robust, although it is actually merging with the others at the textual "crossing" that the river here denotes, becoming more credible even as it becomes more empty and less specific. Darl would like to be disembodied, narrating from all possible positions. His "I" would be the nexus where all parties to reading would merge. Indeed, if we work through the scene of Homer's ghostly "as I lay dying," in which an empty ghost narrates, disembodied, we can discern the aptness of the Homeric image for Faulkner's narrative of consciousness. Narrative is by nature a *bothros*, or pit, that attracts the "speaking dead" who are both dead and living – Hadean ghosts, to be sure, but also joined in a spectral text that centers the reading act, enclosing authors dead and dying with living readers, all within a work that will outlast author and reader. The "I" is the place in the "pit" of narrative that attracts the individuals for whom it is constructed.

Darl suggests that "It takes two people to make you and one to die. That's how the world is going to end" (38). This is in any case how Darl himself "ends." He tries to re-create alone what should require at least "two people," so that his "I" becomes its own concourse and terminal. Darl may be what several critics have called him – "inhuman" or "anti-social" – but it seems clear that by the end of the novel we are meant to have taken Darl's fate as an allegory for how "it takes one [mind] to die." Darl, escaping the socially defined "I," tries to think his way into many viewpoints, but merely ends up back in the solipsism of the "I," incorporating all grammatical persons into the "one" and not the "many":

> Darl has gone Jackson. They put him on the train. . . . Darl had a little spy-glass he got in France at the war. In it it had a woman and a pig with two backs and no face. I know what that is. "Is that why you are laughing, Darl?"
> "Yes yes yes yes yes yes."
> Darl is our brother, our brother Darl. Our brother Darl in a cage in Jackson where, his grimed hands lying light in the quiet interstices. . . . "Yes yes yes yes yes yes yes yes."
> (243–4)

In this example, Darl has collapsed the speech circuit, and no longer has an addressee. Darl has become not only "I" but also "you" and "him." He is literally "feeding back," in the manner of a microphone or camera recycling its own output in eerie repetitions. He has not lost his identity, as some have claimed, but simply will not have his place taken by any one pronoun. Vardaman also rebels against being "shifted" by particular pronouns:

> I am not crying now. I am not anything. Dewey Dell comes to the hill and calls me. Vardaman. I am not anything. I am

quiet. You, Vardaman. I can cry quiet now, feeling and hearing my tears. (55)

Despite all the striving to escape pronoun, name, and definition, the search is futile: no matter how much Darl, Addie, and Vardaman try to escape names, their sections have their names as titles.

These considerations should reveal *As I Lay Dying* as an inquest into the source of "voice" in narrative. For finally the novel poses one unanswerable question: who is speaking the "I"? Hence the banal, though common, criticism of the novel's diction – that its poor white sharecroppers do not speak like themselves, but with words that are too long, suspiciously like Faulkner's – can be put to rest.[23] The so-called "inconsistent" uses of dialect in *As I Lay Dying* suggest that Faulkner's project resembles Darl's in a less radical way. Asserting narrative verisimilitude, Mark Twain explicitly differentiates between several classes of dialect in the prologue to *The Adventures of Huckleberry Finn*. Opposed to this practice, Faulkner's tone approximates the act of reading, and not exclusively any landscape "out there." Recordings of Faulkner reading from *As I Lay Dying* show that, whether reading neutral descriptions or the voices of characters, he keeps his tone utterly flat, ignoring diacritical marks, including quotations marks and italics. Reading, for him, is not representation – except of the act of reading. *As I Lay Dying*, Faulkner's first experiment in multiple perspectives, employs a ubiquitous voice while feigning written separation of characters.

The conflation of the various "I"s has led to severe confusions. Many readers have attempted to diagnose Darl's and Addie's language as "pathological" or "schizoid." Indeed, some specialists have even produced diagnoses of Darl, Addie, Vardaman, and Dewey Dell, together with full-scale critiques of Faulkner's psychoanalytic acumen![24] We should recognize that the narrative voice here proposes, as an alternative to Darl and Addie, a possible way (short of death or madness) for a writer, and even a reader, to escape the prison-house of language: the text, as "vessel," fills up with the "not-I" and the "dead I," both still preferable, for now, to the socially recognizable "I."

Addie: the empty "I"

But linguistic segregation and not narratological integration is the lot of Faulkner's most lonely "I"s. There are at least three kinds of verbal "separation" in *As I Lay Dying*: the dialects separating the poor white Bundrens from the town; the hermetic references that only the family grasps (such as the name "Jewel," which designates Jewel as his mother's favorite); and idiolects that characters such as Darl and Vardaman use to sketch out a quasi-magical reality. The self becomes lost in language, even in speaking. Addie wants to escape the anterior, ready-made classifications of gender, pronoun, and name, even if through dying. Addie, of course, does not willingly die or commit suicide (even if the cause and moment of her death are curiously absent), yet her "dying" detaches her speech from the false normalcies of a society that "is the villain."[25] Women, generally, voice the most trenchant complaints about this state of things. "What all the female characters in the novel have in common is that each is *used*": one may apply this statement to almost every one of Faulkner's women characters, but Addie may be an exemplary figure.[26]

Darl would appear to be an exception to the idea that women intuit sooner than men the death of the "I." But Darl, like Quentin Compson in *The Sound and the Fury*, deviates from common definitions of manliness. In fact, one critic contrasts "the femininity of Darl" with "Jewel's fierce masculinity."[27] Both Darl and Addie, for different reasons, have rejected a societal baptism into glib divisions and behaviors. Both, in consequence, spend their lives alone. Cora mentions "Addie Bundren, dying alone" (22), even though she died with most of her family around her. Cora and the other women live by false clichés of "community," "intimacy," and even "love." But society, which compartmentalizes by nature (and by calling compartmentalization "natural"), tries to validate community, not by creating it, but by repeating the word "community." Such empty repetition makes the words' and community's decrepitude all the more blatant.

Rachel rarely complains, but when she does she complains about men: "I just wish that you and him and all the men in the world that torture us alive and flout us dead, dragging us up and down the country . . ." Rachel wants to fill the gap, probably wishing "that you and him and all the men in the world" would "drop dead" – a sentiment worthy of Clytemnestra – but she fearfully or tactfully omits her wish. Addie is not alone among Faulkner's women in suffering from "loneliness" – not just the effects of language, which men delude themselves into thinking they can master, but also the additional separations of society wherein women, as we have seen, are to "mind the house, the garden, and ourselves." The young Addie believes she can overcome loneliness by relying on men and family, but later lampoons these conventions of marriage and happiness: her wedding dress is her cerement; her marriage has been a living death. For attaining wholeness in a world of other selves is impossible: "In any case, man cannot aim at being whole . . . while ever the play of displacement and condensation to which he is doomed in the exercise of his functions marks his relation as a subject to the signifier." A doubled isolation rather than innate neurosis may be the source of Addie's "aloneness." The "chronic and original state of self-insufficiency" that afflicts the psyche deepens in the case of women. "The subject, through his relations with the signifier, is a subject-with-holes," but the holes must be, and usually are, filled with something.[28]

In Addie's case, the filler consists of the name of the husband, as we have seen, but also words: "Love . . . pride or fear. . . . I realised that I had been tricked by words" (164). These abstract words, like personal pronouns and names, have done nothing to eliminate her loneliness:

> He had a word, too. Love, he called it. But I had been used to words for a long time. I knew that that word was like the others: just a shape to fill a lack; that when the right time came, you wouldn't need a word for that anymore than for pride or fear. Cash did not need to say it to me nor I to him, and I would say, Let Anse use it, if he wants to. So that it was *Anse or love; love or Anse*: it didn't matter.
>
> I would think that even while I lay with him in the dark and Cash asleep in the cradle within the swing of my hand. I would think that if he were to wake and cry, I would suckle him, too. *Anse or love*: it didn't matter. My aloneness had been *violated* and then made whole again by the *violation*: time, *Anse, love*, what you will, outside the circle. (164; my italics)

Addie "violates" figures of authority by revealing them as purely rhetorical. She can rearrange them, thus undermining the previous direction of their intent ("Anse or love; love or Anse. . . . Anse or love. . . . violated . . . violation . . . Anse, love"). She goes "outside the circle" and finds her life.[29] Addie, "outside the circle," suspends society's symbolic triangulations of self and desire, and defeats the attempt to encase the world in narcissistic dimensions.

As I Lay Dying recaptures a sense of the real by the figure of litotes, or "double negation." Litotes pretends to enact positivity by negating negatives. Any double negative invents a purely psychological satisfaction, compiling a condition without fulfilling it. Addie's desire to be "made whole again by the violation" turns not on actual wholeness, but (as in Quentin's "unvirgin" in *The Sound and the Fury*) on the lack of the lack that makes the real.

> But then I realised that I had been tricked by words older than Anse or love, and that the same word had tricked Anse too, and that my revenge would be that he would never know I was taking revenge.
>
> Sometimes I would lie by him in the dark, hearing the land that was now of my blood and flesh, and I would think: Anse. Why Anse. Why are you Anse. I would think about his name until after a while I could see the word as a shape, a vessel, and I would watch him liquefy and flow into it like cold molasses flowing out of the darkness into the vessel, until the jar stood full and motionless: a significant shape profoundly without life like an empty door frame; and then I would find that I had forgotten the name of the jar. I would think: The shape of my body where I used to be a virgin is in the shape of a   and I couldn't think *Anse*, couldn't remember *Anse*. It was not that I could think of myself as no longer unvirgin, because I was three now. And when I would think *Cash* and *Darl* that way until their names would die and solidify into a shape and then fade away, I would say, All right. It doesn't matter. It doesn't matter what they call them. (164–5)

Addie, "emptying out," embraces the lack. She does not pretend that "love" has made her whole. "Violation" is inevitable in life. But the remnant – her insight and her violation – is hers. Women have the opportunity to understand better than men the real violations of language and society. Even if many do not, that is their privilege.[30] Addie has discovered how to manipulate the powerful tropes of reversal ("revenge") and multiple negation ("no longer unvirgin") to her own ends. As she says, "my revenge would be that he would never know I was taking revenge."

Addie may even see that her genitals, which first "mark" her, may allow a clever reversal. They are the means whereby society has marked her, but they represent an absence: "the shape of my body where I used to be a virgin is in the shape of a   ." Convention and custom violate and impregnate women with the sign of "absence," opposed to male "presence." So the mark, the writing of Addie's female gender, the "shape of a   ," is absence for males. This paradox, an absence that is the presence of otherness and gender, appears here as a white space, even as black skin is the presence that denotes societal absence – otherness and racial difference.

Nietzsche's aphorism, "Not that you lied to me, but that I no longer believe you, has shaken me" (*Beyond Good and Evil*, 93), well describes Addie's discovery of violation. The lack of the word, the white space, annihilates the name of the husband: "I couldn't think *Anse*, couldn't remember *Anse*." Addie no longer tolerates deceit in words or names – she empties out the name, yet the male name tolerates no spaces. Addie's insights are radical, but private; Anse never hears them. He maintains his illusory independence: "I wouldn't be beholden to no man." Addie has, here as in the beginning, let Anse believe in his dominance:

And then he died. He did not know he was dead. I would lie by him in the dark ... hearing the dark voicelessness in which the words are the deeds, and the other words that are not deeds, that are just the gaps in peoples' lacks. ... I believed that I had found it. I believed that the reason was the duty to the alive, to the terrible blood, the red bitter flood boiling through the land. I would think of sin as I would think of the clothes we both wore in the world's face. (166)

Addie feels "the duty to the alive, to the terrible blood," not to lie. This compulsion also gives her a kind of freedom: she withdraws from Anse sexually and has an affair with Reverend

Whitfield, whose "illegitimate" child is Jewel. Before she dies, she sentences the family to a long ordeal: they must act out her last "will" to the letter. Anse knows her last will, but not her former deeds. Even were he to do so, they would be sins for men, but not for her; for Addie, conventional moral standards are as much a matter of custom as a woman wearing a wedding dress to a marriage – they are "the clothes we both wore in the world's face." When she dies, she has increased, paradoxically, her freedom – she loses, for instance, her confining gender; now Darl and others no longer refer to Addie as "her" but as "it": "It's laying there, watching Cash whittle" (18).

"It was not that I could think of myself as no longer unvirgin": Addie no longer merely uses litotes, or *double* negative, but actually now *triples* the negative. "No longer unvirgin" uses a double negative to suggest a return to a purity already lost. Yet one could suggest that the very terminology of gender division which precedes physical violation already constitutes a kind of rhetorical violence; the opposition "virgin/unvirgin" already posits the existence of "male/female" division. Addie cannot be pure even through litotes: the trope of the "no longer unvirgin" has also failed to satisfy. The limits on her purity are not physical but linguistic. It was not that Addie could think of the state of being "no longer unvirgin, because I was three now." Purity, oneness, lack of division: all cease as soon as the child learns of gender. Dead, Addie can sing with Shelley – and no less perversely – "No more let life divide what Death can join together." Living, Addie battles against imposed divisions by explicating linguistic "nots" ("not-Anse"). In rare moments of rebellion, when her sons' "names would die and solidify into a shape and then fade away, I would say, All right. It doesn't matter. It doesn't matter what they call them."

In this way Jewel, Whitfield, Addie, and Anse construct a circle of lies that underlies the novel. We have already followed the plot of fraud and trade between Jewel, his horse, and Addie. There is an even more complex knot of deceit between Whitfield, Addie, and Anse. Addie says: "Then I would lay with Anse again – I did not lie to him: I just refused. . . . Then I found I had Jewel" (167). Addie's final refusal to lie, like all double negatives, does not actually introduce a positive term. She does not lie to Anse, but she also does not tell him the truth; she does not deny that she has slept with Reverend Whitfield – but she also does not tell him that she has. She simply stops having sex with him: "I just refused." The birth of her child, Jewel, gives the lie to society and its language of deceit. Whitfield refers to Jewel as "a living lie" (169), but perhaps "living lie" is already a pleonasm: to live is to lie. Whitfield gets it wrong here. Jewel appears, and Jewel lives, not a "lie," but the living truth, for Jewel's father is "not-Anse."

Whitfield has Addie's word "that she would never tell . . . the tale of mine and her transgression," but that word is a lie. She has given her word that the truth will never "come from her lips." She does "keep her word" to Whitfield: she "restrained the tale from her dying lips as she lay surrounded by those who loved and trusted her". Yet, despite her vow of silence, Addie tells the tale in a posthumous monologue; she keeps her word, yet gives it away to everyone. Perhaps this is one aspect of the text's wit: Addie, even as she "lies" dead, "lies" with the truth.

Anse has given Addie his "promised word in the presence of the Lord" to transport her body to Jefferson, but he also breaks his word. The truth of Anse's "word" remains concealed until the ending of the novel, and perhaps this cover-up is what is comic about the novel: "the truth of the subject, even when he is in the position of master, does not reside in himself, but . . . in an object that is, of its nature, concealed . . . to bring this object out into the light of day is really and truly the essence of comedy."[31] Anse, in telling everyone that he is determined to get "his wife buried" (107), is neither lying nor telling quite the whole truth. Anse's word, like Addie's, is both given and kept. The lie is in the omission. Anse, like Addie, fails to mention other goals: the teeth, the gramophone, and the wife whose new name, "Mrs Bundren," ends the novel. So Addie and her ring of admirers – Anse, Whitfield, and Jewel – all keep the "words" they give, but also break them. It becomes apparent that the novel largely concerns the potential deceit in any giving of words. For Addie, deception brackets life and death. Darl says, "It was as though, so long as the deceit ran along quiet and monotonous, all of us let ourselves be deceived, abetting it unawares or maybe through cowardice" (127). Addie's life and death confirm this insight. She lavishes all her love upon the counterfeit Bundren whose name begins the novel, "Jewel," while the novel ends with the name of the counterfeit Addie, "Mrs Bundren."

Discourse of the dead: the "neuter"

Finally, let us examine whether the stylistic innovations of *As I Lay Dying* have formal significance for Faulkner's later prose. The tale consists of a family trekking forty miles to bury a corpse: its plot is in fact the absent thing the family buries. The route to Jefferson is a horizontal journey interrupted by two slopes (the descent and ascent from the river), the outline of Addie's coffin itself – "I made it on the bevel," Cash says. The performance of the journey, as in the rite Odysseus performs, elicits the telling voice of the "dead."

Whenever identities empty out, narrative lives. From its first sentence, *As I Lay Dying* exhibits a narrative voice overflowing with identities, yet lacking in identity. The death of the particular "I" seems to reinvigorate its presence as a category, almost in the manner of standard ghost narrations told in the first person. Poe's "Ms. Found in a Bottle" is one of the few examples in American fiction of a "voice from the dead" in which the narrator is not a talking ghost but a posthumous narrative text. The story has its source in the narrator's death, where the text breaks off. Hence the story can only be read because death has stopped the living writer's hand. Hence, the written "Ms." itself, and not any pretended "I," is the speaking "ghost" of Poe's story. In Maurice Blanchot's terminology, *As I Lay Dying* is a ghostly text that could be said to be at the "neuter," the "neither/nor" limit of narrative, for which the proper metaphor would indeed seem to be a speaking corpse. Another emblem of the "neuter" in the novel might be the copulation that Darl recalls in his "neither/nor" state of semi-madness: "a woman and a pig with two backs and no face." Faulkner takes this phrase from Shakespeare's description of a racially *mixed* couple, Othello and Desdemona. They are, in their coupling, neither black nor white, neither male nor female: a neuter pairing, in the literal sense of "neuter."

As I Lay Dying is "the intrusion of the other – understood as neuter – in its irreducible strangeness, in its wily perversity. The other speaks. But when the other speaks, no one is speaking."[32] "Storytelling brings the neuter into play. . . . In this respect, the narrative voice is the most critical one that can communicate unheard. That is why we tend, as we listen to it, to confuse it with the oblique voice of unhappiness or the oblique voice of madness."[33] The narrative's "focalization" must be Addie's corpse itself, a center that is a far cry from "an authoritarian and complacent 'I' still anchored in life and barging in without any restraint." Similarly Faulkner gives the narrative to the voice of a more literal "neuter" in *The Sound and the Fury*, Benjy, whom the unpublished introduction to the novel describes as lacking "thought or comprehension; shapeless, neuter, like something eyeless and voiceless . . . when I wrote Benjy's section, I was not writing it to be printed."[34] Death, idiocy, and madness, at "the limits of the world," of *nous*, now become states, and not merely themes, of narration.

In *As I Lay Dying, Absalom, Absalom!*, and *The Sound and the Fury*, only the missing is real. Shortly after Addie's discourse on "unhappiness," just before Darl descends into "madness," the corpse simply vanishes. There is no burial scene. Addie's corpse slips into its plot. The novel is not merely an ironic allegory of self-discovery or self-destruction, though such suggestions have been offered.[35] Rather, the narrative wishes to show how much inertia (in the sense of "momentum") there is in the desire of death, which is also the desire to fill an absence, hole, or "plot" – often with blood. Addie's desire to be buried with her relatives in Jefferson gets the plot under way; the mission of the Bundrens is also the desire of Agamemnon to move to a proper completion. Personal and societal inertia, I believe – and not "becoming," "honor," or "death and rebirth" – creates the tensions of this text.[36] Section succeeds section; but a final success is threatened even as the narrative stutters along. We race ahead, like Jewel through the flames, to our goal, even if to reach it means to reach the limits of life.

As I Lay Dying seems to illustrate the "deathness" of language, but promises the life and coherence of a special style. These family novels, *As I Lay Dying* and *The Sound and the Fury*, have been seen as Faulkner's "most ambitious stylistic experiments," and his "only substantial adventures in 'stream-of-consciousness' techniques." Faulkner made fun of this conception from the moment Random House first proposed that his fifth and sixth novels be published in one volume: "It's as though we were saying 'This is a versatile guy: he can write in the same stream of consciousness style about princes and then peasants.'" But the question here, as in *The Sound and the Fury*, is quite serious. Is there a style that can encompass divided social classes? Faulkner, writing "about all the kinds of people in Miss. in the same style," seems to promise equality in language if nowhere else. What would be the style of such an integration? Its attractions and dangers would seem clear, particularly in view of the impossibility in 1929 and 1930 of any other variety of "integration."[37]

By making the novel's style fragmentary, in a quasi-Joycean portrayal of inner thoughts, Faulkner crystallizes into form the issue of social rupture. Yet his rendering of relations between human beings only points to their prior violent rendings. The narrative style that pretends to join actually functions by division – textual spacings, separation into fifty-nine "sections"; collapse of normal syntax; fragmentary conversation. This paradoxical handling notifies us that the style of *As I Lay Dying* is disingenuous, much like the conventional figures of societal division. For discrimination in society says one thing and does another. Community falls apart because community wishes not to be merged. Faulkner formalizes divisions as modes of narration that seem to eliminate separations – realism, interior monologue, stream-of-consciousness – but which only encourage further separations. The lesson learned here is startling and even revolutionary: the reader must conclude that the apparent lack of mediation between classes in the real world also results from an overarching design of intentional repetition, reduction, and repression under the cover of unifying, community-building rhetorics. Natural separations, based on human behavior or human anatomy, turn out not to have been natural after all, but only the fruit of rhetorical flowers.

Faulkner's tentative solution treats the empty "I" of fiction, the narrative voice, as the renovation of commonwealth. The all-inclusive emptiness of that voice seriously challenges, on a verbal field, society's plot of separation. Yet Faulkner finally criticizes his own "solution." He suggests, in *Light in August* and *Absalom, Absalom!*, that breaking down the narrating act itself can substitute for trying to break down the narrative "I."

Faulkner shows in his next set of novels how hearsay narratives, though shared, risk repeating fatal errors. *Light in August*, and *Absalom, Absalom!* question the relationship of truth to oral narrative. Is truth at all representable in that discourse of the dead, shared or unsharable, called "writing"?

Notes

1 Reed speaks of the novel as an "autobiography of consciousness" (Joseph W. Reed, *Faulkner's Narrative* (New Haven: Yale University Press, 1973), p. 163). Slatoff cannot fathom Addie—"we are given none of the details which might help us to understand why her torment is so great . . . her torment is also perplexing . . . we do not know why pregnancy should be so horrifying to her"—and Darl undoes him entirely: "No matter how hard we search, he remains essentially a mystery. . . . Darl's mind is disordered. . . . Darl is queer in certain ways": Walter J. Slatoff, *Quest for Failure* (1960; Westport, Conn.: Greenwood Press, 1972), pp. 164–5. Millgate speaks of "a developing internal drama" and "the intense psychological drama of [Faulkner's] major characters": Michael Millgate, *The Achievement of William Faulkner* (London: Constable, 1966), p. 107.

2 William Faulkner, *Faulkner in the University* ed. Frederick L. Gwynn and Joseph Blotner (Charlottesville: University of Virginia Press, 1959), p. 112.

3 Homer's *Odyssey*, trans. William Marris (Oxford: Oxford University Press, 1925). Carvel Collins first suggested that the phrase "as I lay dying" derived from this translation of *The Odyssey* in "The Pairing of *The Sound and the Fury* and *As I Lay Dying*," *Princeton University Library Chronicle*, 18 (1957), p. 123.

4 One is reminded of a similar transformation and "cleansing" of the spirit in "Nigger Hollow," section 4 of *The Sound and the Fury*, and the "Freedman's Town" of *Light in August*. Also, the "self-emptying" of Christ into the world, a paradigmatic act in Christian mysticism, may also be an analogy here: "Christ . . . emptied himself, taking the form of a servant": Philippians 2: 7.

5 William Faulkner, *As I Lay Dying* (New York: Vintage, 1964), p. 76. All subsequent quotations from this edition will be cited by page numbers in parentheses in the text.

6 Thomas Hobbes, *Leviathan*, in *The English Philosophers from Bacon to Mill*, ed. with an intro. by Edwin A. Burtt (New York: Modern Library, 1939), chapter 4, "Of Speech," pp. 140–1.

7 Reed, op. cit., p. 87.

8 Richard Forrer suggests the same idea, speaking of *Absalom, Absalom!*: "The harder these people struggle to communicate with each other, the more isolated they become, miring themselves in a quicksand of sentences": "*Absalom, Absalom!*: Story-Telling as a Mode of Transcendence," *The Southern Literary Journal*, 9, 1 (1976), pp. 25, 37–8. Also Reed, op. cit., p. 87.

9 Fredric Jameson, *Marxism and Form: Twentieth Century Dialectical Theories of Literature* (Princeton: Princeton University Press, 1971), p. 256, where Jameson discusses Sartre's "baptism" notion in *Critique of Dialectical Reason*.

10 Arthur F. Kinney first comments on this anagram, in *Faulkner's Narrative Poetics* (Amherst: University of Massachusetts Press, 1978), p. 173, but I do not agree that Anse's saneness illustrates "the essential rightness of the forces of life. He and his children, like his crops, live." I reject any naturalization of an idea such as "essential rightness" – the sanctioned "sanity" from which Addie is trying to escape.

11 In his *How to Do Things with Words* (New York: Oxford University Press, 1962), p. 147, J. L. Austin contrasts "constative" utterances (assertions that are true or false descriptions of facts) with "performative" utterances, such as a marriage ritual or christening, in which the speech "does something." Jacques Derrida takes on, but does not adopt, this notion in the article "Signature, Event, Context" in *Margins of Philosophy*, trans. Alan Bass (Chicago: University of Chicago Press, 1982), pp. 309–30.

12 For an example of ring composition in Homer, see his *Iliad*, XII, 14 ff. Also, for further discussion of "ring composition" in Homer, see S. E. Basset, *The Poetry of Homer* (Berkeley: University of California Press, 1938); A. Parry (ed.), *The Making of Homeric Verse*, collected papers of Milman Parry :(Oxford: Oxford University Press, 1971); and Kossia Orloff, "Homer and Faulkner: A Study in Ring Composition," *Compass*, 5 (Spring 1980), pp. 1–20.

13 From "Time and Faulkner: *The Sound and the Fury*," in Frederick J. Hoffman and Olga W. Vickery, *William Faulkner* (East Lansing: Michigan State College Press, 1951), p. 183.

14 See "The Tropics of History: The Deep Structure of the *New Science*," in Hayden White, *Tropics of Discourse: Essays in Cultural Criticism* (Baltimore: Johns Hopkins University Press, 1978), pp. 197–217.

15 Theodor W. Adorno, "Subject and Object," in Andrew Arato and Eike Gebhardt (eds), *The Essential Frankfurt School Reader*, intro. by Paul Piccone (New York: Continuum, 1982), p. 501; German title, "Zu Subjekt und Objekt," in *Stichworte: Kritische Modelle 2* (Frankfurt a. M.: Suhrkamp, 1980).

16 Jacques Lacan, *Ecrits*, trans. Alan Sheridan (London: Tavistock, 1977), p. 67; also pp. 199, 217, 310, 314.

17 Faulkner first connects death and sleep, of course, in the notion, repeated in the voices of several different characters, that Cash's sawing of Addie's coffin "sounds like snoring." He is "sawing wood," or, in common parlance, "snoring," but his sawing creates a bed of death – Faulkner, an admirer of the Metaphysical poets, may well be alluding to Donne's "rest and sleep" here. The image of sawing wood to build a coffin recurs in *Absalom, Absalom!* (New York: Vintage, 1972), p. 151.

18 Roman Jakobson, *Selected Writings*, vol. II: *Word and Language* (The Hague: Mouton, 1971), p. 131.

19 John Stark, in an article entitled "The Implications for Stylistics of Strawson's 'On Referring,' with *Absalom, Absalom!* as an Example," *Language and Style*, 6 (1973), suggests that Faulkner exploits the shifter to concentrate the attention of the reader. He says that "the thought-provoking quality that many critics have ascribed to Faulkner's prose is created to a larger extent by the high proportion of expressions that he uses to refer . . . unlike descriptions, references force Faulkner's readers to master the context." But I would assert that precisely such coercion questions the automatic reliance on the fact that in fiction, as in society, the defining context will be there.

20 Cleanth Brooks, *William Faulkner: The Yoknapatawpha Country* (New Haven: Yale University Press, 1963), p. 145.

21 Max Horkheimer, "The End of Reason," in Arato and Gebhardt (eds), op. cit., p. 45.

22 Irving Howe says, "any final interpretation must be our own, for there is no detached observer who speaks for Faulkner": *William Faulkner* (1951), 3rd edn (Chicago: University of Chicago Press, 1975), p. 184. Edmund Volpe agrees: "No single character can be designated as a spokesman for the author": *A Reader's Guide to William Faulkner* (New York: Farrar, Straus and Giroux, 1964), p. 129. Others choose Addie: she is "at the center of *As I Lay Dying*, and it is in her lone monologue that we catch the essentials": Constance Pierce, "Being, Knowing, and Saying in the 'Addie' Section of Faulkner's *As I Lay Dying*," *Twentieth Century Literature*, 26 (1980), p. 295. Slatoff says, "After Addie, the most important character in the book is Darl," yet for him Cash carries the crucial message: "his comparatively compassionate attitude towards Darl, and his philosophizing toward the end of the book all suggest that we view him . . . as a kind of moral or ethical center" (op. cit., pp. 164, 171), a choice which Waggoner echoes: "It is not Addie but Cash who has the last word in the book . . . he

is also, for most readers I suspect, the most sympathetic character in the book": Hyatt H. Waggoner, *William Faulkner* (Kentucky: University of Kentucky Press, 1959), p. 84.

23 Helen Swink suggests that Faulkner developed a "prose style that seems to create for the reader an illusion of 'voice,' i.e., the illusion of an oral storyteller": "William Faulkner: The Novelist as Oral Narrator," *The Georgia Review*, 26 (1971), p. 183. Yet this description does not solve the questions of consistency and presence of "voice" raised by the "oral storyteller" image. Stephen M. Ross's rewarding article " 'Voice' in Narrative Texts: The Example of *As I Lay Dying*," *PMLA*, 94 (1979), tackles the assumptions under which by "criteria of verisimilitude the narrative discourse is inconsistent and implausible, so much so that Faulkner has been accused of botching the first-person point of view." Like Ross, Peter Brooks arrives at the insight that in Faulkner "the 'voice of the reader' has evicted all other voices from the text": "Incredulous Narration: *Absalom, Absalom!*," *Comparative Literature*, 34, 3 (Summer 1982), p. 263.

24 Kinney wavers between calling Addie "a nascent psychotic" and being reminded "of R. D. Laing's recent description of a schizophrenic" (op. cit., pp. 170–1). Other all too typical examples of this kind include Leon Seltzer, "Narrative Function vs. Psychopathology: The Problem of Darl in *As I Lay Dying*," *Literature and Psychology*, 25 (1975); Deborah Ayer Sitter, "Self and Object Representations in *As I Lay Dying*," *Hartford Studies in Literature*, 12 (1980).

25 In Constance Pierce's Heideggerian language: "a person's Being, or what Addie seems to be longing for as Being, is what he is before he begins to think about, or objectify, it (Addie Bundren before she is aware of being Addie Bundren)" (op. cit., p. 294). The search for this state, as Pierce says, "accounts in part for Addie's fragmentation – her loathing of the human world of death-word in which she has to exist (or of consciousness – knowing, saying, aloneness – perhaps close to what Heidegger means by absence) and her longing for a state of unconsciousness (or even preconsciousness) including all her notions of being and wholeness . . . (and the impossibility of merging her life with that of any other human in a bond that has no need of language)", (ibid., pp. 295–6). I agree with the general diagnosis here, without, however, accepting with Pierce the possibility of such a state of "wholeness" or "a bond that has no need of language".

26 Elisabeth S. Muhlenfeld, "Shadows with Substance Exhumed: The Women in *Absalom, Absalom!*," *Mississippi Quarterly*, 25, 3 (Summer 1972), p. 290.

27 Millgate, op. cit., p. 105.

28 Jacques Lacan, "The Signification of the Phallus," in *Ecrits*, p. 287; Anika Rifflet-Lemaire, *Jacques Lacan*, trans. David Macey (Boston: Routledge & Kegan Paul, 1977), p. 59; and Lacan, "The Partial Drive and its Circuit," in *The Four Fundamental Concepts of Psychoanalysis*, trans. Alan Sheridan (London: Hogarth, 1977); French title: *Les Quatre Concepts fondamentaux de la psychanalyse, Le Séminaire, Livre XI*.

29 Indeed, the "circle" metaphor encloses an entire string of allusions: "In Addie's section the dominant mode is geometrical: circles, verticals and horizontals, diagonals, and curves are the objects of the controlling collective metaphor." Reed over-specifies here, since throughout the novel, and not just in this section, Anse has been associated with the "vertical" and "stationary," and the rest of the family with the "horizontality" of the journey. Reed also later misconstrues the "slant." Far from representing "the unknown" or "the unpredictable," the "slant" or "tilt" figures "dying" itself, both foreshadowing and recalling Addie's death: Reed, op. cit., pp. 100–3. For example: Darl's wagon tilts into a ditch the moment Addie dies; the coffin is built "on a bevel" and is often seen slanting; the very site of the Bundrens' house, "tilting a little down the hill"; the slant of the guy-rope in the river-crossing.

30 Women seem able to interpret signs of absence and presence better than men. Cora reads correctly that the sudden appearance of Peabody's loose horses signifies the death of Addie; Dewey Dell notices that the absence of her period is a "sign when something has happened bad."

31 Lacan, *The Four Fundamental Concepts*, p. 5.

32 See Maurice Blanchot, "The Narrative Voice," in *The Gaze of Orpheus and other Literary Essays*, trans. Lydia Davis (Barrytown, NY: Station Hill Press, 1981), p. 134. The term "focalization" is Gérard Genette's refinement of "point of view," as defined in *Narrative Discourse*, trans. Jane E. Lewin (Ithaca: Cornell University Press, 1980), p. 10. Compare these notions with the more traditional definition of "point of view," as given by Percy Lubbock: "The whole intricate question of method, in the craft of fiction, I take to be governed by the question of the point of view – the question of the relation in which the narrator stands to the story," from *The Craft of Fiction*, quoted in John Hersey (ed.), *The Writer's Craft* (New York: Knopf, 1974), p. 58.

33 Blanchot, op. cit., pp. 140–1, 143.

34 William Faulkner, "An Introduction to *The Sound and the Fury*" (1933), in *Mississippi Quarterly*, 26 (1973), p. 414.

35 See Elizabeth Kerr, "*As I Lay Dying* as Ironic Quest," *Winsconsin Studies in Contemporary Literature,* 3 (Winter 1962). The frequent mythic interpretations of the novel take its various hints at fertility (eg. Dewey Dell's "I feel like a wet seed wild in the hot blind earth"; 61) as some redemption myth featuring Demeter (Addie), Kore (Cora), and Persephone (Dewey Dell), culminating in "a ruefully humorous conviction that no matter what happens life goes on": Richard P. Adams, *Faulkner: Myth and Motion* (Princeton: Princeton University Press, 1968), pp. 73, 83.

36 As in Reed, op. cit., p. 94; C. Brooks, op. cit., p. 143; Adams, op. cit., p. 82. Rather, Peter Brooks's formulation concerning *Absalom, Absalom!* again applies well to this text: "the reader's desire inhabits the text and strives towards the fulfillment of interpretation" (op. cit., p. 263).

37 Millgate, op. cit., p. 104; William Faulkner, *Selected Letters,* ed. Joseph Blotner (New York: Random House, 1977), p. 228. Considering such a stylistic search, one might bring up William Empson's idea of the "essential trick of the old pastoral, which was felt to imply a beautiful relation between rich and poor": William Empson, *Some Versions of the Pastoral* (1935; New York: New Directions, 1974), p. 11. Irving Howe confirms that Faulkner is trying, like his predecessors, to put "the complex into the simple": "An American epic, *As I Lay Dying* is human tragedy and country farce. The marvel is that to be one it has to be the other": Howe, op. cit., p. 191. But Faulkner's "pastoral" or "country" conception complicates rather than simplifies. Its very efforts only reveal that there is no verbal linkage between or even within the various stations of society. Whatever the social "station," no one is receiving any signals.

4

Light
in
August
(1932)

Faulkner, faced with the problematics of racial division and himself seeking figures of merging and synthesis, presents in *Light in August* a man both masculine and feminine, both black and white, a "tragic mulatto," an American double-being who breaks all the semiotic codes of society. In his novels of his mid-30s, Faulkner seems to be working out the question whether such a reconciliatory, almost mythical figure might transcend in fiction the dire antagonisms of life.[1] In the already "conventional" anti-traditionalism of the modern era, we have seen that vision begins with figures of merging: "The attraction of reconciliation is the elective breeding-ground of false models and metaphors."[2] But it must be added that "false models and metaphors" are also the feeding-ground of most great writing. In more traditional Western thought, merging is considered a chaotic condition which threatens the structures of society, language, and identity. Joe Christmas, Charles Bon, and Lucas Beauchamp (the central figures of *Light in August*, *Absalom, Absalom!*, and *Go Down, Moses* – all mulattoes), far from being ideal solutions to racial polarity, come to seem exactly those points of chaos that threaten to destroy every plot of false serenity. Insofar as Joe Christmas and Charles Bon cannot signify any one thing, they must finally undercut the very possibility of unitary significance. The tragic realization of these novels may be that a kind of semiotic discrimination is as necessary to reading as it is, deplorably, for the whites of Jefferson, Mississippi.

Having depicted and arrived at this brink, Faulkner – no less than Jefferson – shows a conservative compulsion to impose order. In the killings of Joe Christmas and Charles Bon, society represses by violence the proofs of its own brokenness, yet cannot erase the double debris – both of its initial collapse and of its violent repressions. In other words, the post-modernist reconciliation in Faulkner culminates precisely in the destruction of that which had seemed to remedy modernism's atomizations. Yet this destruction cannot but seem a restoration of the past and as such not a promising Second Coming, but rather a very weary *déjà vu. Light in August* presents a cyclical movement: the town goes from certainty about what race signifies and what signifies race, through an experience that disrupts that surety, and back again to a forced reestablishment of certainty. Christmas and Bon give the promise of reconcilement, but also remind of an original, violent, sundering. Therefore they must be eliminated. But to murder them does not restore a unified past; it simply repeats a former separation by force.

What the town knows

Consensus arises in the performative mode. The early pages of *Light in August* overflow with tropes of domination in the town's common parlance: "Starting in at daylight and slaving all day like a durn nigger"; "Well, maybe some folks work like the niggers work where they come from."[3] Lucas Burch repeats this simile later on, referring to himself: "Slaving like a durn nigger ten hours a day" (408). This trope would engrave in language by repetition the economic connection between blacks and "slaving" – a class rigidification that has ensured the economic stability of Jefferson and, more generally, American society. Hearsay would virtually write behavior, making it inflexible in the reality of these commonplaces. Byron Bunch says of Joanna Burden: "they say she is still mixed up with niggers. . . . Folks say she claims that niggers are the same as white folks" (48). What "they say" may be true or false, but because "they say it" it seems the truth.

We have seen just a few examples of significant reference points in Jefferson language. A black is a certain thing; a black does certain jobs. To find these rhetorics in well-socialized speakers is one thing, but it is quite another to find them in the voice of the narrator. Faulkner gives us the choice to be racists in a very cunning way: do we passively accept the truth of the narrator's judgment and thereby ourselves join the town's consensus? Or do we suspend our own judgment for the sake of fairness? There is, for instance, the text's repeated notion that blacks smell different from whites: "before he knew it he was in Freedman Town, surrounded by the summer smell . . . of invisible negroes" (106); "He could smell Negro" (109); "the same children, with different names; the same grown people, with different smells" (131). Outrageously the narrator wants bodily odor here to replace the visual signifier of race that Joe Christmas has now made defunct (dark skin color), but his subterfuge is transparent. Umberto Eco includes *olfactory signs* among the possible components of a general cultural semiotics, citing Baudelaire's notion of a "code of scents," or Peirce's notion of smell as an "index" – hence olfactory signals are as apt to be abused by socio-economic "marking" (presumably, they designated a "natural" difference) as any other sort.[4]

Earlier, we have read the following sentences:

He [Armstid] got into the wagon and waked the mules. That is, he put them into motion, since *only a negro can tell when a mule is asleep or awake.*

None of them knew then where Christmas lived and what he was actually doing *behind the veil, the screen, of his negro's job at the mill* . . . even the ones who bought the whiskey did not know that Christmas was actually living in *a tumble down negro cabin* on Miss Burden's place, and that he had been living in it for more than two years.

Hightower knew that the man would walk all the way to town and then spend probably thirty minutes more getting in touch with a doctor, *in his fumbling and timeless negro fashion,* instead of asking some white woman to telephone for him. (8, 31–2, 68; my italics)

The italicized statements demonstrate a highly revealing yet suspect alternation of ignorance and knowledge. The first shows that "a negro" knows whether a mule is awake or asleep – no doubt because of a connection "they say" exists between blacks and the natural world of animals. In the second, "everyone" ostensibly knows what a "negro cabin" is: the kind of cabin where a Negro would live. But here the narrator even seems to know more than "they" do. He sees "behind the veil" of a job that "everyone knows" would ordinarily be a "negro's." In the third example Hightower knows the future behavior of blacks already, as if sequence were reversed, and future action had preceded the present. But these statements, which seem absolutely correct versions of reality, are quite duplicitous. For example, if "only a negro" can really know a mule, then the Negro knows more than both the white narrator and Hightower. In the second example, the narrator does not simply say "job at the mill" but "negro's job at the mill." Joe Christmas hides his "blackness" behind the screen of a "negro's job": he pretends to "slave like a negro" so no one will think he is one. But the very category of "Negro" ("negro's job . . . negro cabin") may be seen as a screen, a veil of only apparent difference that society may be using to disguise actual similarities. Therefore, the narrator has yet to see through "Negro," even though he has seen through the "job." Possibly the whole white society, like the "white" Christmas, is hiding behind the veil of "Negro" (recall Quentin's "a nigger is . . . a form of behaviour; a sort of obverse reflection of the white people he lives among"). One citizen says, "That nigger murderer. Christmas," but says in the next breath, "He dont look no more like a nigger than I do, either" (328). Finally, Hightower, in the third example, predicts that any black will "naturally" hesitate under certain circumstances. Yet he selectively omits to mention that such hesitation comes from the standard consequence – lynching and castration – of a black male "asking some white woman" anything, even "to telephone for him": "Now you'll let white women alone, even in hell," Grimm says over Christmas's emasculated corpse, "flinging behind him the bloody butcher knife" (439). Hightower, typically for Yoknapatawpha, represses society's threats and acts of violence, while highlighting what are blacks' "natural" and "timeless" "fashions." He shows a willed ignorance (akin to Freudian dream censorship) that must ultimately condition all questions of knowledge and ignorance in the novel.

Light in August, *Absalom, Absalom!*, and *Go Down, Moses* treat, more informatively than their predecessors, the relationship between language and knowledge. At question is, above all, what the town knows, what it thinks it knows, what it knows but must conceal, and finally what it can never know because the knowledge would imperil its ability to know anything. In *Light in August* Faulkner diverges from Fielding's omniscient narrators or Conrad's and James's unreliable ones by exposing omniscience as unreliability. The unreliability is an active deception. There is no deficiency, of either intelligence or perspicacity: the narrator is actively creating error. Society here turns arbitrary codes of dominance into "fact." To make matters worse, the reader helps accomplish the entire process.

The narrator wishes to surpass in accuracy a malleable "oral" account, claiming to know what others do not. Oral tales are flexible, subject to skepticism: Lena says, "most of what folks tells on other folks ain't true to begin with" (49). The novel is quite knowledgeable about lack of knowledge in others: "it is possible that she did not know this at the time" (2); "they did not know who he was . . . none of them had the sense to recognise it" (28–9); "they still do not know for certain if Christmas is connected with it . . . some of them know that Christmas and Brown both live in a cabin" (41–2). Oral accounts strive – as written narrative does – for rigidity and invariance leading to credibility. "They say" always yearns to become "it is written." The written always vaunts authority over the told, which it must place within quotation marks.

Habit and misrecognition

Reading and gossip seem to offer something new to be told, but both operations essentially involve recognizing the old in the new, hence misrecognizing what one sees. *Light in August*, despite its "emphasis on perception," is actually about what people fail to perceive. Most often, characters remain ignorant either because they cannot look, or because they think they do "not need to look to know." The assumption that omniscience is a real prediction of the future turns out badly. Christmas represents the aporia that comes when real events do not replicate social expectations. All the ways of custom and habit are blocked or at best circular.

Perception seems particularly difficult between races and sexes. Martha and her husband Armstid, for example, seem in different worlds:

> He does not look in that direction; he does not need to look to know that she will be there, is there. . . . He does not watch her. . . . He does not need to. . . . He does not look at her. . . . He begins to wash, his back to her. . . . Mrs Armstid does not look around. . . . And he can feel her looking at him. . . . He cannot tell from her voice if she is watching him or not now. . . . And now he knows that she is watching him. (12–14)

Habituation (akin in this context to an optical effect: persistence of vision) tends to obscure whatever it fixes. Lena and her male driver never look at each other; each knows what the other "is": "Apparently he has never looked at her. . . . Apparently she has never looked at him, either. She does not do so now" (24–5). Byron and Burch mirror each other when they speak, called "the one" and "the other": "Byron thinks that this is just the reflection of what he himself already knows and is about to tell. . . . He is not looking at the other now" (74–5). At times, distraction is the culprit. When the young couple stop their car for him, Christmas does not actually register their words: "Christmas did not notice this at the time. . . . Christmas did not hear this either. . . . But again Christmas did not notice . . . he was not even paying attention" (267–8).

Misrecognition, whether caused by oversight or self-delusion, is the central theme in *Light in August*, and the novel shares this concern with *Don Quixote*, which Faulkner invariably listed among those books that had influenced him most. Readers misperceive before anyone else, as at the beginning of chapter 2: "the group of men at work in the planer shed looked up, and saw the stranger standing there, watching them" (27). Our immediate temptation is to think that "the stranger" is Lucas Burch, whom Lena Grove has been seeking in chapter 1. But "the stranger" is Christmas, whom we meet here, unnamed, for the first time. Christmas himself misperceives crucial moments in his life, such as when the dietician offers him "hush money": "When he saw the hand emerge from the pocket he believed that she was about to strike him. But she did not; the hand just opened beneath his eyes. Upon it lay a silver dollar" (116). Joe seems generally unable to understand the visible and audible signs of society: his mother puts "into the can beneath his round grave eyes coins whose value he did not even recognise" (158). Christmas misunderstands Max and Mame: "it was as if they talked at and because of him, in a language which he did not understand" (182–3); "Perhaps he heard the words. But likely not. Likely they were as yet no more significant than the rasping of insects beyond the closedrawn window, or the packed bags which he had looked at and had not yet seen" (201).

Joe Christmas's ignorance is also a kind of sexual innocence. As a boy, his older friends know about sex. The younger ones, Christmas included, "did not know that. They did not know that all girls wanted to, let alone that there were times when they could not" (173). He misunderstands the name "Bobbie," calling it "A man's name" (168). Bobbie Allen has two men's names, and as a result helps create Joe's general confusion about gender. Forgetting what he had learned about menstruation, Joe listens to Bobbie saying to him that she cannot go to bed with him: " 'Listen. I'm sick tonight.' He did not understand. He said nothing. Perhaps he did not need to understand" (176). Bobbie Allen is also a prostitute, but Joe does not seem to understand:

> "I thought you knew," she said.
> "No," he said. "I reckon I didn't."
> "I thought you did."
> "No," he said. "I dont reckon I did." (187)

Joe wrongly thinks that Max and Mame reject him because of his sexual designs on Bobbie Allen: "Very likely until the last he still believed that Max and Mame had to be placated, not for the actual fact, but because of his presence there" (185). But Joe has misread the telltale signs of prostitution; he cannot read the language: " 'I dont even know what they are saying to her,' he thought, thinking *I dont even know that what they are saying to her is something that men do not say to a passing child*" (165).

Signifying "X"mas

Joe finds the world puzzling, but the world in turn finds him indecipherable. *Light in August* depicts how Joe Christmas resists signification, while showing that we cannot tolerate anything that does not signify. Like Jefferson, readers seem compelled to supply anything that makes Christmas significant, even what is not in the text. It is as revealing as it is embarrassing to consider how many readers fall into the same racist mentality as Jefferson, even despite Faulkner's own admonition that Christmas "himself didn't know who he was – didn't know whether he was part Negro or not and would never know." Early critics, especially, insisted on calling Christmas a "harried mulatto" or a "white Negro." Some credited Gavin Stevens's intentionally ludicrous "blood" theory, discussing "a sinister figure haunted by knowledge of his negro blood." Others described "the conflict in Christmas of the white and the negro blood." Cleanth Brooks is correct to say "we are never given any firm proof that Joe Christmas possesses Negro blood" – indeed, at one point Joanna asks Joe how he knows one of his parents is "part nigger." Joe answers, "I dont know it" (240). The simple basis of "not knowing" about Joe's race (onto which others project would-be knowledge) is the chief rhetorical prerequisite for interpreting the novel.[5] The novel poses a challenge to our own self-reading: do we comply with or resist the signification of Joe Christmas as "nigger"?

Throughout the novel, Christmas is the sign of resistance to fixed signs. He is the quintessence of indeterminable essence. He is ambiguous from his first description: "the stranger . . . looked like a tramp, yet not like a tramp either" (27). We never actually discover his true age.[6] Even his name can be written

"Christmas" or "Xmas" (and is, within three lines; 53). He symbolizes the frustration and resistance that knowledge encounters whenever it wants to become permanent, or "written." In the context of the town, he is above all a matter of "rumor," and the chief episodes involving his flight and capture come to us as oral conjecture or "telling." Conjecture and oral narration are key modes here because so much knowledge in Jefferson is partial. Consequently, we immediately assimilate the town's hearsay narrative. One might even suggest that the town wishes to capture and confine Joe's meaning more than his actual body.

Critical conjecture about the meaning of the Joe Christmas figure and its containing narrative attests to this wish. The reception of Joe Christmas by the town resembles the reception of the novel by the critical community, whose general perplexity revolves around the problem of "unity of plot." The "unity" problem has close ties with the "abstraction" issue, about which there is considerable disagreement. One critic can say that Joe Christmas is an idea rather than a person, a character who "remains almost completely opaque," while another claims that "Christmas seems immediately and indisputably real."[7]

Bobbie Allen watches Joe leave her sight, and misperceives what she seems to see: "As he faded on down the road, the shape, the shadow, she believed that he was running. . . . He was not running" (177). He is an elusive shadow. Writing is Faulkner's metaphor here, and Joe Christmas avidly resists the properties and effects of written imprintation. He escapes the purview of his father McEachern by climbing down a rope "with the shadowlike agility of a cat . . . passing swift as a shadow across the window" (159). Later "Joe, descending on his rope, slid like a fast shadow across the open and moonfilled window. . . . McEachern did not at once recognise him or perhaps believe what he saw" (189). McEachern has just been trying, upon pain of whipping, to get Christmas to "take the book" – or learn by heart excerpts from "an enormous Bible" and "a Presbyterian catechism." Rote memorization uses Pavlovian conditioning by repetition in order to "imprint" the written text upon the mind. It is no wonder, then, that McEachern's voice "was just cold, implacable, like written or printed words" (139). He manifests a Protestant literalism that must, upon pain of death, see the world in black and white terms.

Joe is the uncertainty that resists being made into writing. He is more an absence than anything else. From childhood, he has willed insufficiency: "Once he had owned garments with intact buttons. A woman had sewed them on. . . . With his pocket knife . . . he would cut off the buttons which she had just replaced" (100). A woman completing the "intact buttons" of his garment also stands for the marital bond and its social sanction. If "postponement" of gratification and fear of punishment are the controlling tenets of civilization, then Joe counters them by rejecting all deferments – particularly of punishment, hating the kindness of his mother who "would try to get herself between him and the punishment," a mediation of pain that "must give it an odor, an attenuation, and aftertaste" (157). He has exempted himself from the prolongation of touch that extends the memory of suffering.

Joe's social exclusion typically becomes a sexual alienation from which his difficulties with women may derive. While most commentators agree that Lena is a kind of "good anima" or "fertility figure" or "earth mother", few have been able to explain her place in a novel with Joe Christmas, whose "chief problem was not nearly so much his black blood or repressive upbringing as that world of women." Brooks even goes so far as to describe Christmas's "distaste for women" and "antifem-inine attitude" as "a latent tendency" towards homosexuality. It seems clear, however, that, rather than seeing Lena as the "integrity and wholeness by which the alienated characters are to be judged" and opposing this "integrity" to Joe's "latent tendency," both Joe and Lena must be seen as responses to the society from which they spring. In other words, Lena's final triumph over conventions of male–female relationships is just a happier way of dealing with the same problems that Christmas fails to solve.[8]

Joe resists writing, but he must be written. He cannot be a total absence. He dislikes traces, but he leaves them everywhere. The posse are chasing a "shadow," but an imperfect one: "They could even see the prints of his knees and hands where he had knelt to drink from a spring" (310). In a society in which everyone is part of a "social text," socialization paradoxically means to become as white as paper.

This fact applies most of all, ironically, to the blacks. The black is a shadow, and Joe is another version of what the white mind thinks a dark mystery. Blacks leave a "mark" or "trace," be it color or smell, even despite society's efforts to erase them altogether, to make their blackness a signifier of what Ellison in *Invisible Man* calls a social "invisibility." Joe senses that he is like blacks as he walks among them:

> In the wide, empty, shadow-brooded street he looked like a phantom ... before he knew it he was in Freedman town, *surrounded by the summer smell and the summer voices of invisible negroes. They seemed to enclose him* like bodiless voices murmuring, talking, laughing, in a language not his. ... About him the cabins were shaped blackly out of the blackness. ... *On all sides, even within him, the bodiless fecundmellow voices* of negro women murmured. (106–7; my italics)

The effaced black is meant to be the background for society's "writing" – like a carrier wave that you are not supposed to sense, the essential yet unperceived thing that carries the "message." Hence Christmas's flesh is "a level dead parchment color," especially in the scenes where McEachern's voice, "like written or printed words," tries to get him to repeat a catechism. Yet Joe rejects being inscribed until the very end. Late in the novel the fugitive can still leave behind, "wedged into a split plank on the side of the church, a scrap of paper." This "pencilled message" is "raggedly written, as though by an unpractised hand or perhaps in the dark. ... It was addressed to the sheriff by name and it was unprintable – a single phrase – and it was unsigned" (309): the last white scrap of Joe's black defiance is still "unprintable" and "unsigned."

As Christmas becomes more "Negro," he becomes less vague, less "parchment-colored." Society flattens him into a backcloth that must become one or the other color:

> He watched his body grow white out of the darkness like a kodak print emerging from the liquid. (100)

> vanishing as he ran, vanishing upward from the head down as if he were running headfirst and laughing into something that was obliterating him like a picture in chalk being erased from a blackboard. (195)

the black abyss ... into which now and at last he had
actually entered, bearing now upon his ankles the definite
and ineradicable gauge of its upward moving. (313)

The townspeople accept Burch's claim that Christmas is a
"nigger" mainly because it explains the inexplicable. But the
narrator, while sharing this fiction, often needs to call Joe
"white": "Sometimes the notes would tell him not to come
until a certain hour, to that house which no white person save
himself had entered in years"; "Then they saw that the man
was white. . . . Then they saw that his face was not black" (245,
305). The vacillation between white and black in the "kodak
print" and "blackboard" similes is like the confusion in the
last example about whether "not black" always means white,
or even whether white always means "white." The final
misrecognition must be that the "dark complected" (46, 50)
Lucas Burch most likely has a darker skin than Christmas,
whom he betrays as a "nigger."

Burch, a criminally and blatantly distorted character, supplies
the town with a sense of coherence by introducing at the right
time divisive racial classifications. Dividing Joe Christmas
from white folks immediately solves the town's problems. He
restores the town's sense of identity and thereby escapes his
own quandary by intensifying Joe's. Like the falsely knowledgeable narrator, Burch pretends to assert his own superior
knowledge against the town's stupidity:

> "You're so smart," he says. "The folks in this town is so
> smart. Fooled for three years. Calling him a foreigner for
> three years, when soon as I watched him three days I knew
> he wasn't no more a foreigner than I am. . . . He's got nigger
> blood in him. I knowed it when I first saw him. . . . One time
> he even admitted it, told me he was part nigger."
>
> "A nigger," the marshal said. "I always thought there was
> something funny about that fellow."
>
> "Well," the sheriff says, "I believe you are telling the truth
> at last." (92)

Lucas Burch is Christmas's darker double. He looks more like a
"foreigner" and "nigger" and "murderer" than Christmas does
(he has a "little white scar by his mouth"; 51, 74, 258, 285), and
yet Christmas is the "nigger" whom the community sacrifices.

In fact, by the time the lynch mob is aroused, actual color makes no difference: the "countrymen . . . believed aloud that it was an anonymous crime committed not by a negro but by Negro and [they] knew, believed, and hoped that she had been ravished too: at least once before her throat was cut and at least once afterward" (272). The intentional humor of this excerpt is matched only by its absolute horror. Given that Joe and Lucas are really each other's "dark doubles," sharing every duty and function, it must follow that the "dark complected" Lucas, and not Joe Christmas, is likely to have "black blood." This assumption would explain why he is so anxious to "darken" and destroy Joe. Lena Grove's child, fathered by Burch, will be another mulatto in a long string of uncertain progeny that here, as in *Absalom, Absalom!*, ravels out into an uncertain future.

White Jefferson constitutes hearsay as authority, and has formed the hearsay into fixed figures to which force lends validity. For Christmas to become part of that society, he has to become one thing or an other. But he is neither/nor: neither black nor white, neither background nor writing – he is, no less than Darl or Addie, socially neuter. Joe Christmas must become the object of a signifying violence. *"We'll see if his blood is black. . . . We'll need a little more blood to tell for sure"* (205), say the men who come to brutalize him; they certainly wish to harm Joe, but their motives are in large part definitional. Yet even their expedient of violence does not help. The more blood is spilled to distinguish black from white blood, the more difficult it is to see the difference; at a considerable price it becomes clear that black and white "blood" are the same.

The fate of Christmas demonstrates that the town signifies "natural" value by force. There is no natural way to know what Christmas is, but this is precisely what annoys the town:

> He dont look any more like a nigger than I do. But it must have been the nigger blood in him. . . . He never acted like either a nigger or a white man. That was it. That was what made the folks so mad. . . . It was like he never knew he was a murderer, let alone a nigger too. (331)

He has not been socialized; he does not "know" what his "I" signifies. At their moment of outrage, the men of the town choose a murderous sort of coherence. In *Absalom, Absalom!*

Mr Compson says of the "white Negro," Charles Etienne Bon, "he was, must be, a negro" (198).

The moral of *Light in August* – that "when anything gets to be a habit, it also manages to get a right good distance away from truth and fact" (69) – has yet another test-case: Gail Hightower. He deludes himself thoroughly, becoming the victim of his own self-delusions. By interposing himself in Christmas's place, he almost prevents the mob's ritual murder of Christmas at the end, yet he comes short. In almost the same sense as Christmas, he is the town's scapegoat. He is marginal, living in a "small, brown, almost concealed house ... on what used to be the main street" (53–4). Faulkner makes it quite clear that someone living in a "high tower" of thought can communicate with few in the outside world. Even "the sign, carpentered neatly by himself and by himself lettered" (53), attracts no patrons. His sign, advertising "Art Lessons / Handpainted Xmas & Anniversary Cards / Photographs Developed," has "fading letters." Hightower, like his sign, suffers from the same malaise of communication as Joe does:

> [The fading letters] were still readable, however; though, like Hightower himself, few of the townspeople needed to read them anymore. ... So the sign which he carpentered and lettered is even less to him than it is to the town; he is no longer conscious of it as a sign, a message ... it is just a familiar low oblong shape without any significance at all. (53–4)

Gail Hightower (like Emily Grierson) wants to be "sheltered from the harsh gale of living" (453), but it is too late for him to return to the seminary and too soon for him to die.

The town has destroyed Hightower's life in a way that almost exactly parallels its victimization of Christmas. But his relations were already corrupted by his own misrecognition of his grandfather's heroism. He "grew to manhood among phantoms, and side by side with a ghost" (449). Faced with the unknown or indefinable nature of history, Hightower invents a repetitive ideology of the past:

> Then Sunday he would be again in the pulpit, with his wild hands and his wild rapt eager voice in which like phantoms

God and salvation and the galloping horses and his dead
grandfather thundered, while below him the elders sat, and
the congregation, puzzled and outraged. (60)

The public accepts his heroization of the past while remaining
somewhat uncomfortable with it; they adopt the idea that his
grandfather was "shot from the saddle of a galloping horse in a
Jefferson street" (452). Public opinion, however, cannot digest
the idea that his wife has a lover in Memphis. Hearsay fulfills
itself: "the ladies . . . maybe wondering if he knew what they
believed that they already knew" (58). "The town," "the
neighbors," "the ladies," begin to construct their own version
of things. They ignore Hightower's "slatternly" wife; their
fictional constructs even change what they see: "And soon it
was as though she were not there; as though everyone had
agreed that she was not there, that the minister did not
even have a wife" (61). When "Sunday morning's paper" says
"she had jumped or fallen from a hotel window in Memphis"
(62), it confirms the narrative that "everyone had agreed" upon
already. Agreement about reality contributes to creating
reality. Through his wife's death, Hightower learns important
lessons about how the town will construct "facts" later, in Joe
Christmas's case (and, by implication, in its overall handling of
any undefined otherness): "that was all it required: that idea,
that single idle word blown from mind to mind" (66). Fictions
seem inevitable, and their "ingenuity" recalls the constructs of
Don Quixote, the *ingenioso hidalgo*. Hightower thinks that
"ingenuity was apparently given man in order that he may
supply himself in crises with shapes and sounds with which to
guard himself from the truth" (453): by now he knows this
statement is apt, and most of all apt in his own case.

Joe's end: the "coherence" problem

Yet we must ask at the end to what extent Faulkner himself
hides from a truth he has uncovered, mainly by encasing it in
an overcomplex, even dual, narrative structure. Let us turn to
the most frequently encountered critical crux of the novel, the
"coherence" problem. The peculiar quality of *Light in August*
derives from the manner in which it encloses an indeterminate

character within a construct that struggles to give that character's life and death a significance. Faulkner, answering the criticism that his novels were merely short stories patched together, assured Ben Wasson after writing *Light in August* that "this one is a novel, not an anecdote," but less than a year later F. R. Leavis was to call the elements of the novel "unrelated organically." Another critic suggests that the "difficulty has always come with the attempt to relate the various episodes so as to show a coherent pattern of meaning. Critics so generally sympathetic as Conrad Aiken and George Marion O'Donnell find the novel a failure because of lack of unity."[9] It should be clear by now, however, that such a project of creating an organic "unity" or "coherent pattern of meaning" would involve us in the very same procedure of misrecognition that society uses to force Christmas to be "one thing."

As in *The Wild Palms*, and to an extent *Go Down, Moses*, Faulkner would "freeze" the meaning of an indeterminate signifier. The very cyclicality of the enveloping Lena Grove story is striking. The symbolism of her circular road ("My, my. A body does get around," she repeats) is an apparently redemptive counterpoint to Joe's linear, fateful, and "tragic" road to death. The powers of darkness and bigotry would, according to this interpretation, be overturned by the forces of fertility, the "fundamental permanence of the earth" represented by Lena.[10] The novel ends with the tale of how Lena sexually excites and then restrains Byron Bunch. The comic narration here is told by a furniture dealer to his wife in bed. The fact that the teller "shows" his wife what Bunch "wanted to do" with Lena – he makes love to her, rather than telling her "Bunch wanted to make love to Lena" – may represent a victory of deeds over words, activity over sterile talking. Even this final possibility, however, explicitly cancels out any sense that a verbally communicable lesson may be learned from the Christmas story.

Instead of the "tale later," the furniture dealer's wife gets "action sooner," yet the need to create meanings sooner or later is powerful enough that no one can claim to have escaped, not even Christmas himself. Joe Christmas learns that he has to be black, because "If I'm not, damned if I haven't wasted a lot of time" (241). He lives among blacks, "trying to breathe into himself the dark odor, the dark and inscrutable thinking and being of negroes . . . trying to expel from himself the white blood and the white thinking and being" (212). But even here the narrator has learned nothing. The narrator, unable to suspend judgment about Joe's true "being," says "white blood."

Despite the comic denouement, Christmas's tragic death provides the true climax of the novel. Interestingly syntax becomes suddenly ambiguous in this scene. The uncertainties surrounding the meaning of Joe Christmas's murder implicate author, town, and reader in the same web of guilt. We all owe a debt, of sorts, to any victim. Manifestly, in this case, his observers have crucified Christmas (or allowed him to be crucified), and his death has made a good yarn for the public:

> Then his face, body, all, seemed to collapse, to fall in upon itself, and from out the slashed garments about his hips and loins *the pent black blood* seemed to rush like a released breath. *It* seemed to rush out of his pale body like the rush of sparks from a rising rocket; upon that *black blast* the man seemed to rise soaring into their memories forever and forever. *They* are not to lose *it*, in whatever peaceful valleys, beside whatever placid and reassuring streams of old age, in the mirroring faces of whatever children *they* will contemplate old disasters and newer hopes. *It* will be there, musing, quiet, steadfast, not fading, and not particularly threatful, but of *itself* alone serene, of *itself* alone triumphant. (439–40; my italics)

This long excerpt may be the most important passage in the novel for tracing Faulkner's ambiguous conclusions. At least two things are striking in this tableau of Joe Christmas's martyrdom. In the first place, the various fatal ambiguities concerning "white" and "black" blood come to a head, without being at all resolved. What is "the pent black blood?" Whether "black" is here a figurative or literal term is crucial, but impossible to determine. Does this idea of "black blood" share in Calvin Burden's idea of a curse of blackness "staining their blood and flesh" (234) or Gavin Stevens's elegant schematics of "white blood" and "black blood" (424)?[11]

Moreover, the "blood" would seem to be the antecedent of "It" in the next sentence. "It" is the "black blast" upon which the figure of Christmas rises, apotheosized into an elegiac mode of memory. Faulkner has made the scene into a tableau, a "frozen moment," in which we would preserve in "memory" what he deems important.[12] This "memory" is above all the written text, and the lesson, such as it is, has been made at the expense of a life. Certainly, though, the image that has been "fixed" here as permanent and self-sufficient ("not fading ... of itself alone triumphant") only leads to more instability – particularly in the interpretation of "black blood." Who are the "They" of this excerpt? Who actually remembers the death of Christmas? "They are not to lose it. ... It will be there, musing, quiet, steadfast." "They" must certainly refer to the same people as in "their memories." But the memory is as ambiguous as the "they" who remember. Either "It" may be a condemnation of the inhumanity, or "It" may be a warning to the "niggers" of Jefferson – as such murder/castrations tended to be – about how *not* to behave with whites in general and white women in particular. "Pantaloon in Black" gives a similarly striking example of Southern "pedagogy" for blacks, an unwritten education by violence. After the black hero Rider kills a white man, we find "the prisoner on the following day, hanging from the bell-rope in a negro schoolhouse about two miles from the sawmill" (*Go Down, Moses*, p. 154). The blacks in Jefferson can be expected to remember every nuance of the Christmas story, including the fact that Joe was probably white. "The town," on the other hand, while remembering the tableau, will probably repress how and why Christmas died, as Hightower does above. This forgetting would be in accord with the general style of the town. As Adorno suggests, "all reification is a forgetting": Jefferson cannot remember the truth without losing its flattering and fixed self-image. For the town, Joe Christmas will always be "the nigger" who slit the "white woman's" throat and "got what he deserved."

In the end, the town, which seems "peaceful" and "placid" soon after the murder, does not choose between possibilities. The "memory" is only a potentially recapturable trace. Once we extend the possible referent of the "they" to Faulkner's readers, we can perhaps account for the confusion about the meaning of *Light in August*. With few exceptions, such investigations into "coherence" remain unsatisfying as descriptions of the "It" that Faulkner has promised will not even need justification ("of itself alone triumphant"). The ironic thing – which no doubt did not escape Faulkner – is that if we actually follow his narrator here, who offers a "serene" and "triumphant" recollection of a vigilante murder, then we have but murdered Joe Christmas once again.

Notes

1 Faulkner borrows, for the "tragic mulatto" figure, chiefly from abolitionist writers such as Stowe, Hildreth, and Trowbridge. See Walter Taylor, "Faulkner: Nineteenth Century Notions of Racial Mixture and the Twentieth Century Imagination," *The South Carolina Review*, 10 (1977), p. 59, and also Judith R. Berzon, *Neither White nor Black: The Mulatto Character in American Fiction* (New York: New York University Press, 1978), pp. 81–98. His enterprise may be a fictional working out of the subject–object, master–slave relations in other senses too. As Theodor Adorno says in his article "Subject and Object," "If speculation on the state of reconciliation were permitted, neither the undistinguished unity of subject and object nor their antithetical hostility would be conceivable in it; rather, the communication of what was distinguished": in Andrew Arato and Eike Gebhardt (eds), *The Essential Frankfurt School Reader* (New York: Continuum, 1982), p. 499.
2 Paul de Man, *Allegories of Reading: Figural Language in Rousseau, Nietzsche, Rilke, and Proust* (New Haven: Yale University Press, 1979), p.5.
3 William Faulkner, *Light in August* (New York: Vintage, 1972), p. 39. All subsequent quotations from this edition will be cited by page numbers in parentheses in the text.
4 Umberto Eco, *A Theory of Semiotics* (Bloomington: Indiana University Press, 1976), p. 9.
5 William Faulkner, *Faulkner at West Point*, ed. Joseph L. Fant III and Robert Ashley (New York: Random House, 1964), p. 83; Irving Howe, *William Faulkner* (1951), 3rd edn (Chicago: University of Chicago Press, 1975), p. 201; Robert Penn Warren, "T. S. Stribling," *American Review*, 2 (February 1934), pp. 483–6, quoted in John Bassett (ed.), *William Faulkner: The Critical Heritage* (Boston: Routledge & Kegan Paul, 1975), p. 161; Jean Stewart, "The Novels of William Faulkner," *Cambridge Review*, March 10, 1933, pp. 310–12, in Bassett (ed.), op. cit., p. 150; F. R. Leavis, review, *Scrutiny* (June 1933), in Bassett (ed.), op. cit., p. 144; Cleanth Brooks, *William Faulkner: The Yoknapatawpha Country* (New Haven: Yale University Press, 1963), p. 50.

6 See Sally Padgett Wheeler, "Chronology in *Light in August*," *The Southern Literary Journal*, 6 (1973), p. 23.

7 See, for instance, Brooks, op. cit., p. 99; Walter J. Slatoff, *Quest for Failure* (1960; Westport, Conn.: Greenwood Press, 1972), p. 175; Richard P. Adams, *Faulkner: Myth and Motion* (Princeton: Princeton University Press, 1968), p. 84; Slatoff, op. cit., p. 185; Howe, op. cit., p. 204.

8 See, respectively, Adams, op. cit., p. 164; David Williams, *Faulkner's Women* (Montreal: McGill/Queen's University Press, 1977), p. 184; Michael Millgate, *The Achievement of William Faulkner* (London: Constable, 1966), p. 134; Slatoff, op. cit., pp. 176, 182; Brooks, op. cit., p. 56. Gail L. Mortimer, *Faulkner's Rhetoric of Loss* (Austin: University of Texas Press, 1983), p. 25, repeats the "homosexuality" suggestion.

9 William Faulkner, *Selected Letters*, ed. Joseph Blotner (New York: Random House, 1977), p. 66, letter to Ben Wasson, September 1932. The Leavis reference is from an untitled review in *Scrutiny*, 2 (June 1933), quoted in Bassett (ed.), op. cit., p. 143. See also Brooks, op. cit., pp. 48–9.

10 Faulkner calls Joe Christmas "one of the most tragic figures I can think of," yet the Lena story is essentially comic; the linear/cyclical opposition here represents the basic difference that Northrop Frye, among others, sees between a tragic and a comic plot. See his *Anatomy of Criticism: Four Essays* (Princeton: Princeton University Press, 1957), pp. 158–239. See also Millgate, op. cit., p. 135.

11 See Taylor, op. cit., p. 64, for a typically glib resolution of this ambiguity.

12 Such a "fixing" of a fleeting reality is a standard technique of Faulkner's later fiction, and is certainly inspired by the sensibility of Keats's "Ode to a Grecian Urn." Similar "frozen moments" occur during the river-crossing in *As I Lay Dying*, in the death of the bear in the short story of the same title, and in the scene where Henry shoots Charles Bon in *Absalom, Absalom!* See Karl E. Zink, "Flux and the Frozen Moment," *PMLA* (June 1956).

5

Absalom, Absalom! (1936)

Faulkner called his ninth novel "a manifestation of a general racial system in the South which was condensed and concentrated ... a constant general condition in the South, yes."[1] Having in *The Sound and the Fury* and *As I Lay Dying* rejected escape through a narcissistic return to oneness (by madness or death), and having in *Light in August* predicted ever newer acts of social violence whenever signifiers of difference fail, Faulkner now reveals through his characters the joints of racism's plot, joints that may well end up as sprains.

In *Phaedrus*, Socrates praises the dialectician who can "survey scattered particulars ... make a regular division and discover a characteristic mark of each class," and who can divide the classes "into species according to the natural formation, where the joint is" (sec. 281-4). The "joint," in *Light in August*, *Absalom, Absalom!*, and *Go Down, Moses*, is where one human class can be distinguished from another, and it is the natural place of contrast where a clean separation can be made. But with color there are no clean separations; where does white end and black begin? The "joint," as such, is where the racial plot of the South both holds together and threatens to fall apart. Since in racial discrimination "the characteristic mark of each class" is visual, and since all blood looks the same, both visual and "blood" distinctions destroy their own verifiability precisely at their "joint." Division's dialectician surveys "scattered particulars," finding skin color an apt visual signifier of difference. Subject and object take up conventionally fixed places: the viewers decide on a characteristic mark which becomes the static denotation of the viewed. Calling this classification "natural" hides its sources in fear, not nature, and attempts to underplay the arbitrariness of the mark.

When Socratic rhetorical division is applied to social organization, it becomes clear that skin color is among the significations that have historically allowed human beings to be ranked, properly or improperly, within a hierarchy of oppositions. Fredric Jameson says that "The realm of separation, of fragmentation . . . exists, as Hegel would put it, not so much *in itself* as rather *for us*, as the basic logic and fundamental law of our daily life."[2] Color is perhaps the most deceitful of all characteristic marks, because it seems self-evident, a division *in itself* – common sense says that everyone can agree upon the color of skin. Yet, compared to what all humans have in common (arms, legs, hair, blood, eyes), race is somewhat trivial, belonging to the category termed "deception" by Socrates himself: "When will there be more chance of deception – when the difference is large or small?" "When the difference is small," Phaedrus correctly replies (sec. 280).

Sigmund Freud noticed that individuals decide upon small differences as the principle of individuation. In "The Taboo of Virginity," he notes that "every individual distinguishes himself from others by a 'taboo of personal isolation' . . . it is exactly the small differences, alongside an overall similarity, that were the basis for the feelings of strangeness and enmity between them." Freud's *Group Psychology and the Analysis of the Ego* suggests that human social relations might be constituted by what he calls "the narcissism of small differences":

> Closely related races keep one another at arm's length; the South German cannot endure the North German, the Englishman casts every kind of aspersion upon the Scot, the

Spaniard despises the Portugese ... greater differences ...
lead to an almost insuperable repugnance, such as the Gallic
people feel for the German, the Aryan for the Semite, and *the
white races for the coloured.* (my italics)

But even these "greater differences" constitute an example of
an anatomical fallacy that would systematically tie external to
internal attributes.[3]

Absalom, Absalom!, like its predecessor *Light in August*,
thoroughly undercuts the outside–inside equation that the
deceitful signs of race and gender are supposed to cement.
Their incorrigibility – which Freud bemoans – comes from the
fact that they share what Paul De Man calls the "property of
language ... the possibility of substituting binary polarities ...
without regard for the truth-value of these structures ... this is
precisely how Nietzsche also defines the rhetorical figure, the
paradigm of all language." The crucial difference here is that
Southern segregationist discourse wishes to "freeze" figures
that link gender or skin color with value in coded signifier–
signified pairs. For Nietzsche such rhetorical figures are unable
to support a stable equivalence of exterior and interior – after
all, the trope is exactly that which turns. As De Man suggests:
"Rhetoric is a *text* in that it allows for two incompatible,
mutually self-destructive points of view. ... Considered as
persuasion, rhetoric is performative, but when considered as a
system of tropes, it deconstructs its own performance."[4]
Faulkner's Charles Bon, like Joe Christmas, is a "black
Caucasian" or "white Negro." Any conceptual configuration
of strict racial division develops sprains in the light of real
oxymoronic figures such as these.

Against chaos: repetition and division

Miss Rosa is the model of the reducing, signifying drive of
reading, and she begins the novel as if to center the narrative's
reducing efforts. Vladimir Propp argues that the signifying
value of crucial plot objects derives from their relation to
desire.[5] If a character desires (lacks) an object, then that object
will signify the reader's desire for narrative completion. Sutpen

is first of all important to us because he is important to Rosa. But he is important to Rosa not as a man, but as the epithetic center of a longer narrative. It is not enough that Rosa has a desire. Her desire for the other must attain a *Vorstellungsrepräsentanz*, in Freud's terms, a "representing" language of images or fantasies.

Rosa has been exposed to the greatest possible historical and personal chaos, judging from her life-span (1845–1910). The Civil War, and the deprivations, triumphs, and retreats it brought to pass – Shiloh, "Chickamauga and Franklin, Vicksburg and Corinth and Atlanta" (345) – are arguably the cause of much of what goes on in *Absalom, Absalom!*, but perhaps also the result. Does Sutpen's design fail because the South lost the war, or did the South lose the war because its design was as intrinsically callous and corrupt as Sutpen's? The role of the Civil War in Sutpen's narrative is important but not definitive. The confusions over dates and even the jumbled sequences of each narrative suggest that *Absalom, Absalom!* is not primarily about particular historical events, but rather about how actual historical events are transformed, often retroactively, into deceptive fictive, mythic, and ideological constructs.

Rosa is 15 or 16 when her world of men virtually vanishes. She is not yet 20 when her father dies, and in the next year Henry kills Charles Bon and the South loses the Civil War. One year later, Sutpen asks her to "breed" with him, and the match will end in marriage if the offspring is a male. Her story establishes for the reader the novel's repetitive structure of violence returned for violence given. She begins to change others into the objects they had hoped to mold her into. For Rosa, value no longer derives from physical satisfaction, but from significations of thwarted desire. She is a ghost, one of the "also-dead," and repeating her "outrages," she freezes the repetitions into offprints of the missing fulfillment. Hence for her, every incident or person becomes an epithet. She changes the complexity of "Sutpen" into "an ogre or Djinn," "demon," "brute," "shadow," or "devil," epithets which now designate absent commodities.

abstract

indeed, the very process of *abstraction* itself is in its very essence a reduction, through which we substitute for the four-dimensional density of reality itself simplified models, schematic abstract ideas, and thereby of necessity do violence to reality and to experience.[6]

Miss Rosa's abstractions are mental prostheses that abut severed stumps. Like phantom limbs, they only recall an itch that cannot be satisfied.

But, almost as soon as Miss Rosa starts making Sutpen into epithetic narrative, she becomes her own narrative's victim, calling herself repeatedly "an orphan . . . and a pauper" – she is a bit of both, but is hardly reducible to either. Yet she reduces herself to them, and soon Mr Compson follows her lead: "Now Miss Rosa was not only an orphan, but a pauper, too. . . . So Miss Rosa was both pauper and orphan."[7] As much as Miss Rosa, Mr Compson now assumes the reductive discourse of the town. In almost every case (with Shreve and Quentin providing the exceptions), *Absalom, Absalom!*'s narrators tend to adopt verbatim the tag-like leitmotifs that others have relayed, without peering behind them for any "rounder" truths of character. Most reductive of all, of course, is the narrative of "the town" itself, which believes "the stranger" equals superficial signifiers of "a horse," "two pistols," a "short reddish beard," "the roan horse," "teeth," and "wild beasts." The outward man and inward man are, by a semantic violence, one.

After the chaos of the Civil War, Rosa, like many of her countrymen, opted for an extreme version of signifying differences. Faulkner does not err in depicting this extreme need for division as sexual in origin. The paradox that fuels Faulkner's major novels here emerges: the South's fear of racial mixing involves an element of undefined sexual desire for the denied other, a conscious fear of merging with the other, and finally a fetishization of the other's intangibility. Rosa's frenetic self-separation from Sutpen (also a dark, unknown other, as we shall see) dooms her to cling forever to him as her lost object of desire, just as the radical separation of the races only ensures that their fates will forever be, peacefully or violently, intertwined.

Miss Rosa represents extreme separating tendencies. Her "eternal black," juxtaposed to her pale skin, makes her something of a semaphore of racial sequestration. Yet, in advertising the separation of black and white, she paradoxically has to don the black that she would banish. The subject/object dominance she proclaims has allowed the white male to reduce women, blacks, and nature to servants and seconds. Sutpen drags "house and formal gardens violently out of the soundless Nothing," or, as Rosa says, "*Tore violently a plantation*" (9), or, again "dragged house and gardens out of virgin swamp, and plowed and planted his land with seed cotton which General Compson had loaned him" (40). Land exists for Sutpen as "virgin," to be inseminated with the old seed of the Old South, represented by General Compson's loan of "seed cotton." Women are "adjunctive or incremental" (240) to men's designs, and at best may become "the anonymous wife" or "the stainless wife" (51).

In this world, blacks, women, and poor whites, insofar as they represent only their economic value as labor, might as well signify beasts as humans, as Sutpen thinks, looking at

> his sister pumping rhythmic up and down above a washtub in the yard, her back toward him, shapeless in a calico dress and a pair of the old man's shoes flapping about her bare ankles and broad in the beam as a cow, the very labor she was doing brutish and stupidly out of all proportion to its reward: the primary essence of labor, toil, reduced to its crude absolute which only a beast could and would endure. (236)

Beasts in human form do the work of the South, yet the South cannot integrate labor into its formulation of what is human; blacks and beasts are both inhuman, "the primary essence of labor, toil, reduced to its crude absolute which only a beast could and would endure." Henry's "entire cosmopolitan experience ... consisted probably of one or two trips to Memphis with his father to buy live stock or slaves" (335); Sutpen chose his slaves "with the same care and shrewdness with which he chose the other livestock" (61). Slaves are "other livestock": the animal/human opposition aligns with the black/white one, a trope made necessary by the role of animals and blacks alike in the economic system as labor. Sutpen's innocence comes from an ignorance of the link between social and economic division:

> So he didn't even know there was a country all divided and

fixed and neat with a people living on it all divided and fixed
and neat because of what color their skins happened to be
and what they happened to own, and where a certain few
men not only had the power of life and death and barter and
sale over others, but they had living human men to perform
the endless repetitive personal offices . . . that all men have
had to do for themselves since time began. (221–2)

"All divided and fixed and neat" aptly communicates the
double moments of separation ("divided") and orderly habituation ("fixed and neat") upon which such a system depends. The
reduction of the individual to the "barter" value of his or her
"labor" may be the chief underlying reason for strict large-
scale separations; figures of division collude with a general
system of economic exploitation.

For racial identity is reciprocal. The black, as the white's
"shadow" – borrowing Otto Rank's notion in *The Myth of the
Birth of the Hero* of the "double" who figures the distance
between ego-ideal and reality – evokes love (the black, seen by
the white as an offprint of himself) but also hate and fear (being
a copy with a difference). *Absalom, Absalom!* illustrates that
barriers between the races are logically, psychologically, and
sexually permeable. Freud suggests that, in an "erotic" state in
which "the boundary between ego and object threatens to melt
away," we wish to reintegrate what has been separated. The
loss of identity is a wish as well as a threat, belonging to "an
earlier state of things" – the Urchaos of the womb ("the
restoration of limitless narcissism"), a time when there were
no social (or any other) divisions.

As in every conceptual system, racial opposites rely on the
other's signifying difference in order to mean anything at all.
Society typically disregards this interlinkage, covering up the
quantum of debt and guilt that each race must bear for the
other. Charles Bon, in speaking to his innocent half-brother
Henry, exposes as false the independence of white women
from black "slave girls." He refers to "the chasm which could
be crossed but one time and in but one direction . . . slave girls
and women upon whom that first caste [white virgin women]
rested and to whom . . . it doubtless owed the very fact of its
virginity." The system permits crossing "in but one direction":
white men may molest black women, but black men may not

even glance at white women, as if "trope" did not mean "turn." In short, the twin sexual taboos of the white Southern male – against racial mixing, and against premarital sexual relations with white women – have become, in the face of *eros*, mutually exclusive. The "debt" that the virgin caste owes to despoiled black women also creates a residue of "guilt" in which the seeming polarities of white virgin and slave concubine inextricably commingle.

The most insidious operation of division is its self-erasure as "nature." Sutpen discovers that division "had never once been mentioned by name" (231), yet stereotypes based on dialect, skin color, smell, and gender signs are "the natural thing for any Southern woman, gentlewoman" (86) to maintain. Rosa and the town find in their shared ability to equate outside with inside a so-called "community." Miss Rosa thinks herself part of the community, "a woman who . . . had already established herself as the town's and the county's poetess laureate" (11), but she remains marginal in her "little grim house's impregnable solitude" (88). She has walled herself into a sort of hermetic lifelessness: "a dim hot airless room with the blinds all closed and fastened for forty-three summers" (7), "as if there were prisoned in it like in a tomb all the suspiration of slow heat-laden time which had recurred" (10). Time "recurs," yes, but nothing changes; Rosa calls it "the office because her father had called it that" (7).

Shreve may be right that the South is "something you live and breathe in like air" (361). Such hermetic stuffiness is powerful; even the cold northern air becomes, as Shreve and Quentin reconstruct Sutpen's story, "tomblike: a quality stale and static and moribund beyond any mere vivid and living cold" (345). To tell the story is to breathe the contagious southern air, "the air which he had once walked in and breathed" (202), "the same air in which the church bells had rung on that Sunday morning in 1833," even the same air "where descendants of the same pigeons strutted and crooned or wheeled in short courses" (31). Miss Rosa's "frozen time" would reify persons and relations lest they cause her any further harm. Freezing would give them a surface demeanor, unblurred and forever static, "a sort of lifeless and perennial bloom like painted portraits hung in a vacuum . . . the originals of which had lived and died so long ago that their joys and griefs must now be forgotten" (75).

Miss Rosa speaks in the rhetorical figures that her reductive fixings mandate. The best rhetorical term for her discourse would be chiasmus or *anti-metabole*, demonstrated in the form and content of what the narrator says of Quentin: "He was a barracks filled with stubborn back-looking ghosts . . . looking with stubborn recalcitrance backwards" (12); the chiasmus (A : B : : B : A) always looks backwards, in stubborn protest against the new. Rosa's verbal fixations show a marked inability to carry a grammatical progression beyond an initial assertion. Speech, blocked, stumbles. Often in Rosa's case the hindrance is not actually a willed separation from future, but a historical blockage that sentences her to the past. Rosa's repetitions are "graphs" – possibly even "scratches" of a phonograph record beyond which the needle may not progress, the scars that repeated outrage has left behind. Consider, for example, the following passages, beginning with the scene in which Clytie blocks Miss Rosa from ascending the staircase:

> Yes, I stopped dead – no *woman's* hand, no *negro's* hand, but bitted bridle-curb to check and guide the furious and unending will – I crying not to her, to it; speaking to it through the *negro*, the *woman*. (139, 140, my italics)

> That was I. I was there. (152)

> One day he was not. Then he was. Then he was not . . . he was absent, and he was; he returned, and he was not . . . and he had never been. (152–3)

> Oh, I hold no brief for Ellen: blind romantic fool . . . youth and inexperience . . . blind romantic fool . . . blind woman mother fool . . . youth or inexperience. . . . Yes, blind, romantic fool. (15)

Especially in the last example, Rosa's thoughts return in an elliptical curve to their unchanged origins, killing any promise of novelty.

Most critics agree that Sutpen begins as an underprivileged white on the periphery of privileged society, who learns to classify others, and hopes to build up his fortunes and "respectability." Sutpen is the outsider made good, but outsider he remains. He embodies the falsity of an American rags-to-riches myth which claims that the "social structure of the South has always been more fluid than outsiders suppose."[8] Yet Sutpen, intruding from without, might have been the breath of air that could have saved Miss Rosa. She sees Sutpen as her redeemer; just as the poor white Wash Jones (even more clearly in the precursor short story "Wash," written in 1934) views Sutpen as the apotheosis of lower-class dreams. Sutpen rouses in Rosa and Wash the vain hope that they are not in the same circle as the "niggers" whose social elevation the community has permanently barred. Yet Thomas Sutpen violently excludes both Rosa and Wash, each in a cruel way.[9] In all respects, the novel affirms that the "nigger" is just an exaggerated and special case of the way whites treat each other: as long as there are any "niggers," whites run the risk of being treated like them.

If one must read Sutpen as "a version of the American Dream," a myth of rags-to-riches elevation, then clearly the American Dream of advancement deconstructs its own performance. Something is wrong if, even after the white outsider learns the text of segregation, something bars his acceptance into white society. Brooks asserts that "Sutpen does remain outside the community," and Ilse Lind agrees: "To be sure, he never becomes an integrated member of his community."[10] When such a society systematically excludes, the overall notion of "community" becomes degenerate and impracticable, even for the most persistent strivers. Whenever the woman (Miss Rosa) or the poor white (Sutpen) try on the mask of segregation, they merely define themselves as enigmatic; even though they learn to dominate others, they can never shed their signification as subordinate.

Figures of merging

Despite a general tendency to separate and reduce in Yoknapatawpha, we find in *Absalom, Absalom!* a seepage between ostensibly discrete social cells. For instance, the siblings' relationship throughout mocks strict sexual definition, "the two of them, brother and sister, curiously alike as if the difference in sex had merely sharpened the common blood to a terrific and almost unbearable similarity" (172). Male and female roles interweave without warning. Henry, young heir to the masculine hegemony of the Sutpen line, runs "screaming and vomiting" from the fights his father has with the "wild niggers," while his sister Judith watches "with the same cold and attentive interest with which Sutpen would have watched Henry fighting with a negro boy of his own age and height" (120). The daughter, Judith, and not Henry, the son, copies the father's roughness. Even within Rosa's family, her aunt is a "strong vindictive consistent woman who seems to have been twice the man that Mr Coldfield was and who in very truth was not only Miss Rosa's mother but her father too" (63). Rosa sees herself as "androgynous" (146) and "not as a woman, a girl, but as the man which I perhaps should have been" (144). Sutpen, Charles Bon, Charles Etienne Bon, Mr Coldfield, Mr Compson, and Quentin – in short, all the major male characters in the novel – spend great portions of time in a state that Faulkner at one points calls "some hiatus of passive and hopeless despair" (197), a "feminine," passive mode. Bon, in particular, seems "feminized." Rosa dreams of him as the romantic "white male" lover, yet he wears an emblematic "flowered, almost feminized gown" (95), and one cannot be certain whether Ellen, Judith and Rosa love him more because he is a man or because he resembles a woman.

Mergings of black and white are still more striking. In a society that defines black skin as a signifier of absence or "invisibility," it seems remarkable how often the supposedly reliable white males are absent. Rosa's father disappears into an attic for three years, never to come out. Sutpen, from the outset a shadow, returns from his Civil War absence a "sonless widower" (155), that is, defined by what he lacks, a son and a wife. In Rosa's eyes, he "seemed to project himself ahead like a mirage . . . he himself was not there. . . . The shell of him was there. . . . Yes. He wasn't there" (160). Henry is "the absent male" (158). Bon's "substanceless" traces include the "invisible imprint of his absent thighs," "a name . . . a photograph"; "an echo, but not the shot," of the gun that kills him before he can "leave even the imprint of a body on a mattress" (152). Rosa's desire for Bon to have "left some seed, some minute virulence in this cellar earth of mine" (146), would apparently revivify the insemination metaphor (Sutpen

had "plowed and planted his land with seed cotton which
General Compson had loaned him"; 40), and links it with the
problems of global meaning in *Absalom, Absalom!* Bon and all
the other absent white males have left seed, but not a seed
that "inseminates." Rather it is "seed" that "disseminates,"
in Derrida's term, and this sowing leads to the prolific
repeatability "of always different, always postponed meanings."
But in this book of ghosts the success of Bon's dissemination is
articulated as an *absence* of seed. The project of finding
meaning in the novel is akin to Rosa's sensing the fallowness
of indeterminate seed left "in this cellar earth of mine."[11] No
wonder that Bon wants proof of his identity "on paper": "He
would just have to write 'I am your father. Burn this' . . . Or if
not that, a sheet, a scrap of paper with the one word 'Charles'
in his hand. . . . Or a lock of his hair or a paring from his finger
nail" (326). The white male, who has disinherited and effaced
the black other, has in consequence become his invisible
servant's white double, equally absent and equally seedless.

The vagueness of racial identity, in key moments, affects the
ability even of whites to characterize themselves as anything
at all. Miss Rosa, who on the surface represents white
spinsterhood, is more "mixed" than she knows. She wears
"eternal black" and sits in the darkness in a "black bonnet
with jet sequins" (88). She imagines herself as a child "standing
motionless beside that door as though trying to make myself
blend with the dark wood" (27). On childhood trips to Sutpen's
Hundred, Rosa's aunt "would order her to go and play with her
nephew and niece" (62), meaning Henry and Judith. Rosa's
aunt does not mention Rosa's step-niece, Sutpen's black
daughter, Clytie. In her turn, Rosa also rejects her familial
connection with Clytie. During her visits to Sutpen's mansion,
Rosa "would not even play with the same objects which
[Clytie] and Judith played with . . . the very objects [Clytie] had
touched" (140). Despite the aunt's hysterical precautions,
Judith and Clytie have "even slept together, in the same room
but with Judith in the bed and she on a pallet on the floor
ostensibly." Rosa's "ostensibly" entails a further falsehood: in
fact they are not lying separately side by side, but in the same
bed: "I have heard how on more than one occasion Ellen has
found them both on the pallet, and once in the bed together"
(140). Proximity becomes intimacy. Before long, even Miss

Rosa has merged with her once tabooed step-niece, Clytie: Judith, Clytie, and Rosa lived

> not as two white women and a negress, not as three negroes or three white, not even as three women, but merely as three creatures ... with no distinction among the three of [them] of age or color. ... It was as though [they] were one being, interchangeable and indiscriminate. (155)

The most striking breakdown of racial division comes in the figure of Sutpen himself, about whom Faulkner cleverly leaves open the question of exact origins:

> he didn't know just where his father had come from, whether from the country to which they returned or not, even if his father knew, remembered, wanted to remember and find it again ... he did not know within a year on either side just how old he was. So he knew neither where he had come from, nor where he was nor why. (223–7)

It soon becomes clear that Sutpen has produced in Clytie what Rosa calls the "Sutpen coffee-colored face" (136), a black "replica of his own [face] which he had created and decreed to preside upon his absence" (138). Yet, like Charles Bon, Clytie, the replica, results from an intercourse of the races that, according to society's official view, may not exist. Given the overall valence of Sutpen in the novel as an absence that does not exist, it would seem that, far from Clytie's being a dark replica of his whiteness, Sutpen himself is the source of a certain censored blackness in the narrative. Sutpen introduces a kind of demonic "otherness" that seems to force open Jefferson's sureties of plot or language as if by fate or by accident. He is, in fact, the carrier of an originless blackness that clandestinely inserts its way into the presumably pure genealogies of Southern whiteness.

Ignorance of his origins is but one respect in which Sutpen exactly mirrors his own "originless" son, Charles Bon. Sutpen rejects Bon, his son, just as the "nigger" servant rejected him as poor white. Here we have another Faulknerian "merging": the servant supports the system as the *Doppelgänger* for the white master, an example of Freud's "identification of the suppressed classes with the class who rules and exploits."[12] Sutpen, like Benjy in *The Sound and the Fury* and blacks generally in

Absalom, Absalom!, is a "carrier," a medium for messages he does not create or share. Blacks are frequently messengers in Yoknapatawpha: Rosa summons Quentin "by the hand of a small negro boy" (10); one of the "wild negroes" carries Ellen's wedding invitations "from door to door by hand" (54); the messages from Henry and Bon to Judith make "weekly journeys by the hand of Henry's groom" (105) and "The nigger groom that fetched the mail back and forth each week" gives Bon's letters to Judith (268); the New Orleans lawyer keeps "a special nigger in the lawyer's anteroom to do nothing else but carry" his faked reports to Bon's mother (304); Henry waits for a letter from Bon "each time the nigger rode over from Sutpen's Hundred" (326); Bon writes "by the first nigger post which rode to Sutpen's Hundred" (322); finally, Henry and Bon dispatch the fatal proposal to Judith "by hand, by a nigger" (342).

The black servant rejects the young Sutpen as if he were just another black messenger boy, just as Henry later rejects his half-brother Charles Bon's approach to their sister Judith. Both rebuffs take the form of a physical obstacle that enforces socially impassable divisions.[13]

> He didn't even remember leaving. All of a sudden he found himself running and already some distance from the house, and not toward home . . . like when you pass through a room fast . . . and you turn and go back through the room again and look at all the objects from the other side and you find out you had never seen them before. (232, 230)

But now a physical rebuff has caused a psychic and verbal regression, as in Rosa's chiasmus-filled prose. Nothing can ever be the same until the rejection is reversed.

The rejection–initiation scene at the door exactly parallels Sutpen's first exposure to writing. Blacks cannot write; Charles Etienne's "coal-black" wife puts down an "X" for a signature – analphabetism constitutes but one more link between Sutpen and blacks, and one more factor separating them from their white superiors. Sutpen's mother "never did quite learn to speak English" (241). When Sutpen listens to his teacher reciting about the West Indies from a book, he asks: " 'How do I know that what you read was in the book?' . . . I had not then learned to read my own name" (242). Perhaps in the end he learns to read his own name but Sutpen consistently

favors oral modes. Hence Bon's wish to receive a "written
note" from Sutpen is doomed from the start. Even on the boat
to the West Indies, the young Sutpen had "no more way of
knowing whether the men who said the ship was going there
were lying or not than he had of knowing whether or not the
school teacher was telling the truth about what was in the
book" (244). Once in Haiti, Sutpen sets out to master the
blacks' "dark and fatal tongue" (36), "that tongue which even
now a good part of the county did not know was a civilized
language" (56). His black driver speaks to his team in
"something without words, not needing words probably, in
that tongue in which they slept in the mud of that swamp"
(24). This is the language with which Sutpen can hold "his wild
negroes with that one word" (57).

Sutpen represents the perfect middleman; his mastery even
seems hermeneutical. He is lord over the written and the oral,
able to interpret worlds black and white. No white is like him.
Rosa, for instance, expresses her estrangement from Clytie and
all blacks in terms of language: "we might have been not only
of different races (which we were), not only of different sexes
(which we were not), but of different species, speaking no
language which the other understood" (153). Clearly Sutpen's
linguistic intercourse with blacks extends to the fact that "he
named them all himself" (61), including "Charles Bon. Charles
Good" (265), even if the black wife's name was "Eulalia Bon"
well before she met Sutpen. His act of re-naming Eulalia after
God's "it was good" puts him in the place of her own father,
who was also presumably named "Bon." Insofar as "Bon"
signifies her "black blood," Sutpen's act of naming merges him
with the black donor of that blood and that name.

Sutpen and blacks are twinned versions of what no system
can either repress or signify for good. Sutpen's youth depicts
the rejections that one typically finds in the lives of young
blacks in white society. By the time Sutpen is older and arrives
in Jefferson, he has almost completely merged with the "wild
negroes," who "belonged to him body and soul" (40): they are
"distinguishable one from another by his beard and eyes alone
. . . the bearded white man and the twenty black ones and all
stark naked beneath the croaching and pervading mud" (37).
He fights "naked chest to chest" (253) with the blacks, "both
naked to the waist and gouging at one another's eyes as if they

should not only have been the same color, but should have
been covered with fur too" (29). Sutpen is a "public enemy"
(43) and a "runaway slave" (48). It becomes increasingly
difficult, it seems, for any narrator to separate Sutpen from the
"wild negroes." Both habitually show their teeth, and indeed
in one case we see "his face exactly like the negro's save for
the teeth (this because of the beard, doubtless)" (23). The
"teeth" image is also the last we see of Sutpen: Judith helps
carry his corpse home, "quiet and bloody, and his teeth still
showing in the parted beard" (185).

These mergings would be less noteworthy if they did not
culminate in Sutpen's merging with the one black whom he
most wants to distance, his son Charles Bon. Sutpen's
characteristic "expression almost of smiling where his teeth
showed through the beard" (57), his "something like smiling
inside his beard" (279), and his final "looking at Henry with
that expression which might be called smiling" (357) resonate
in "Bon's teeth glinting for an instant" (113). The accidental
repetition echoes a fundamental harmony. At one point Judith
says:

> you are born at the same time with a lot of other people, all
> mixed up with them, like trying to, having to, move your
> arms and legs with strings only the same strings are hitched
> to all the other arms and legs and the others . . . all trying to
> make a rug on the same loom only each one wants to weave
> his own pattern into the rug. (127)

Her textual metaphor links society and Faulkner's narrative.
Writing pretends an isolation of narrative strands that cannot
last. Patterns intertwine: *en route* to college, Henry and Bon
were "only in surface manner of food and clothing and daily
occupation any different from the negro slaves who supported
them" (97). Sutpen and Bon express, as the novel's key
figures, tragic symmetries: both knock at closed doors and are
rejected; both marry without knowing their wives are part
black; both abandon their wives and sons; both are alternately
active and passive; both are named and "nameless" shadows;
both are present and absent; both are futile avengers of prior
affronts.

If Bon is one of "the white men" as he says (115), then the
reversal of the novel's standard reading is complete. It is

incorrect to say that the white Thomas Sutpen rejects his black son Charles Bon. Rather, Sutpen (like Burch in *Light in August*) may be considerably "blacker" than we thought – and perhaps most black where he wishes to be most white. In turning his "black Caucasian" son away from his door, Sutpen has simply merged with the same "monkey-dressed nigger" who first rebuffed him at a front door as a child. He, the father, has become black by turning back his putatively black son (we never learn whether in fact Bon has black blood). The climactic scene in the novel, the meeting between the aging Henry and Quentin, also figures a chiasmus structure, a turn of plot all the more compelling because it uses as its pivot exactly what has been made absent: the black. Faulkner's text illustrates that American caste and economic relations revolve around the black, the source of the paradoxes in Sutpen's story, and American society's most volatile subject.

For we have gone from the "unbroken perpetuity" of reductive social distinctions to a shifting and merging of these roles based on narrative exchange. Indeed, the narrative is the trickiest space of all, as Mr Compson inadvertently exemplifies when he "raised his feet once more to the railing, the letter in his hand and the hand looking almost as dark as a negro's against his linen leg" (89): even as he speaks, he "blackens"! So Mr Compson need not verbalize what the account is doing to him and to his characters; the account itself does so:

> We have a few old mouth-to-mouth tales; we exhume from old trunks and boxes and drawers letters without salutation or signature, in which men and women who once lived and breathed are now merely initials or nicknames. ... Yes, Judith, Bon, Henry, Sutpen: all of them. They are there ... they are like a chemical formula exhumed along with the letters from that forgotten chest, carefully, the paper old and faded and falling to pieces, the writing faded, almost indecipherable ... you re-read ... you bring them together again and again and nothing happens. (101)

The external rearrangements of fading letters makes combination and merging, not separation and division, the generators of narrative meaning. Quentin sees that "the mere names were interchangeable and almost myriad" (12); Mr Compson speculates that Miss Rosa sees Sutpen's face "like the mask in

Greek tragedy, interchangeable not only from scene to scene, but from actor to actor" (62) – which is to say that his reduction to a mask has invalidated any prayed-for adequation of outside to inside.

The main actors in the Sutpen story, by following logical steps forwards from illogical premises, have created the sort of chaos they were hoping to dispel. They have reduced life to "jigsaw puzzle integers ... inextricable, jumbled, and un-recognizable yet on the point of falling into a pattern" (313). The energy of creating "a pattern" will always seem "on the point of" success, but instead "nothing happens." We are back to Judith's textual imagery of people "all trying to make a rug on the same loom only each one wants to weave his own pattern into the rug." Making solipsistic plans, as if this were not a world of interconnection, risks disastrous conclusions. Willed forgetting of others does not at all erase the other. Herbert Marcuse suggests that "the *return of the repressed* makes up the tabooed and subterranean history of civilization," and *Absalom, Absalom!* precisely illustrates such a return: the return of the black.

Withholding the black: racism and narrative omission

The "absenting" of society's repressed member becomes the place of greatest structural weakness in the social narrative that Shreve and Quentin, in the latter part of the novel, try to reconstruct seam by seam. The omission of the central reference point, the black, disturbs as if by seismic influence the other coordinates that should be connected in normal narrative; everything makes sense when the effaced of society are brought back into the picture; without them, the picture "makes no sense." Judith's "loom" imagery recalls an excerpt from Freud's "The Forgetting of Dreams":

> If the account of a dream seems at first difficult to understand, I ask the narrator to repeat it. This then rarely happens in the same words. But the places where he has altered the form of expression have marked themselves as the weak points of the dream disguise; they assist me like Hagen was assisted by the embroidered mark on Siegfried's cloak.[14]

Freud's textual or narrative "hiatus" is indeed the Platonic "joint" where the dominant/subordinate divisions of the South stand ready to be slain. The repetition of the seemingly seamless text exposes the gap, the false assertion of autonomous pattern. The first telling repeats omissions; the second telling inserts truth as difference. The tale turns on the differences created by its omissions and later by forced re-insertions of black presence.

Sutpen's "innocence" is a general innocence in white American society: in the first place, innocent or ignorant about the violence that guarantees its sense of identity; secondly, innocent after the prior innocence is outgrown, because it believes that prior innocence can still be feigned. Sutpen, a victim of omissions, arrives repeatedly at a "withholding," a factual gap he cannot go beyond: "they deliberately withheld from me the one fact which I have reason to know they were aware would have caused me to decline the entire matter ... this new fact rendered it impossible that this woman and child be incorporated in my design" (274). Narrative "withholding" has been discussed frequently in the criticism of this novel (from Conrad Aiken's "deliberately withheld meaning" (1939) to Peter Brooks's "dilatory space" (1982)), without, however, having been seen in relationship to a general censorship and effacement of the black's importance within the American social narrative. In his perplexity, Sutpen recounts

> an arrangement [with his first wife's father] which I had entered in good faith, concealing nothing, while the other party or parties to it concealed from me the one very factor which would destroy the entire plan and design which I had been working toward, concealed it so well that it was not until after the child was born that I discovered that this factor existed. (274)

Sutpen's innocence here ("concealing nothing") is feigned: he has, in fact, concealed his entire design from his future father-in-law. We see above that Sutpen ends his own narrative with a hiatus. He never says explicitly that the withheld "factor" is race. His wife (Eulalia Bon) and child (Charles Bon) turn out to be black, but Sutpen withholds this fact from General Compson just as it has been withheld from him. General Compson faithfully and unquestioningly passes that omission or self-destruction of antagonists; sexual linkages between apparent racial opposites; the joining of hero and quest-object. A final merging is also fatal, because absolute merging – as we have seen in *The Sound and the Fury* or *As I Lay Dying* – betokens the death of identity.

Merging is in every sense "the end of narrative," and operates under the collapse of the "appearance/reality" or "deception/truth" pairs, wherein crossing over to the suppressed term must compromise both the opposition and the story built upon it.[16] Texts first correctly repeat an order, then challenge it through a dialectical routine, and finally the antagonisms of plot lead to a terminal resolution or dissolution of once strictly competitive sides. The relationship between what Faulkner calls "the general racial system in the South" and this compositional principle is just the reverse: social logic encounters undifferentiated entities, divides them into "species," and then transmits these classifications as an exactly repeating narrative.

Transmitting errors/errors of transmission

At one point, Mr Compson describes the plot of *Absalom, Absalom!* as follows: "We have a few mouth-to-mouth tales; we exhume from old trunks and boxes and drawers letters without salutation and signature." For Mr Compson, the proper model of oral narration is actually logocentric: the oral tales are to be treated as written "letters." The voice of the father transfers an oral account to the son, who must repeat it without alteration to his son. Oral histories exhibit a compelling need for exact repetition. Their mouth-to-mouth tales should, as if written, survive the distortions of time and space. The teller transmits culture as a life-or-death proposition.[17] The teller enforces exact transmission through the repetitive "conditioning" of the listener (recall McEachern's Pavlovian methods in *Light in August*): fidelity is rewarded and deviation is punished. In a classical example of this procedure, Hermes typically repeats Zeus's commands in *The Iliad* and *The Odyssey*. Indeed, Hermes is the paradigm of the medium who carries, but does not formulate, the message. The oracular voice also presents a passive conduit through which

⟶ 122

on to his son, Mr Compson, who passes it on to Quentin. The omission that actually interrupts Sutpen's narrative, then, the effacement of race, allows the narrative to continue. Sutpen's dark hiatus is an aporia as well – the shadow of blackness beyond which Shreve and Quentin venture at their peril. The importance in psychoanalysis for such a juncture merits these rare italics of Freud in "The Forgetting of Dreams": "*Whatever disturbs the continuation of the work is a resistance.*" Resistance or obstacles represent the reality which the patient's repetitions of false narratives continuously try to avoid.[15]

The aporias here – figures of repeated confrontation and blockage – all occur when the repressed blacks (the "nigger servant," Clytie, Charles Bon, and his son Charles Etienne Bon) break out unpredictably into white "respectability" and awareness. The dominant viewpoints from which we first encounter the Sutpen narrative (Rosa's and Mr Compson's) require the expectation of a stable and unitary perspective point (the Cartesian "I" or "eye"). We do not expect what ophthalmology calls *stereoscopic vision*, which perceives depth by disparity or the slight *difference* between the images. In all cases, the repressed presence of the black, while adequate for the social text, causes interruptions of difference in the Sutpen narrative which prevent it from making sense. Sutpen, the "boy symbol," has already been surprised by the silencing of racial division in the social text: racial segregation "had never once been mentioned by name, as when people talk about privation without mentioning the siege, about sickness without ever naming the epidemic" (231). The "unnameable," the absence, the "withheld" here is exactly the repressed black double that, by forcing differences into repeated narratives, returns to soil and spoil the point of view of white autonomy and dominance.

Although any story must select and withhold at times, *Absalom, Absalom!* reveals a social law through a narrato-logical insight: society and the tale at first seem to function, but soon falter if one element is omitted consistently. Sutpen is like John Sartoris and Old Carothers McCaslin; he creates by sexual union black offprints or "replicas" of himself whose legitimacy he then tries to deny. The drive to suppress again and again a self-created double approximates the narrative's postponement of its promised final joinings: reconciliation the otherworldly message "breathes." Shelley's poet-prophet (or *vates*) epitomizes such a "carrier." Homer's bard, Phemios, escapes the wrath of Odysseus, claiming that he is only a carrier: "deep in my mind a god shaped all the various ways of life in song" (*Odyssey*, XXII, 347–8). Several communities in the south today still employ the techniques of oral narration that characterized the Homeric tradition and pre-literate societies in general.[18] Yet the notion of passive verbal carriage quickly translates, under certain conditions, into a sanction for moral obtuseness. Since neither listener nor teller may alter the story, neither need question its ethical messages. The transmitting carrier has no moral responsibility for the message content.

The attempt to transmit exactly what has come before clashes with another approach to oral transmission, the interpretive approach. In the second half of *Absalom, Absalom!* Shreve, mainly, begins to pose embarrassing questions about the inherited narrative, in a "creative treason" enacted against its handed-down form: " 'creative treason' as we understand it does not really add anything to the work of art. It is simply a shifting of values, a rearrangement of the poetic pattern."[19] Against the insistence of prior generations on "exact transmission," subsequent carriers feel the rebellious pressure of a tendency to review the narrative in a semi-automatic readjustment of belief, adapting it to the needs of the present. By this model, the oral narrative wants to be revised, and indeed cannot avoid revision. Despite the exactness that each new version feigns, the very goal of each telling would be to alter the prior one.[20] The joy of the revision is akin to that of play – Shreve at one point cries: "Let me play a while now" (280). Yet even this ludic practice does not arrive at the "complete story." Rather, it is a dialectical relationship between a handed-down tale and the revising tellers, a relationship that inevitably represses some elements even as it unearths others. The narrative cannot be complete as long as time continues to pass. Each revealment, then, also leaves something unsaid. The oscillation between the emergence and the fading of credible truth would guarantee the story's present vitality. Such a reworking of material can even be gratuitously antithetical. At one point, Shreve says to Quentin without any evidence, "your old man was wrong here, too! . . . it was not

Bon, it was Henry who was wounded at Shiloh" (344).

Miss Rosa says she "wants it told," but Quentin discovers too late, if at all, that turning the "told" into the "exactly told" destroys what was to have been preserved. Quentin thinks of such exact transmission as a kind of writing, even though he realizes that even writing is a "faint spidery script . . . which might fade, vanish, at any instant" (129). Quentin sees himself as carrying a fixed text, not a malleable story; he has become "the blank face of the wall" onto which a "scratch" or an "undying mark" has been written. Hence he risks the same "fading" as all the other "carriers" in the novel – he is "the Quentin Compson who was still too young to deserve yet to be a ghost, but nevertheless having to be one for all that" (9).

The white mind now divides within: Quentin, carrying the tale, feels unable to alter it, despite the pressures of the present context. Hence he is alienated from his message, from his environment, and from himself. Exactly as in Lacan's definition of Freud's *Spaltung*, the (prior) subject of the utterance is split from the (present) subject of the enunciation.[21] Quentin hears at a distance an internal dialogue between what he automatically memorized as a child, and his mature criticisms as a young man:

> he would seem to listen to two separate Quentins now – the Quentin Compson preparing for Harvard in the South . . . and the Quentin Compson who was still too young to deserve yet to be a ghost . . . the two separate Quentins now. . . . *It seems that this demon – his name was Sutpen –* (*Colonel Sutpen*) *– Colonel Sutpen.* (9)

At this early stage of the novel, one of the two "Quentins" still honors the wishes of Mr Compson and Rosa to repeat their narrative exactly, while the other only dimly wishes to change it, to end its spurious withholdings. Hence Quentin can hardly engage the kind of corrective dialectics that Shreve will in due course have to introduce.

To insist on exact transmission of an oral narrative (as if it were a kind of writing) debases both message and carrier. For in exact transmission it seems that neither message nor carrier is as important as creating a line of authority whose stability guarantees a consistency. Conversely, as long as the message can be transmitted exactly, the line of authority is verifiably intact. It is no accident, then, that the young Quentin Compson responds to the narrations of his elders (Miss Rosa and Mr Compson) with the word "Yes" and little else. He senses but does not fully grasp what is happening to him: "*Yes, I have had to listen too long*" (193). He even addresses himself as a passive object, telling himself about his own inertness: "*But you were not listening, because you knew it all already, had learned, had absorbed it already without the medium of speech somehow from having been born and living beside it, with it, as children will and do*" (212). He has listened too long, but by now the presence of the voice itself has habituated him to that listening: "[Rosa's] voice would not cease, it would just vanish ... the voice not ceasing but vanishing ... listening, having to listen ... his very body was an empty hall echoing with sonorous defeated names" (8–12). Quentin is practically an addict to authoritative voices now; he craves the *ex cathedra* decrees of Mr Compson and Rosa – he does not know why, and does not understand why he does not know.

By extension, Jefferson too has confused a wish for minimum distortion with a need to transmit its mythologies of white purity and natural superiority without alteration. Its story-tellers have become addicted to the story's presence and its ability to silence its hearers.[22] Despite Shreve's demands for meaning ("Tell about the South. What's it like there. What do they do there. Why do they live there. Why do they live at all"; 174), Quentin cannot really make sense of what he has memorized, since the tale really preserves not "sense" but the authority of the telling voice.

Mr Compson, through a certain attitude towards storytelling, really aims at asserting his authority over Quentin – hence Quentin feels that he really does not have to listen:

> what your father was saying did not tell you anything so much as it struck, word by word, the resonant strings of remembering. You had been here before ... been familiar with how it would look before you even saw it. (212–13; italics removed)

Such oral exactitude at first intended to ensure correct transmission, but now aims at establishing the superiority of an authoritative voice. Believing that the "logos can be infinite and self-present . . . can be *produced as auto-affection*, only through the *voice*," the father wishes to conjure up authority by telling stories.[23] To the process of transmission, the personality of the "carrier" is as unimportant as the content of the message. Hence "tellers" – Sutpen, Judith, Miss Rosa, etc. – tend to choose "carriers" – General Compson, his wife, Quentin – at random: "[Judith] . . . knowing no more why she chose your grandmother to give the letter to than your grandmother knew" (126).

Walter Benjamin's third thesis on the philosophy of history would seem to encourage the notion of exact transmission: "only for a redeemed mankind has the past become citable in all its moments."[24] By this logic, a message is valuable exactly by overcoming the mutations of time and space. But it is clear that Benjamin's brand of "citability" never canonizes. Rather, it attests to an intrinsic fragmentariness of all man-made meaning. Benjamin's mystically "pure" language emanates – as in the Homeric example – from a divine source. For modernity, however, the exact citation of any message usually seems intentionally mechanical and therefore makes the messenger appear ridiculous, particularly when much has changed between the scene of the utterance and the occasion of the enunciation. Where the Sutpen history becomes most laughable to Shreve, its gaps become most apparent to Quentin.

Précis as process

Summary and précis are habits of narrative that lead to the omission of blacks. One of the basic requirements for narrative must be the ability to tell which of the myriad details does and does not belong to the story. So the need to omit details gives to narrators the same license of exclusion that Southern society enjoys with respect to its darker and poorer members. Withholding, then, becomes not merely the vagary of the individual consciousness, or the bad luck of the social outcast, but rather a mechanism of all narrative, one not immune from being abused as social censorship. The expectation that a narrator will formulate the universal in the shape of a text results from the audience's (here, Jefferson's) need for a consensus narrative in which it recognizes, as if in a flattering mirror, its own face. But the drive for self-recognition often means a refusal or inability to recognize others. Such a refusal, however, hides under the normal requirement for plot to withhold what does not belong.

Plot formation touches questions of history and time as well as of meaning. Creating a précis means reorganization, in a retrospective sense. But the reflective exercise of looking backwards reverses events, producing the illusion that history itself can, by acts of performative language, be revised. Sutpen thinks that "in the restoration of that ring to a living finger he had turned all time back twenty years and stopped it, froze it" (165). In the timelessness of the psyche, history can seem a mere trope, reversible by raconteurial caprice. In general, the novel treats actual historical dates and Civil War events as secondary to the ability of the narrator – for reasons of evasion and censorship – to reorder the sequence and revise the significance of any given event.

Précis formation involves the censorship of memory (Freud's "waking redaction"). The reduction of variety brings coherence; the précis systematically omits marginal figures. Sutpen suppresses the role of women in his design, failing to realize that he cannot achieve his dynasty without them. Moreover, the poor white, Wash – the laboring "nobody" of the South – must finally slay Sutpen, his erstwhile benefactor and friend. Reduction to epithet and précis fails beause the repressed returns in the précis as *the idea of absence*. The manifold "shadows" and "ghosts" of Rosa's narrative are the blacks whom narrative *précision* (actually, "*im*precision") has rendered invisible, and whose invisibility finally thwarts all efforts to understand the "why" of Sutpen's life: "it just does not explain. . . . Yes, Judith, Bon, Henry, Sutpen: all of them. They are there, yet something is missing" (101). The repetition of blacks' absence makes the exactly transmitted narrative incredible until Quentin and Shreve, as a last resort, restore the black, whose import as repeated absence everyone had overlooked all along.

But any such omission of the past quickly becomes a standard for the future. The normative tale becomes the social norm. There is more at stake here than simple narrative inaccuracy. Whatever it is said that people "usually do" will soon emerge as "what people must do" (the German *pflegen* and *Pflicht*, from the same root, have exactly these meanings). For many people, the step from what is done to what should be done, from the normal to the norm, is taken for granted. So the errors of omission that society hands down are probably inseparable from and simultaneous with a hoped-for social order. Yet racial separation destroys rather than creates order, and this may be the true moral of the Sutpen story. A shared paraphrase of events that excludes the black would be impossible without a consensus about reality that mirrors the unison participation of teller and listener. Perhaps for this reason it takes a Canadian, Shreve, to make the sense of the Sutpen story for which Quentin so desperately longs.

We have seen the importance of the précis in narrative transmission. Now let us look at the epithets which facilitate the memorization of plot by reduction to simple marks. An epithetic plot, though exclusive, seems precise and well formed. The town's epithetic Sutpen narrative at the start of chapter 2 is instructive:

> It was the Chicksaw Indian agent with or through whom he dealt and so it was not until he waked the County Recorder that Saturday night with the deed, patent, to the land and the gold Spanish coin, that the town learned that he now owned a hundred square miles of some of the best virgin bottom land in the country, though even that knowledge came too late because Sutpen himself was gone, where to again they did not know. (34)

Sutpen's "hundred square miles of some of the best virgin bottom land in the country" later becomes "Sutpen's Hundred." Later, the Civil War reduces "Sutpen's Hundred" to "Sutpen's One," according to Miss Rosa. "Sutpen's Hundred" joins the "Chicksaw agent," the "Spanish coin," the "patent," the "roan horse," the "wild niggers," and "the French Architect" as acceptable narrative abstractions of Sutpen's rise to power. Finally the name "Sutpen" is a reduction of what it concerns: Mr Compson says "that nobody yet ever invented a name that somebody didn't own now or hadn't owned once" (267), and "Sutpen" could be anyone – his story is "about something a man named Thomas Sutpen had experienced, which would still have been the same story if the man had had no name at all, if it had been told about any man or no man over whiskey at night" (247). The name "Sutpen" is exactly a mnemonic epithet itself, a simplifying index for the town's vicarious experiences.

Since the name needs no specific tether of reference, it too may be exchanged, and the more this occurs, the more acute the experience. Notice, for example, the erasure of names during the showdown between Bon and Henry:

> the one saying to Henry *I have waited long enough* and Henry saying to the other *Do you renounce then? Do you renounce?* and the other saying *I do not renounce* ... the one calm and undeviating ... the other remorseless with implacable and unalterable grief. . . . They faced one another on two gaunt horses, two men, young ... the one with the tarnished braid of an officer, the other plain of cuff. (132–3)

Under this summary supervision, Bon and Henry are "the one" and "the other." Likewise Quentin and Shreve, mesmerized by the story's reducing effects, become "as free now of flesh as the father who decreed and forbade, the son who denied and repudiated, the lover who acquiesced, the beloved who was not bereaved" (295).

Perhaps the most clever instances of plot reduction are exactly like the one above, since the duplications of "son," "brother," "sister," "daughter" are perfect opportunities for narrative duplicity. Miss Rosa's concise plot summary – "the son who widowed the daughter who had not yet been a bride" (11) – tells us everything we need to know, but reveals precisely nothing. A few pages later, she repeats the epithetic plot: "the daughter who was already the same as a widow without ever having been a bride ... and the son who repudiated the very roof under which he had been born" (15). By now, Miss Rosa has allowed the abstractions to replace the names; it is Quentin's problem to fill in the blanks. Even when Miss Rosa supplies certain names, she leaves out more important ones: "I saw Henry repudiate his home and birthright and then return and practically fling the bloody corpse of his sister's sweetheart at the hem of her wedding gown" (18). If she had said "brother" instead of "sweetheart," we would already know of the censored incest. But this narration employs the cloaking epithet "sweetheart."

Blacks are epithets ("nigger"), not persons. "Nigger" in the social text means unalterable abjectness rather than narrative terseness. Even the epithet "nigger" may be removed by parenthesis, so that we no longer even think of the reduction. When, for example, Sutpen and Quentin's grandfather go with the "wild niggers" to hunt the "French architect," we read that "the niggers had made camp and cooked supper and they (he and Grandfather) drank some of the whiskey and ate and then sat before the fire drinking some more of the whiskey and he telling it over" (247). The parenthesis removes one of two possible grammatical ambiguities here, and does so in order to disconnect "the niggers" from "he and Grandfather" as possible referents of "they" – indeed, it wishes to make the ambiguous pronoun "racially pure." The other personal pronoun, "*he* telling," remains equally ambiguous, but here there is no threat of interracial reference. More frequently, though, blacks vanish without even being named (or unnamed) by epithets. The town claims that Sutpen "lived out there, eight miles from any neighbor, in masculine solitude" (39), but later we learn that two (black) women were indeed present in Sutpen's "masculine solitude": "Miss Rosa didn't tell you that two of the niggers in the wagon that day were women? . . . He brought the women deliberately; he probably chose them with the same care and shrewdness with which he chose the other livestock" (61).

Quentin shares in the narrative erasure of blacks. At one point he describes Sutpen's "two children – no, three" (259), but soon afterwards he says "Yes, the two children, the son and the daughter" (262). In fact, Sutpen has (at least) four children: one visibly black (Clytie); the other visibly white but called "black" (Bon); and two others who are "pure" whites (Henry and Judith). Shreve surmises, "So he just wanted a grandson" (217), but in fact Sutpen's designs were less temporally remote and less racially neutral: he wanted a "pure white" son.

From the above discussion it should be obvious that the Sutpen story hides its truths in seemingly guileless forms – everyday figures of speech, innocuous habits of expression, sudden forgettings. For instance, the town speculates on the relationship between Bon and Henry: "They would be seen together in the carriage in town now . . . which certainly would not have been the case if the quarrel had been between Bon and the father, and probably not the case if the trouble had been between Henry and his father" (79). Already the difference between "the" and "his" "father" conceals the fact that the father in both cases is the same person. When Mr Compson says "that Bon's intention . . . was apparently to make his (Henry's) sister a sort of junior partner in a harem" (119), his bracket removes the possibility that Judith is Bon's half-sister, by clarifying "his" as "Henry's." Such clarification, however, increases rather than decreases what Socrates in *Phaedrus* calls the "deception" of reductive classification.

Even if the epithet successfully reduces, omits, and repeats the social plot, still "it just does not explain" (100), because logical coherence has given way to relations of dominance and submission. Following a traditional sequence of actions from cause to effect is impossible in *Absalom, Absalom!*, but this fact should hardly be taken as a criticism of Faulkner's literary skill. For his narrators interchange and rearrange epithets at will without harming the essential purpose of the story, which is finally neither to relay historical facts and dates, nor to describe a linear sequence of logically coherent events, but rather to establish a narrational regimen that allows a particular story to be told repeatedly in a certain way.

Absalom, Absalom! is not primarily either about Sutpen or about Harvard or Jefferson in 1909. The narrator of the novel "sets" us in these contexts, but the individual narrators hardly mention the physical setting in which they find themselves relating their stories. Quentin, Rosa, Shreve, and Mr Compson engage their listeners but ignore their environments. Indeed, the Sutpen story might "be told about any man or no man" (247), because the telling of the story is really a sort of induction rite, testing the novitiate's ability to learn and tactfully transmit the secret sleight of hand upon which racial classifications are based. The story both hides and exposes "two hundred years of oppression and exploitation" (251) of the black, as well as the continued exploitation of those victims' children and grandchildren, refusing to speak of things that are plain to see. As an apprentice, the listener should never betray the mechanics of such racial legerdemain. For the parable says to its white Southern auditors: "ignore that the black is deeply implicated in all you do, and ignore that the story makes no sense when you ignore the black." The initiate and listener both escape despair at this message by transmitting it automatically without questioning or even understanding its true injunction. Shreve has punctured this smooth fabric, saying that the story makes sense if you restore the black, but it fails otherwise"; but even by mentioning the black he has already failed the story. And Quentin has failed even more grandly, because he and his Southern informants have failed to impose through their narrations the South's influential magic upon the shrewd Canadian listener.

The hiatus: interruption and interpretation

The "loving partnership" of Shreve and Quentin occurs as they dismantle the Sutpen story and restore the black to his rightful place in the Southern narrative. Their "partnership" takes place, like the ending of *Light in August*, in bed. Shreve's "naked torso pink-gleaming and baby-smooth, cherubic, almost hairless" (181) and his "pink naked almost hairless skin" (275) prepare us for the notion that he and Quentin share "that state of virginity which is neither boy's nor girl's" (324). They have indeed passed into the "marriage of speaking and hearing" (316), yet this seeming reciprocity – and even the idea that Shreve lets a little "Northern" air into the tale – is compromised by the fact that these are *men* in bed speaking to each other (as opposed to the male–female storytelling couple at the end of *Light in August*). While not remotely what some have called it – "mildly homosexual" or "homosexual attraction" – the "marriage of speaking and hearing" indicates a union that is no longer just an empathy of joint narration.[25] The linkage of Shreve and Quentin, while it reveals some important truths, threatens to turn into a solipsistic or hermetic male bond that perpetuates myths of white male paranoia; "the Jim Bonds are going to conquer the Western hemisphere" (378), as a closing statement, seems to negate by its racial panic all the lessons the boys have just painstakingly uncovered.[26]

Shreve finds the black in the most intimate circles of Southern and Northern white society – "in a few thousand years, I who regard you will also have sprung from the loins of African kings" (378) – but his "admission" seems a non sequitur. Even were the black to be restored, the "carrier" would resist total signification here, as in *Light in August*. To Rosa, Clytie has an "inscrutable coffee-colored face" (138); Sutpen cannot "read" the truth about his first wife from her "parchment-colored" face (335); the parchment is written in an ink that was black until society made black invisible. Bon, the most "invisible" black, becomes real only by crossing the black shadow of the fence posts. "Crossing the fence" in every sense means the death of the black. Dead, he vanishes: "I never saw him. I never even saw him dead" (150).

The final message to be suppressed by the chain of carriers is that the tale, like the "natural formation" of color designation, contains hiatus-like joints, each of which may sooner or later develop sprains, challenging its latent inaccuracies, particularly concerning its black figures. In order to dramatize visually where the spoken transmission might fall apart, Faulkner exploits typographical presentation. Well-regulated and consistent font, proper spacing, punctuation, margins, and spelling guarantee that print and paper will not hinder our climb to "pure meaning": they are to be ignored so long as they retain their composure; exact repetition assures their future pertinence. Predictability in print is the first tool of the realist pretense, although it is the least "real": we pretend in the literary as in the social text that the polarities of black/white and print/background are normal rather than normative.

Faulknerian style, with its periodicity and chain-like assemblies, lends itself to sprains. Some have called Faulkner's prose in this novel "baroque and involuted in the extreme, these sentences: trailing clauses, one after another, shadowily in apposition, or perhaps not even with so much connection as that; parenthesis after parenthesis, the parenthesis itself often containing one or more parentheses." The baroque era begins at the high Renaissance and "reaches a culmination at about 1630," but both the *style coupé* and the "loose style" are periodic, and both continue through most of the eighteenth century. Morris Croll's article, "The Baroque Style in Prose," describes a periodic style used by two of Faulkner's literary influences, Milton and the King James Bible. A comparison between the highly periodic prose of Defoe or Swift and Faulkner might also be profitable. As Swift does in *A Tale of a Tub*, Faulkner disturbs typographical convention to get at unconventional truths. Swift calls the frequent gaps in his text "Chasms" – a word that aptly underscores their power to lay bare chaos. He glosses one such hiatus, "I cannot conjecture what the Author means here, or how this Chasm could be fill'd, tho' it is capable of more than one interpretation."[27] What Shreve does best in Quentin's hopefully seamless narrative is not to give it a sense of an ending, but rather to open up chasms to "more than one interpetation."[28] Faulkner's typographical gaps serve the same purpose. The hiatus is that normally unnoticed juncture in every page, paragraph, and sentence where things threaten to fall apart. Above all, the hiatus represents the death of meaning. It lets in a momentary silence as the visible absence of print.

As we have seen, gaps in oral narrative are just as threatening: Freud sees them as the most valuable outlets for the repressed materials of the psyche. Like sealant under pressure, the patient's neurotic narration plugs for a time these weak points. Truth emerges by comparing many separate tellings in order to account for disparities. Similarly, Walter Benjamin says in *The Origin of German Tragic Drama* that "Truth, bodied forth in the dance of represented ideas, resists being projected, by whatever means, into the realm of knowledge." Geoffrey Hartman suggests that "Juncture is simply a space, a breathing-space: phonetically it has zero-value, like a caesura ... it dramatizes the differential or, as de Saussure calls it, diacritical relation of sound to meaning."[29] The last half of the novel shows Shreve opening unexpected chasms of interpretation in the transmitted text.

Quentin's despair, Rosa's hysteria, and Sutpen's vagueness all come from their having confused oral with "permanent" written discourse in order to freeze the social hierarchy. But Shreve, unlike Quentin, never answers with the reverent "Yes" or "Oh" but repeatedly interrupts Quentin's inherited narrative. Quentin cannot reverse his own submission to the story. He has no future, yet Shreve is dismembering his past. Shreve sees conversation as living communication, not as a fixated ritual of authority. He repeatedly uses what Roman Jakobson calls the *conative* mode ("Wait"; "Go on"), as well as making sure the partners are in contact ("Dont tell me. Just go on"), the *phatic* mode. Agonizingly for Quentin, narrative gaps seem to show black and white – not just white paper and white skin, but black blood. But Shreve turns tradition to invention, being above all a Canadian and unafraid of a merging between himself and Quentin, Henry, and the "nigger" Bon.

Shreve becomes the tale's only authoritative teller, not as a prior knower of the plot, but as one who usurps by imagination the power that Quentin should have had by inheritance. In order to interpet, Shreve interrupts. So he develops the "Wait!" Quentin tells Shreve "Wait" only once during all their conversation, significantly, when he realizes that he is losing control: " 'Wait, I tell you,' Quentin said. . . . 'I am telling' " (277). But he fails to silence his listener. So he tries to weave himself into Shreve's inventions, "taking Shreve up in a stride without comma or colon or paragraph" (280), hoping that perhaps their corporate narrative might be at least as seamless as the one inherited from his elders has failed to be:

"And Father said –"
   "Oh," Shreve said. "After you and the old aunt. I see. Go on. And father said –"
   "– said how he . . ." (266)

". . . running –"
   "Wait," Shreve said; "wait. You mean that he had got the son at last that he wanted, yet still he –"
   "– walked . . ." (286)

But, after a time, Quentin gives up. Shreve even supplies the "wait" in his own narrative:

"– wait," Shreve cried, though Quentin had not spoken. . . . Shreve said Wait. Wait. before Quentin could have begun to speak. (321)

"– and listen," Shreve cried; "wait, now; wait!" (344)

In the last words of the novel, Quentin seems doomed to return to habitual Southern rhetorics: denial; double negatives; omitted or ambiguous references; and repetition: "I dont hate it. . . . I dont. I dont! I dont hate it! I dont hate it!" (378) – here the Sutpen narrative, divested of every frill, betrays its true figures of division.

That there is a possibility for revolution in language, and perhaps an abrupt one, is the major premise of Faulkner, particularly in his novels between 1929 and 1940. Principles of order and regulation, enforced by modes of exact repetition, can also be dismantled by repetition with a difference. Blacks, as the center around which social figures of division revolve (even as white society denies blacks' presence), furnish for Faulkner the proper emblem for revealing the duplicitous formation of social narratives. The black could be the social correlative of differential repetition on the literary level, since the repeated omission of the black in Sutpen's story enables a continuous narrative to admit after a time its own latent discontinuities. So, while the rhetoric of race remains the same, Faulkner's text undermines the South's social equations.

While Joyce, Beckett, Pound, and Eliot were thematizing and otherwise exploiting at this time the estrangement of signifier from signified, Faulkner had traced in his "county" and "country" the social ramifications of what other writers thought a largely aesthetic quandary. Man's separation from his fellow men and his labor, as Faulkner saw, is an inevitable result of the attempt to overlook the economic factors that underpin semiotic discrimination. By making orthography strange, and by showing social orthography to be constructed like a narrative, *Absalom, Absalom!* opens up the dangerous domain of alternatives. Rosa has given Quentin the charge in the beginning – "maybe some day you will remember this and write about it." Quentin thinks "she dont mean that . . . she wants it told" (10). Changing Rosa's "write" to "told" is his first and last attempt at interpretive freedom in the novel. But Quentin's single act of interpretation ultimately dooms him. Precisely in the gap between "write" and "told" is where *Absalom, Absalom!* and, ultimately, Quentin must live and die.

Notes

1 William Faulkner, *Faulkner in the University*, ed. Frederick L. Gwynn and Joseph Blotner (Charlottesville: University of Virginia Press, 1959), p. 94.

2 Fredric Jameson, *The Political Unconscious: Narrative as a Socially Symbolic Act* (Ithaca: Cornell University Press, 1981), p. 40.

3 Sigmund Freud, "The Taboo of Virginity" (1918), in *The Standard Edition*, ed. James Strachey (London: Hogarth Press, 1953–74),

vol. 11, p. 199; "Das Tabu der Virginität," *Studienausgabe*, vol. V; p. 219. *Group Psychology and the Analysis of the Ego* (1921), *Standard Edition*, vol. 18, p. 101; *Massenpsychologie und Ich-Analysis, Studienausgabe*, vol. IX; p.95. See also I. A. Newby (ed.), *The Development of Segregationist Thought* (Homewood, Ill.: Dorsey Press, 1968), pp. 164–75, on the false application of color and anatomy to social division.

4 Paul de Man, *Allegories of Reading* (New Haven: Yale University Press, 1979), pp. 108, 131.

5 Vladimir Propp, *The Morphology of the Folk Tale*, trans. Laurence Scott (1928; Austin: University of Texas Press, 1968), pp. 101–9.

6 Fredric Jameson, *Marxism and Form*, (Princeton: Princeton University Press, 1971), p. 222.

7 William Faulkner, *Absalom, Absalom!* (New York: Vintage, 1972), p. 84. All subsequent quotations from this edition will be cited by page numbers in parentheses in the text.

8. Cleanth Brooks, *William Faulkner: The Yoknapatawpha Country* (New Haven: Yale University Press, 1963), p. 12.

9 The plot of Wash's revenge on Sutpen resembles in many respects that of Anderson's *Poor White* (1920), as John B. Rosenman makes clear in his article, "Anderson's *Poor White* and Faulkner's *Absalom, Absalom!*," *Mississippi Quarterly*, 29 (1976), p. 437.

10 Brooks, op. cit., p. 297; Ilse Dusoir Lind, "The Design and Meaning of *Absalom, Absalom!*," in Frederick J. Hoffman and Olga W. Vickery, *William Faulkner* (East Lansing: Michigan State College Press, 1951), p. 299; Joseph W. Reed, *Faulkner's Narrative* (New Haven: Yale University Press, 1973) p. 146.

11 Jacques Derrida, *On Grammatology*, trans. Gayatri Spivak (Baltimore: Johns Hopkins University Press, 1974), "Translator's Preface," pp. lxiv–lxvi.

12 Sigmund Freud, *The Future of an Illusion* (1927), *Standard Edition*, vol. 21, p. 13.

13 The class implications of this scene are clearer in its original version, the short story "The Big Shot" (1930), in which the white master, not the black servant, comes to the door: "Anyway the boss came to the door himself. Suddenly he – the boy – looked up and there within touching distance for the first time was the being who had come to symbolise for him the ease and pleasant ways of the earth: idleness, a horse to ride all day long, shoes the year round. And you can imagine him when the boss spoke: 'Dont you ever come to my front door again.' ... He didn't deliver the message at all": in William Faulkner, *Uncollected Stories of William Faulkner*, ed. Joseph Blotner (New York: Random House, 1979), p. 508. "Idleness," for Sutpen, as also for Marcuse, is the sign of the difference between rich and poor. See Herbert Marcuse,

Eros and Civilization: A Philosophical Inquiry into Freud (1955; Boston: Beacon Press, 1966), pp. xiv–xv. Leisure and therefore wealth in Western society were signified until quite recently by being "white," or owning a "pale-white" pallor like Miss Rosa's, which meant that she survived without having to work in the sun. The modern "tan" also signifies not having to toil, but now in an interior workplace, the office. The next major signifier of wealth and "idleness" is literacy, with the concomitant leisure time to read books – quite pertinent to Sutpen's case, as we shall see.

14 Sigmund Freud, *The Interpretation of Dreams* (1900), *Standard Edition*, vol. 5, pp. 515–16; *Die Traumdeutung* (1900); *Studienausgabe*, vol. II, pp. 493–4.

15 Freud, *Standard Edition*, vol. 5, p. 571; *Studienausgabe*, vol. II, p. 544.

16 Reconciling false opposites brings about the *telos* of narrative by puncturing the weak points of its disguise. In simpler narratives, such as *Aesop's Fables*, or *Grimms' Fairy Tales*, this paradigm holds true. Aesop's "The Lion in Love," for instance, contains uncanny parallels to the Sutpen–Judith–Bon story. In this fable, the Woodman tells the lion, "You must have your teeth drawn and your claws pared before you can be a suitable bridegroom for my daughter." As soon as he does this, and the threatened breakdown of the human/animal opposition (among others) draws near, the Woodsman slays the lion. In the Grimms' "Frog-Prince" the identity of the "animal-frog" with the "human-prince" is what the plot repeatedly hides until the ending. Here, the iconography of the princess's golden ball (her nascent sexuality – the frog fetches it from a deep well) merges with the imagery of the golden sun (emblem of her quasi-incestuous ties with her father the king – the sun "rises" the morning after their first night together). As soon as these "suns" elide, she and the now human "frog-prince" become one in marriage: the tale is at an end. "The Fisherman and his Wife" ends as soon as the ambitious wife's request for ever greater powers threaten to merge her with the power of her benefactor, the magical fish – at this point, she encounters a rebuff from the fish: "Go home to your ditch again."

17 Jack Goody and Ian Watt, in their well-known article "The Consequences of Literacy," put it this way: "The transmission of the verbal elements of culture by oral means can be visualized as a long chain of interlocking conversations. ... Thus all beliefs and values, all forms of knowledge, are communicated between individuals in face-to-face contact": in *Language and Social Context: Selected Readings*, ed. Pier Paolo Giglioli (1972; Harmondsworth: Penguin, 1977), p. 313.

18 Jonathan Swift had a rather droll comment on what happens to the

oral message in transmission. In part 4, chapter 9 of *Gulliver's Travels*, we learn that the Houyhnhnms, who know no "fictions" or deviations, "have not the least idea of books or literature. . . . The Houyhnhnms have no letters, and consequently their know-ledge is all traditional. But there happening few events of any moment among a people so well united, naturally disposed to every virtue, wholly governed by reason, and cut off from all commerce with other nations, the historical part is easily preserved without burthening their memories." Here, history does not cross over into memory, but is precisely trimmed to fit the capacity of memory. Jonathan Swift, *Gulliver's Travels* (1726; New York: New American Library, 1960), pp. 254, 294.

19 See Raymond Escarpit, " 'Creative Treason' as a Key to Literature," *Yearbook of Comparative Literature*, 10, repr. in *Sociology of Literature and Drama: Selected Readings*, ed. Elizabeth and Tom Burns (Harmondsworth: Penguin, 1973), p. 365.

20 Goody and Watt, op. cit., pp. 319, 337.

21 Anika Rifflet-Lemaire, *Jacques Lacan*, trans. David Macey (London: Routledge & Kegan Paul, 1977), pp. 75–6.

22 Biblical contacts between God and man will also often involve the forced silencing of the human party, as in the case of Daniel ("And when he had spoken such words unto me, I set my face toward the ground, and I became dumb"; 10:15), or Moses' famous ineloquence (Exodus 4:10). One might call the ability of the dogmatic word to silence unbelievers the "Zacharias complex," recalling that, after the father of John the Baptist doubted the performative efficacy of Gabriel's words, the angel delivers this sentence: "And behold, thou shalt be dumb, and not able to speak, until the day that these things shall be performed, because thou believest not my words, which shall be fulfilled in their season" (Luke 1:20). When the story itself silences or omits dissenting voices, it constitutes truth from that censorship alone. Friday, whom Robinson Crusoe at first teaches only three English words, "yes," "no," and "master," suffers from the Zacharias complex, as do blacks generally, who cannot answer Faulkner's whites in their own language, but who instead seem to speak "some dark and fatal tongue of their own" (36).

23 Derrida, op. cit., p. 98.

24 Walter Benjamin, *Illuminations*, ed. with intro. by Hannah Arendt, trans. Harry Zohn (London: Fontana, 1973), p. 256; German title: *Schriften* (Frankfurt a.M.: Suhrkamp, 1955).

25 Lind, op. cit., p. 283; Richard P. Adams, *Faulkner: Myth and Motion* (Princeton: Princeton University Press, 1968), p. 194.

26 In fact the remaining Sutpen, Jim Bond, is akin to the "remainder" of which Derrida speaks in "White Mythology": Jacques Derrida,

Margins of Philosophy, trans. Alan Bass (Chicago: University of Chicago Press, 1982), pp. 219–20.

> If one wished to conceive and to class all the metaphorical possibilities of philosophy, one metaphor, at least, always would remain excluded, outside the system: the metaphor, at the very least, without which the concept of metaphor could not be constructed, or, to syncopate an entire chain of reasoning, the metaphor of metaphor. This extra metaphor, remaining outside the field that it allows to be circumscribed, extracts or abstracts itself from this field, thus subtracting itself as a metaphor less.

Once more we see the simultaneous subversiveness and indispensability of the black in the construction and deconstruction of social meaning.

27 Hoffman and Vickery, op. cit., p. 137, for the Aiken quote; Swift, *A Tale of a Tub and Other Satires*, ed. Kathleen Williams (1704; New York: E. P. Dutton, 1975), p. 113.

28 Yet these junctures are not gratuitous, as John A. Hodgson, " 'Logical Sequence and Continuity': Some Observations on the Typographical and Structural Consistency of *Absalom, Absalom!*" *American Literature*, 43 (1971), p. 97, and Arthur L. Scott, "The Myriad Perspectives of *Absalom, Absalom!*," *American Quarterly*, 6 (Fall 1954), p. 211, have proposed.

29 Compare Dante's "le mente che non erre" ("memory that does not err"; *Inferno*, II, 6–7) or the Platonic "reminiscence" in *Phaedrus*, by which one recalls "general unerring truth," with the comparison of different versions that both Freud and Faulkner recommend. The former seems the guarantee of cognitive certainty, but also "locks in" error. The latter is dialectical and can never fill all possible gaps. See also Walter Benjamin, *The Origins of German Tragic Drama*, trans. J. Osborne (London: New Left Books, 1977), p. 29; German title: *Ursprung des deutschen Trauerspiels* (Frankfurt a.M.: Suhrkamp, 1963), Another view of junctures comes from Geoffrey Hartman, *Beyond Formalism: Literary Essays 1958–1970* (New Haven: Yale University Press, 1970), p. 341.

6

The Hamlet (1940)

Ten years after *As I Lay Dying*, Faulkner redraws its rural setting with even more attention to nature, the seasons, and eccentric families living by "clan virtues."[1] Faulkner returns in *The Hamlet* to a project already envisaged in 1929, a trilogy (continued in *The Town* and *The Mansion*) narrating the Snopes family history, and especially the rise of its wunderkind, Flem. On the surface, the contrast with Jefferson and Sutpen's Hundred could not be greater; here, it seems, racial difference has been eliminated altogether; blacks and Indians are absent. The state of affairs here contrasts greatly with *The Sound and the Fury*'s abysmal "Nigger Hollow." Similarly, the area Joe Christmas passes in *Light in August*, "the original quarry, abyss itself," with "black, impenetrable," "negro voices" speaking in a strange "language not his," could not be more distant. Will Varner's cook remains "not only the only Negro servant but the only servant of any sort in the whole district."[2] In a county where, according to Faulkner's imaginary census, whites make up only 40 percent of the population, the hamlet is manifestly a white enclave. Such a privileged realm excludes not merely by "clan virtues," but by the threat of Klan violence: "there was not one Negro landowner in the entire section. Strange Negroes would absolutely refuse to pass through it after dark" (5). An all-white hamlet (a suburb of Jefferson, as it were) indeed seems a "pastoral world," a "mythic atmosphere," and a "remote, entranced world" full of people "more simple, more strange, and more elemental than are the ordinary human beings we know."[3] All social strata here – peasant, tenant-farmer, middle-class proprietor, rich landowner – seem to speak the same language; all are white; all understand each other. Verbal accessibility, lucidity, and even familiarity – as embodied in the ritual of exchanging pleasantries – are the liquid assets of this neighborly community. Yet, in spite of these indications, there is trouble even in paradise. Given that Faulkner confines his stories' geographical scope in order to enlarge their symbolic range, it seems that problems of equality between whites and whites, and not just between whites and blacks, will be considered here, in Frenchman's Bend.

"Frenchman's Bend": exclave and enclave

The beguiling vision of "elemental" or "mythic" simplicity in a racially pure enclave quickly turns dark. Separation creates a sense of community by rejecting the "other," but soon wrecks the community it wishes to constitute. The segregated commonwealth discovers itself internally split, not pure.[4] The separationist mentality, developed as an economic and psychological defense against the black, schools some whites in the general tactics of separation and subordination. Faulkner consistently views Southern racism as an ideology that tries to invent natural reasons for economic and power considerations. In opposition to some of the more racially intolerant views he voiced in America (such as the infamous "shooting Negroes" statement in the 1956 London *Sunday Times* interview conducted by Russell Warren Howe "I'd fight for Mississippi against the United States even if it meant going out into the street and shooting Negroes"), Faulkner, when abroad, put the burden of guilt for racial problems upon the white man's economic system. For instance, during a trip to Japan in 1955, he gave a rather radical analysis of racism no less than six different times:

> the white man is afraid that if the Negro has any social advancement his economic status will change . . . now they can raise cotton and get 30 cents a pound for it as a profit, but if the Negro's economic status changes, they can't raise cotton and make a profit of 30 cents. . . . They are the bankers who depend on the mortgages on the cotton, they are the planters who have got to make the crop, with government support, plus Negro labor . . . they're the people who think "if we have this, my dollar is worth six cents less or eight cents less" . . . the whole trouble between the black and the white is not in anything racial [or ethnic]. It's an economic fear that if the white man allows the Negro any sort of advancement whatever, the Negro will take his economy away from him.[5]

Yet, even in the absence of blacks, the same economic injustices reign.

The Hamlet takes place in a quadrant of Yoknapatawpha County diametrically opposite to Sutpen's Hundred; the Sutpen mansion is twelve miles northwest of the courthouse; Frenchman's Bend is twelve miles to the southeast. The frenzied prose of *Absalom, Absalom!* contrasts with *The Hamlet*'s placid first paragraph:

> Frenchman's Bend was a section of rich river-bottom country lying twenty miles southeast of Jefferson. Hill-cradled and remote, definite yet without boundaries, straddling into two counties and owning allegiance to neither, it had been the original grant and site of a tremendous pre-Civil War plantation, the ruins of which – the gutted shell of an enormous house with its fallen stables and slave quarters and overgrown gardens and brick terraces and promenades – were still known as the Old Frenchman's place, although the original boundaries now existed only on old faded records in the county courthouse in Jefferson, and even some of the once-fertile fields had long since reverted to the cane-and-cypress jungle from which their first master had hewed them.

The classical realist narrator here pretends that everything is

known, even what "nobody knew." The narrator satisfies the
reader's passivity, positioning him or her in a continuous,
consistent, and comprehensible topography. The story's loose,
anecdotal style recalls the humorous realism of the "tall tale"
or Twain's comic/serious yarns. Security of time and place
dominates here ("there is a sense of community: no one
entertains any doubt as to what the prescribed values are"), yet
"sense" deceives.[6] The style of this passage constructs a
creditable world by imposing a universal and timeless "written-
ness" onto the particular. Lulled by the realistic "mirroring,"
one misses important gaps and blind-spots. The sober narrator
of *The Hamlet* (originally entitled "the Peasants") inspires
confidence. One critic writes: "One of Balzac's novels is called
Les Paysans, and *The Hamlet* itself opens in almost Balzacian
fashion with a precise and detailed description of the historical,
geographical, social, and economic setting of the novel's
subsequent events." Another says that "*The Hamlet* includes
more social history, economics, and politics than any of
Faulkner's earlier novels. ... [It] owes much to the great
realist enterprises of the nineteenth century ... like them
it is scrupulous in rendering the particularities of its social,
economic, and political milieu, as well as the customs and
folkways of its people."[7] Yet despite such appearances *The
Hamlet* is not a Balzacian, classical realist text. The stylistic
seduction of "scrupulous rendering" is an ideological one. The
narrative relies upon figures of division and unification already
"social, economic, and political" in nature, already distorting
what they describe.

At first *The Hamlet*'s narrator seems to have anticipated all
such objections by his candor. Trustworthy, he lets us share
the hamlet's worst secrets. The "scrupulous" opening comes
with its own philosophy: things get worse with time; the
tremendous plantation is a ruin; the once fertile fields are now
jungles. The citizens scavenge the ruined mansion as long as
they do not have to "climb a ladder" (6) – a delicate admission,
but not beyond our need to know. An implied teleology
compares the present unfavorably with the larger, more
"fertile" past. Will there be a new, well-rendered version of
erstwhile glory now lost? Perhaps Flem will be the remedy:
"Flem's story is basically a progress or history, the story of a
rise and fall, its essential element is change – specifically a

dramatic change in status and fortune."[8] Frenchman's Bend
has gone down in the world, but Flem can, in the novel's last
words, "Come up."

The reliability of the first pages comes from their irony
towards the hamlet. Such blissful cynicism must be correct, it
seems. One imagines oneself the narrator's confidant: things
are not what they used to be, and, if we promise not to tell, we
can be told of the creeping decay. Yet, in this tricky novel,
retailing fraudulent stories for future gain is quite common;
the "reliable" narrator is most certainly a storyteller. By
owning the dilapidation of the Southern myth, the narrative
formulates another. The narration comes to own its reader and
shelter itself from every skepticism.

The initial description of the Old Frenchman's place and the
Frenchman himself contains a buried riddle that may (and
does) swindle the unwary listener:

> his dream and his pride now dust with the lost dust of his
> anonymous bones, his legend but the stubborn tale of the
> money he buried somewhere about the place when Grant
> overran the country on his way to Vicksburg. (4)

The proud Civil War legends of "dreams" and "lost dust" may
be as untrue as "the stubborn tale of the money." Because a
listener has inherited the tale, he might mistakenly think
himself the beneficiary of the money – such a fate befalls
Armstid at the conclusion of the novel. He cannot abandon the
myth of wealth underlying a site he deems original. He takes
the myth of the hamlet even beyond the point of madness,
because, while Flem exploits the tale of the money, Armstid
believes in its underlying meaning: the mansion founds the
truth of the hamlet's very identity. If the money does not exist,
then the Frenchman also did not exist, and therefore the
town's founding moment would have been a lie. By extension,
the very stories America (particularly the American South)
tells about its foundation would also have to be lies. Therefore,
Armstid reasons with perfectly logical error, the money must
be buried where Flem Snopes says it is. Yet the truer version is
there all along, for anyone who cares to look at the ruined and
scavenged hulk of the actual mansion.

The Hamlet critiques "realism" itself, and reveals the links

that, ever since Defoe, the trading, exchanging mentality has
had with exact, realistic description. For realist narration is a
kind of accounting, an inventory of real, material objects (and
persons) that could at some point be owned. Realist "precision
and detail" is a smooth façade seeking to restore an original
moment of intact ownership before time corrupted the original
goods, before it turned the "enormous house" into a "gutted
shell." The narrator's description would exchange the hollow
shell for a hallowed myth of an intact past. As an original
topos, or reference point, the myth of the "Frenchman"
confirms the stature of Frenchman's Bend. The myth allows
the townspeople to return, by a fiction, to a place and time
whose existence the mansion substantiates. The smoothness
of the mythological telling overlooks the unsettled facts at the
heart of the Frenchman's Bend "setting."

The Mississippi landscape is, at best, deceptively idyllic; it
turns "even the horrible into the merely picturesque."[9] *The
Hamlet*'s narrator attempts to do the same. The myth about
the Old Frenchman's original acts is a myth of initiation
invented after the fact to support the present constitution of
Frenchman's Bend.[10] Yet the clues to the myth's tricky
illusions come well before the novel's ending. Faulkner's
tale is actually a register of absences, contradictions, and
discrepancies, and the more one reads the first paragraph, the
more it seems to forge, and not represent, the past. Where are
the animals that were in the stables? Where are the slaves
whose quarters now stand in ruins? Where is "his family"?
And where is the "Frenchman" who gave the place its name?
What was his "original" name? – "Even the name was
forgotten" (4). Even were the name to be recalled, though, it
was an "appellation which those who came after him . . . could
not even read, let alone pronounce." The "Frenchman" may
not even have been "French" (possibly not even "foreign").
The town's "tale" slides without effort from a total absence to
the name that "was gone now, the foreigner, the Frenchman
with his family and his slaves and his magnificence" (3).

The name "Frenchman's Bend" is the trace of what never
was. The "Frenchman" already represents a triple uncertainty:
the cloudiness of his racial identity; the loss of his name – "all
that remained of him was the river bed which his slaves had
straightened for almost ten miles to keep his land from

flooding" (3); the name's foreignness were it ever to be remembered. There emerges from the last quotation a much larger quandary: the "Bend" has been "straightened," nature despoiled by already despoiled naturals, the slaves. So "Bend" is actually a fraudulent term: where the "bend" exists, the "original" land is flooded! No settlement exists until the bend in the river has been eliminated; the hamlet comes into existence by the *removal* of what its name refers to: the "Frenchman's Bend." So the name "Frenchman's Bend," even while trying to give the town stable origins, betrays an original deceit. The name widens, rather than closes, the gap between past and present. The name "Frenchman's Bend" – like the narrator's smoothness – tries to make the unreal seem unquestionable.

"Frenchman's Bend," in the first words of the novel, proclaims a constitutional fraud. The name "Frenchman's Bend" indeed conspires in a general American custom of naming localities after European founders or Indian inhabitants, as if to remove their actual threatening presence by the false homage of the name. Indeed, the name "Yoknapatawpha" is but one example of how appropriating the Indian name allowed white settlers to remove, perhaps with a less guilty conscience, the Indians themselves. By the settlers' usurping a fallacious name, and their believing in what never was – "Frenchman's Bend" – whole epochs of brutality, despoilment, and violence can be forgotten. However, seen more skeptically, such naming seems only to proclaim a loss that keeps being carried forward, a boon that is a liability, an evil bequest that the white settler would rather exchange than expiate.

Spatially, the hamlet is similarly unstable, being not "an original grant and site" but an axis of transition. It is "definite yet without boundaries, straddling into two counties and owning allegiance to neither," separate from Jefferson, yet reckoning distance and time by the Jefferson courthouse. The so-called "original boundaries" exist "on old faded records." The vagueness of "Frenchman's Bend" facilitates rich Aristotelian peripeteiae, both comic and tragic. People might "come up" or be "pulled down" here. Flem Snopes begins his "northwest crawl" to Jefferson in the hamlet. The townspeople dismantle and burn the mansion bit by bit, creating and cancelling their debt to the past (3, 357).

Temporally, the hamlet lies halfway between glory and obsolescence, construct and firewood.

The myth of original stability disguises immediate problems in the hamlet that concern the nature of inequality. As we have seen, *nous* defends itself from chaos by setting up binary oppositions based on significant differences in which one of two terms governs the other. For such a mentality, "original purity" is an established economy that separates the dominant term as far as possible from the polluting other. In this paradoxical but perversely logical movement, relations of division and dominance *between* groups would seem to pave the way for a "sense of community" and equality *within* a particular group. The trauma of separation has its chief compensation in the unity of the clan. Yet it is interesting to see that inequality reappears even where the "other" does not reside.

Equality and exchange

"The Peasants" refers not to the minority, but to the majority of Frenchman's Bend. Will Varner, the folk hero of the hamlet, "merry," "mild-mannered," and even "lusty," seems to be tolerated, even beloved in the community. The fact remains that he "owned most of the good land in the country and held mortgages on most of the rest." He has, in short, almost single-handedly destroyed the hamlet's economic equity, but nevertheless his general store, as a nodal switchboard for commerce and gossip ("retailing" and "retelling"), holds the hamlet together. Frenchman's Bend transforms systematic class inequality into the ideology of economic equation. As we have seen, social and economic exchange is both equal and unequal. The strange toleration of their secondary status among Frenchman's Bend's whites may well derive from a shared belief in a fable: exchange (though always unequal) will always be equal and fair for them because it is the very mechanism that makes Frenchman's Bend a distinct enclave.

Many critics have seen the novel's barters and exchanges only as studies in personal avarice or "greed."[11] But there is something more general awry here, something indeed "definite yet without boundaries" (3). The hamlet's routines of interaction

are no more idiosyncratic than Armstid's ultimate madness –
and the two may be related, as we shall see. To psychologize
them, as if studying solitaries, ignores Faulkner's wider
references. *The Hamlet*, in making explicit statements about
economic exchange, indirectly asks about the kind of equality
that equal access to money and commerce constitutes. The
intrusion of the mediating other, money and coins, already
erodes any notions of wholeness and community. The clash of
mentalities – cash versus community – may be seen in
Faulkner's short story "Two Soldiers" (1941), in which the
narrator wants to swap a "shikepoke egg" for a "ticket to
Memphis" and is somewhat surprised when the clerk insists
upon a "cash basis."[12] Misunderstanding the deleterious
effects of exchanging monetary for personal relationships, the
hamlet builds communal experience upon such exchanges,
unable to grasp that its shared reference points (Varner's store,
the Old Frenchman's house, the Civil War and buried treasure)
are all centrally bankrupt. "What is done to all by the few,
always occurs as the subjection of individuals by the many:
social repression always exhibits the masks of repression by a
collective."[13] Just as the name "Frenchman's Bend" explicitly
wrecks its own authenticity, the hamlet's economic routines
cloak and continue its own longstanding inequalities.

To understand Faulkner's dissection of Frenchman's Bend
and its ideologies, let us examine more closely the idea of
exchange. Exchange is unequal if one partner gives defective or
deficient goods (as in the case of Pat Stamper's horses), or if one
partner must pay another person commissions (Ratliff) or
interest (Varner). Yet the notion of a "fair" transaction, if the
objects concerned are different, cannot be empirically grounded.
One cannot ask "What's it worth?" in isolation. Rather, the
question becomes "What's it worth to you?" or, still more,
"What does everyone else (the market) think it's worth?"
Valuation, although apparently a matter of agreement between
two parties about a tradable good, always engages a silent third
partner – the market. So gossip, rumor, and storytelling
("retelling") are almost as important as any intrinsic quality of
the goods involved, being the psychological or narratological
equivalent of market price. All seemingly dual transactions
also engage a third: unspoken expectations (none of the parties
to the sale of the Old Frenchman's place actually mentions the

legend of the treasure during the sale) or tacit threats (Jody Varner mistakenly believes he can blackmail the Snopeses out of their wages by threatening to expose them publicly as pyromaniacs, but the Snopeses welcome the free publicity). Similarly, Eula Varner's pregnancy facilitates Flem Snopes's admission into the social fabric of the hamlet. She must be married at all costs, and so her "dowry" grows; as an available bachelor, his market value increases without any effort on his part.

The apparent "discontinuity" in the novel's form repeats the hamlet's general evasiveness about waste and value. One critic suggests that "at several points Faulkner's use of the episodic form proves unsuccessful . . . there is looseness in the sense of wasteful construction," another speaks of a "loose collection of spectacular yarns and anecdotes . . . episodic looseness," while the *Times Literary Supplement* reviewer called it "a chaotic narrative," and even Robert Penn Warren found it "loose and casual."[14] The apparent lack of stylistic rigor here may only show, in Fredric Jameson's words,

> the very nature of cultural change in a world in which separation of use value from exchange value generates discontinuities of precisely this "scandalous" and extrinsic type, rifts and actions at distance which cannot ultimately be grasped "from the inside" or phenomenologically, but which must be reconstructed as symptoms whose cause is of another order of phenomenon from its effects.[15]

In his *Politics*, Aristotle attempts to explain how inequality emerges in a theoretically closed two-party agreement. His instincts made him conclude that something was awry in the model of transactional equality, yet, like many who propound self-cloaking ideologies, Aristotle tends to ignore his own conclusions and to *naturalize* this imbalance by overlooking its *systematic* component.[16] Aristotle's analysis of unequal exchange eventually succumbs to an almost antithetical model that naturalizes and hence justifies the origins of profit. The art of exchanging for "profit" or "trade" is "unnatural," yet it somehow derives from "natural" and "simpler" need-related barter. Aristotle never really suggests a source of the "unnaturalness" of profit. Instead he merely proceeds to inject the "natural" back into the "unnatural" without even questioning the reversal:

> the art of getting wealth out of fruits and animals is always natural. . . . There is still a third sort of wealth-getting . . . which is purely natural, but is also concerned with exchange, viz. the industries that make their profit from the earth . . . for example the cutting of timber and all mining. (1258a–b).

By such a turn of argumentation, the unnaturalness of unequal exchange is no longer a problem as long as its *objects* belong to nature. Profit becomes "natural" as long as "nature" is its direct source. In this way the most blatant despoilments of nature – agriculture, animal husbandry, forestry, mining – may be justified as "natural." It is only a short step to the full-scale exploitation of nature for profit:

> The useful parts of wealth-getting are, first, the knowledge of live-stock – which are most profitable, and where, and how – as, for example, what sort of horses or sheep or oxen or any other animals are most likely to give a return. (1258b)

Natural fertility and multiplication seem the proper analogy for money. Aristotle even calls interest ("the most hated sort" of exchange) by the Greek word *tokos*, meaning "offspring," naturalizing by a birth metaphor what he had formerly deemed unnatural – that is, the idea of money reproducing itself.

In Aristotle we see that Western political economy begins with the discovery that profit and wealth accumulation are "unnatural" but goes on at once to justify the domination, suppression, and exploitation of nature for profit. It is not surprising, therefore, that his *Politics* soon afterwards inspects differences between masters, slaves, men, and women, and finally justifies slavery and male supremacy. *Absalom, Absalom!* depicts the intermediate step that Aristotle does not gloss – the movement wherein rhetoric turns the human objects of exchange (mainly, women and blacks) quite literally into "naturals," hence suitable for exploitation as livestock.

Carrying on Aristotle's line of inquiry, *The Hamlet* explores the "Eula phenomenon" whereby the underlings of Frenchman's Bend – especially the poor white "peasants" and women – endure transformation into falsely hypernatural and therefore exploitable beings. Many critics separate the themes of "love and marriage, on the one hand, and of trading and barter on the other."[17] Yet if most of the swaps in *The Hamlet* involve horses, cows, and mules, how interesting that the novel's narrator often transmutes women into barter objects, "cows, heifers" (47). Ike-H-Mope – like Benjy Compson a "natural," immune to social cloakings – literalizes the social figures that divide women from men by grouping them with "natural" animals. Noting quite astutely that the dominant men in society view their women physiognomically and economically as cows, Ike takes for his sexual love object a cow transmuted into a woman.

Arguably, it is the balance-sheet symmetry of exchange that imitates equality. The citizens, blinded by the white balance-sheet, overlook the red and black inks of the profit-and-loss statement. In Jefferson, the racially mixed town, there is scant pretense of equality. Here, the jails are full of "the Negro victims of a thousand petty white man's misdemeanors" (257). With blacks and whites, the rhetoric of "equality" is manifestly fraudulent, and often simply dispensed with, as in the "exchange" Hoake McCarron enacts with his lifelong "sole companion": "he would pay the Negro out of his pocket money at a standard rate fixed between them for the privilege of whipping the Negro, not severely, with a miniature riding crop" (135). The concession whereby Frenchman's Bend establishes its identity entails submission to metaphors of naming and origination that, as metaphors, promise to supply something absent in a relation of equality with something present. Just as the name "Frenchman's Bend" itself has demonstrated, this promise cannot be maintained. Neither was it ever to be maintainable, for the true object of belief all along was not the elements of exchange, but the efficacy of the ideological metaphors that allow economic differences to be channeled into a false sense of sameness – "community."

The metaphor of the "natural" for Aristotle serves a similar function. For Aristotle, both the spurning and the desiring of profit are in some way "natural." Hence, paradox can be suspended under an overarching and presumably prior category called "nature." But even this mythology of "natural profit" collapses after a while, for "nature's" role as both the antithesis and the source of profit will soon lead to nature's depletion and annihilation. Profit, as insatiable and unrelated to need, reveals itself in the long run to have always been "unnatural," despite its momentary disguise. Aristotle's initial admission – that "natural profit" is an oxymoron – asserts itself anew.

Frenchman's Bend has made the act of exchanging much more valuable than either the particular items exchanged or the equity of the exchange. The seemingly totalizing and unifying benefits of exchange as a channel of interaction glaze over its systematic fraudulence. When Ratliff asks Mink Snopes about the sewing machine he has delivered, we get the following verbal exchange:

> "Howdy. Machine still running good?"
>
> "Howdy," the other said. "Why not? Aint you the one that claims not to sell no other kind?"
>
> "Sholy," Ratliff said. . . . "Only it aint quite that, I would put it. I would say, folks names [*sic*] Snopes dont buy other kind." (89)

The reciprocality of the "sell" and "buy" relation presents a kind of game of "tit for tat" (248) wherein both parties agree to deceive, but find this deceiving a reciprocal, hence theoretically equitable, intercourse. To commence the sewing machine deal, Mink Snopes says to Ratliff: "But you aint fooling me any more than I am fooling you" (76). The "any more" denotes the optative vision of equality: no one is getting "any more" than anyone else. Unfortunately, Snopes is not telling the truth, either here or elsewhere. Someone's gain is always someone else's loss. Too often, the hamlet's economic games end up like the checkers game Mink plays with his cousin Flem – Flem wins, but gets clobbered none the less.

Gleichsetzen = 'making equal'

Nietzsche shows inequality to have been there all along, and reveals the mechanism of rhetorical effacement whereby a process of exchange turns the "odd" into the "even." For Nietzsche, all semantic systems – including social, economic, and linguistic ones – are examples not of equal exchange but of *Gleichsetzen*, or "making equal." We are dealing here not with the problem of altering economic relations to distribute wealth more equally in society, but with a selection of ideologies that misrepresent, by the power of metaphor, an already existing inequality as equality. The myth of "racial purity" might also serve this function. For racial purity as a concept relies on the idea of a self-defining, even tautological group from which differences have been banished – a clan "made equal" through its "unequal" treatment of others. Arguably, under a system of racial segregation, after figures of division have done their job, a process of "making equal" would follow, rhetorically restoring the unity within a racially pure enclave that figures of division had sundered from mixed society.

Nietzsche suggests that our concepts derive from an "equalization of things unequal."[18] The *Gleichsetzen* of unequals also suggests the *Gleichnis*, or simile, the respected trope that seems to expand thought even as it flattens and delimits variance. For instance, insofar as the mind conforms all leaves to the concept "leaf," the concept "leaf" becomes a kind of fraud or counterfeit (*Fälschung*) that has gained conventional and current value: "the will to logical truth can be carried through only after a fundamental *falsification* of all events is assumed."[19] To this extent, "*the will to equality is the will to power* – the belief that something is thus and thus (the essence of *judgment*) is the consequence of a will that as much as possible *shall be equal*." "All thought, judgment, perception, considered as comparison, has as its precondition a '*positing* of equality,' and earlier still a '*making* equal.'" The corollary here is that "making equal" erases what might be demonstrated as unequal. Division, we have seen, exploits visible rather than "essential" differences in order to classify. "Making equal," in its turn, pretends to overlook visible differences in favor of setting up an "essentially" homogeneous clan.[20]

Such a moment of equalization must precede economic fungibility. For Frenchman's Bend, *Gleichsetzen* is a metaphor of equal transaction ("barter") that structures the illusion of a pure and egalitarian society ("the hamlet"). Quite literally, the community has agreed to treat the economic equals sign ("=") as a sign of its access to equality. The system of trade in which all have equal share and expect equal treatment does not, however, overturn real social divisions, but only reincorporates in its functioning a systematic imbalance by which some traders always lose, even after closing a "successful" deal:

> the third is necessarily implied in all dyadic contacts . . . as a medium of exchange . . . the parties to the exchange must of necessity have recourse to some external system of equivalence which fills the function of the third. But inasmuch as all direct contact presupposes a common world of some kind, all such contact must necessarily be mediated by a principle of identity which puts the two freedoms, the two totalizations, in equivalence with each other. Normally, of course, language is itself this third party.[21]

The mediating "third" party to these relations is the "barter/ gossip" system itself, the so-called "Varnerism" that interposes a colloquial equivalence upon its practitioners, but whose procedures make "fair" or "equal" exchange chimerical. Fool's gold underlies the self-perceptions of Frenchman's Bend: one myth (equal exchange) rests upon another (racial and communal purity).

Gleichsetzen, therefore, does not ratify an already existing equality. It is rather a kind of "carry over" (the literal translation of the Greek *metaphora*). The German accounting term *Jahresausgleich* ("yearly balance"), from the same family as *Gleichsetzen*, connotes the appropriate meaning. In accounting as in metaphor, the operation of "carrying forward" or "carrying over" allows unequal entities to be fictitiously equated for convenience. The remnant of difference (profit or loss) is then "carried forward" to next year's books with their own version of "equality." Balancing the books eliminates contradiction by decree: the books will balance, whether they balance or not; difference must be postponed indefinitely into the future. Balance-sheet logic requires that a sense of monetary equilibrium and valuational equivalence be perpetuated by handing down from year to year the residual deficit or profit. Although assets and liabilities are not actually equal, all parties to their representational account share in such a global "equalization," as well as in the profit- or debt-ridden inheritance of these inequalities.[22]

Play, gossip, barter

Division isolates Indians, blacks, and women, but not white

men: the white men of Frenchman's Bend feel united in a sort of mock-equality that promises equal access to discourse (speech, writing, laws, courts, contracts) and to trade and barter games – what Ratliff calls "pleasure." Yet there is a price of admission to this select group. *As I Lay Dying* is the first novel where Faulkner analyzed this price in detail, observing in the case of Addie and Darl especially the surrender of self upon entry into society's vicious exchange systems. *The Hamlet* deals with the rite of admission into an unequal and closed enclave, whose veneer of equality certain "foreigners" threaten to destroy. "Foreigners" are feared, for they may break the hamlet's hermetic values, even causing "actual Yoknapatawpha County cash dollars to rattling around loose that way" (34). Contacts with the outside constitute a threat to the hamlet's accounts. They force the system to scan, perhaps for the first time, the living remainders it has constantly generated, and the ignored losses it has automatically carried forward.

The town expects the excluded Snopeses to adopt the hamlet's equivocal truths: horses and cows are like people, and people are like livestock; "admission" means both accepting and being accepted. To "own," it is not enough to be merely white; the newcomer must be a "newsmonger" like Ratliff, but must also learn *praeteritio*, the art of omitting, or not "owning":

> "Huh?" Varner said. "What's that? Burnt barn?"
> "*I never said* he done it," Tull said. "I just said he was kind of involved in it after a fashion *you might say*. . . . It wasn't proved. . . . That's all I know. *I aint repeating nothing.*"
> "I wouldn't," Varner said. "A man dont want to get the name of a idle gossip. . . . Well well well," he said. "A barn burner. Well well well." (9–10; my italics)

Yet even the town's gossipy *praeteritio* can be taken a step further, as Flem Snopes learns to his advantage. He counteracts their partial silences by partial utterances. He has learned that the place of real power in the hamlet is the realm of the unspoken and invisible. As a silent presence that none the less commands the attention of all, he approximates the quality of "originality" that the Frenchman, his house, and property possess in the popular imagination.[23] Mink Snopes, too, has learned the lessons of silence: he does not lie, but simply withholds the information from Ratliff that "Ike-H-Mope" is the legal ward of Flem Snopes and so conceals the tautological worthlessness of the IOU with which be buys Ratliff's sewing machine. Both Flem and Mink have in fact learned to use on their own behalf the habit of omitting whereby the hamlet fashions its ideology of wholeness, common sense, and quasi-equality.[24]

Ratliff's role in this system of equalization is quite peculiar. Critical response to him has been mixed: one reader lauds him as "morally active and admirable," another as "humane," and another calls him "marred."[25] His profession as retailer of sewing machines suggests the textual metaphor, and it seems that he (like Homer's Phemios) is an emblem for the narrative act in operation. Ratliff is able both to weave and "to embroider" his tales.[26] He is the virtual "champion of fabricated meaning in *The Hamlet*," and establishes the "intertextuality" of the Yoknapatawpha region, being in this sense not just a storyteller but also a social reference point. But Ratliff's range and geographical inclusiveness as a roving "I"/eye figure exactly define his value for Frenchman's Bend and for Faulkner's trilogy. Ratliff, while creating the fabric of a sort of communal consensus, is also the shuttle whose course entwines heterogeneous threads. He is both an "internal" and an "external" observer, included in the hamlet and foreign to it. His self-made "neat tieless blue" shirt immediately contrasts with the expected norm of white shirt with tie. His origins are as shady as Thomas Sutpen's in *Absalom, Absalom!* The "Ratliff" seems definite enough, but the initials "V.K." make him literally a deviant from the norm. In *The Town* we learn that "V.K." stands for, of all things, a Russian name – "Vladimir Kyrilytch." Such a title, its foreignness heightened by its unpronounceability, makes Ratliff both foreigner and kin. The outsider, it seems, has the inside line on everyone.

Ratliff's peripatetic rounds are not self-identical, but really represent the literal profit or loss postponed until the next loan installment or carried forward into the next locality. He is a carrier, both of guilt and debt. We see him delivering and collecting debts – and seldom sewing machines. He takes orders and carries obligations, but never seems to touch the goods involved. He guarantees that everyone will get "theirs," but also earns a commission from every transaction. His customers will get a little less than "theirs" so that he can get a little more than "his." Indeed, if the greatest fear of Yoknaptawpha is that an outsider will start "cash dollars to rattling around loose," then Ratliff prevents rattling. If one assumes that Ratliff portrays the community's nature as a repetitive, inbred circuit, then one must examine closely the signs he gives back to the community. He drives around "a sheet-iron box the size and shape of a dog kennel and painted to resemble a house, in each painted window of which a painted woman's face simpered abouve [*sic*] a painted sewing machine" (12). In a narrative with so many crossovers between the human and animal world, it is clear that Ratliff mirrors the community as "cynical" (from the Greek *kunos*, meaning "dog"), or, literally, as residents of a dog kennel living as a fictitious "family" in the fictitious semblance of a "house" (the Frenchman's "mansion"), each happy with the joint ownership of equity in capital goods – specifically, machines that fabricate text(ile)s.[27] The mutuality of ownership, rather than particular machines, is what Ratliff "retails" in a cynical manner.

Already it seems, then, that the very stalwarts and signifiers of "unequal equalization" point to the inevitable intrusion of difference into presumably uniform social texts. Ratliff, for example, seems to get into trouble only when he ventures beyond the immediate circuit of the county where people understand him and each other. For any viewer, Ratliff or the reader, venturing beyond the hamlet's mutual ownership of systematic inequality admits the insight that the system itself, built upon tropes and metaphors, will sooner or later become the source of its own downfall. Ratliff learns this lesson the hard way. An economic bust, of sorts, follows his extravagance:

His route embraced four counties. It was absolutely rigid, flexible only within itself. In ten years he had not once crossed the boundaries of these four, yet one day in this summer he found himself in Tennessee. He found himself not only on foreign soil but shut away from his native state by a golden barrier, a wall of neatly accumulating minted coins.

His mercantile talents almost lead to his mercantile collapse:

> He had oversold himself, selling and delivering the machines
> on notes against the coming harvest, employing what money
> he collected or sold the exchanged articles for which he
> accepted as down-payments, to make his own down-payments
> to the Memphis wholesaler on still other machines, which
> he delivered in turn on new notes, countersigning them,
> until one day he discovered that he had almost sold himself
> insolvent on his own bull market.

The wholesaler from Memphis's "foreign soil" disrupts Ratliff's
tautological system of writing notes and then "countersigning
them." He calls in the debt, demanding paper money, not paper
IOUs. In the event, Ratliff pays off the wholesaler through a
series of exchanges and sales within a quasi-incestuous
network of buyers:

> He sold a machine to the man whom he asked the
> whereabouts of his cousin, he went with the kinsman to pass
> the night at the home of the kinsman's wife's cousin ten
> miles from Columbia and sold a machine there. (55–6).

When metaphoric exchange (equalization) breaks down, the
vendor of illusions has recourse to metonymic, linear resources
(kinship ties). Similarly, Aristotle's model of binary trading
partners could not make profit "natural" by exchange alone, so
Aristotle made it natural by contact, concluding that profit-
making was natural if it derives from natural entities, whose
naturalness then rubs off onto the vendor.

Yet inequality does not derive from one or the other partner
or from the goods, but from the intrusion of the "third," the
exchange system that itself mediates the trading parties.
Aristotle made it natural by contact, concluding that profit-
making was natural if it derives from natural entities, whose
naturalness then rubs off onto the vendor.

mediates between people. Debt and loss, like profit and gain,
must be "carried forward" as a kind of "original guilt" if the
system is to maintain its tautological and holistic aspirations,
yet this "carry forward" into the future by no means eliminates
the unbalancing effects of exchange in the present. Gain, loss,
debt, and inequality in Frenchman's Bend are effects of its very

constitution, not results of deficient morality on the part of certain unscrupulous individuals.

Challenges to *Gleichsetzen*: Flem, Eula, Labove

Because the self-deceptions of Frenchman's Bend are intrinsic, only external forces may challenge them. There are two such challenges in *The Hamlet*: one is to the idea of original and intrinsic value buried in the hamlet's founding location; the other is to the "purity" notion itself, in the form of female beauty.

Most critics view Flem Snopes, particularly in *The Hamlet*, as exemplifying the changing economic order of the South, a man who replaces Varner's folksy, easygoing, approximate barters with mechanical, severe, over-meticulous calibrations of value.[28] To Howe, the "shift of power from Varner to Snopes is, in an oblique sort of way, a social revolution."[29] But another strain of criticism argues the opposite view – that Will Varner and Flem Snopes are really quite similar: "Flem Snopes mimics the manners of the Varner family in a way that is at once comic, pathetic and ominous"; Flem is a "parody" of Will Varner, "merely following established patterns"; indeed, "he may be taken to represent the commercial spirit in its purity."[30] The last quotation inadvertently comments on the sort of "social revolution" that Snopes represents: he is the revolutionary who shatters not by destroying the system, but by taking it to its extremes (indeed, this is an adequate definition for all "parody").

Flem knows the game, but as an outsider cannot and does not have any reason to hide its cost. He represents "the commercial spirit in its purity," but this pure attack brings out impurities that the hamlet has formerly preferred to carry forward. *The Hamlet* seems to concern the struggle between two versions of purity: the town's legend of present equality and prior idyll; and Flem Snopes's deterministic, methodically "pure" progress. Flem's mathematical exactitude competes for semantic space with the fiction of innocence in the past and in the present – Eula; Labove; Ike and the cow; the myth of equality before the law; the belief, especially crucial for the poor, in windfalls; finally, the foundation myth of

Frenchman's Bend itself, the myth of the Frenchman's gold: all fail the test of reality. We recall Addie's and Darl's search for "purity" of self and word, Quentin's struggles with the impossibility of "virginity," and the general search in the apartheid of Yoknapatawpha County for certain examples of white "purity." All seem to founder at the moment of greatest extension.

Flem is the restless center of capitalism, as dangerous to its stability in his own way as Ratliff. Both figures reveal what might be called latent "revolutionary" and disruptive tendencies in the free-market system. The tropological town of Frenchman's Bend, as a "bend" or "turning," is Flem's perfect point of departure, the "ant-heap" from which he begins what Faulkner in *The Town* calls his "northwest crawl."[31] He marks out the points of reversal in the apparently fixed relations of the hamlet, and shuttles between them, earning interest and commission, like Ratliff, from all parties, but thereby destabilizing the fiction of fair exchange. Flem does not represent any such transcendent principle as "honor."[32] Rather he perfects the hamlet's systematic inequality, as the final section of "The Peasants" makes all too clear. Flem Snopes outwits Varnerism (he even outwits the devil in Ratliff's indirectly self-indicting fantasy). He is both head clerk at Varner's store and a loan shark to the poor blacks at Quick's mill, "working the top and the bottom both at the same time," literally encircling the ring of "ordinary white folks in the middle" (71). His "mark," like that of his idiot cousin Ike-H-Mope is an "X," the pre-eminent mark of rhetorical reversal (the rhetorical figure *chiasmus* literally means "X-ing"). On the basis of his example, the last shall be first and the first shall be last, but only within a manipulative system that continues to keep the "peasants" last forever.

The Snopeses are external threats to the hermetic world of Frenchman's Bend, but soon the hamlet accepts them into their commonplace utterance, giving them, even as intruders, a place in the county's stories. "Flem," book 1 of the novel, sketches out the hamlet's earlier stratagems which the Snopeses usurp to gain admission to the hamlet, with Flem Snopes finally replacing Varner on the "throne" at the Old Frenchman's place, the "county seat" of power: "It was Flem Snopes that was setting in the flour barrel" (91). Here, only one-quarter of the way through the novel, Snopesism seems already to have reached its pinnacle of success.

Were the novel only about the Snopeses' rise to power, as many have said, it might easily end here. Instead, there are three more books in which the novel, having shown the mechanisms of unequal "equal exchange," brutally indicts its human costs. More unsettling by far to Frenchman's Bend than the challenges from "outside agitators" are the challenges whereby insiders take societal premises to the point of collapse. By the end of the novel, we learn what the opening paragraphs omitted. The hamlet was never racially pure after all. The first account had said that the mansion only harbored "the lost dust of [the Frenchman's] anonymous bones" (4), but by the fourth section we see that his "anonymous dust lay with that of his blood and of the progenitors of saxophone players in Harlem honkytonks beneath the weathered and illegible headstones" (338). Suddenly, all polar oppositions collapse. A formerly concealed proximity of master and slave, male and female, rich and poor, South and North (Frenchman's Bend spreads a "dust-trail" northwards to "Harlem honkytonks") emerges, as well as their mutual implication in the levelling effects of time, death, and symbolic exchange, whether of words or of money. The notion that Varner has "the only Negro servant" (10) proves to have been false. At the very least, Jack Houston had "a Negro woman to cook although the only other hired cook, white or black, in the country was Varner's" and also at some point a "Negro man to cook" (214–15). Europeans represented an intrusion of heterogeneous nationalitites, but they, too, will be equalized by the dust. Clan purity is at best a short-term hypothesis, since in the end "mother earth" will embrace all clans. A similar sentiment returns in *The Mansion*, when Mink Snopes feels the pull of the "ground already full of folks . . . all mixed and jumbled up comfortable and easy so wouldn't nobody even know or even care who was which any more, himself among them, equal to any, good as any" (435). Time and death mix beginnings and endings, dominant and subordinate. The real threat to the hamlet comes from the self-deconstruction of its own figures of authority, not from the "evil" of the Snopes family, so that the novel's progress intends to show how "Frenchman's Bend reveals more and more its own capacity for self-victimization."[33]

Ratliff, Bookwright, and Armstid return to the underworld, digging for the purest form of equalizing lucre, gold, a natural element now coined into unnatural servitude. The route to the beginning leads underground, but such a retroactive search for origins has its price.[34] Armstid, perhaps the most obvious casualty of the hamlet's economy, ends up in his hole, digging further and further in search of ephemeral sovereigns and receding sovereignty: "I warn you. Get outen my hole" (342). Yet this return to the "true" initiatory wealth of Frenchman's Bend is at best suicidal: the peasants dig their own graves – " 'We're down six foot,' Bookwright said. 'Four foot wide and near ten foot long' " (358).

Where, then, might the hamlet turn for its next ideal, if underground origin seems unreliable? In book 2 ("Eula"), Will Varner's daughter is made out to symbolize feminine beauty or some other transcendent notion of the "*ewig Weibliche*" (Goethe's "eternal womanhood"). Her "commanding beauty," "supernal sex," and "virginal eroticism" connote an "exquisite purity" that "represents a kind of heavy, natural, innocent divinity that is stolen and defiled by Flem's dead wealth."[35] Women are presumably poles apart from man's despoilment of nature and his debasing cycles of business. Eula is the "earth mother."[36] Yet, as we have seen, the "earth" is perhaps not the place to look for pure, natural origins. Something else is at stake in Eula's "purity." It is quite important to note, as David Williams has pointed out in his *Faulkner's Women*, that Eula exists as the *projection* of an ideal onto that which cannot support it: "Eula is shaped for us by minds infected with classicism."[37] Some outside eye may compare her with classical conjurations of bygone beauty, but the key to understanding Eula will be found in the sociopolitical future, not the mythical past. "White womanhood," not just "beauty," must remain "pure." The "impurity" of the white woman could in one generation annihilate whiteness: her purity defends against the black otherness. In Eula, all myths of original purity, welded onto an impure present, will hopefully create a future reality of purity. If this future were to come about, the European races who settle in Frenchman's Bend would at least have their whiteness as a pure evidence of equality (and reciprocity *vis-à-vis* the black). Eula's sanctity represents not just the purity of the "womanly ideal" but a wider self-defense against being overwhelmed by numerically superior non-whites. The mythic use of Eula's body smooths over the issue of inequality within the social system. Elevated to "ideas," not people, women and blacks are demoted to barter objects whose external difference signifies ideational fungibility. At the same time, their distance, signified by their appearance, allows them a certain aura as remote abstractions.

The narrative voice colludes in this purification of origins and must surrender its initial claim to reliability. The language of the hamlet falters in its attempt to encompass an empty center, just as "the youths of last summer's trace-galled mules" ultimately fail "to defend that in which apparently they and the brother both had no belief" (136) – Eula's virginity. The turgid writing during Ike-H-Mope's pursuit of the cow only parodies the hyperbolic images the men of Frenchman's Bend have of Eula: "too much of leg, too much of breast, too much of buttock; too much of mammalian female meat" (100). Grandiloquence here seems born from the woman's silence. Men seem unable to speak unless women, silenced in a "teeming vacuum," listen. As projections of men, women are seen and not heard; at best, they speak imperfectly, as in the case of Linda Snopes (Kohl) in *The Mansion*. Their silence guarantees that they will continue to signify only on the basis of bodily difference. When women write or speak, it means nothing to the social fabric, although it may prove a domestic annoyance to particular men. Indeed, the case of Mrs Tull shows that the woman who speaks the truth in the public sphere will typically sentence herself to defeat: by speaking up in court, Mrs Tull loses her suit. At best, as in the case of the Snopes women, speech is neutral. They speak

> with the loud flat sound of two female voices. They were young voices, talking ... with an unhurried profundity of volume the very apparent absence from which of any discernible human speech or language seemed but natural, as if the sound had been emitted by two enormous birds. (47)

The women are "big, identical, like two young tremendous cows." Having denied the women "human" voices, the narrator makes them "natural" and then turns them into animals: one does not have to consult Aristotle's *Politics* to guess the next transformation.

For the white male observer, women stand for "fertility," "nature," "the body," and a literal "earthiness," but so do blacks. The stereotypical attributes of black males and white women merge, even though society does its best to keep them separate. Eula exists as two opposed qualities: she is the most perfect version of the qualities "white" and "woman," yet she is such an abstraction that she represents the "too much," or the all-too-perfect concept that transcends polarity itself. She is self-sufficient, needing "no playmate, no inseparable girl companion." Her position is "impregnable" (114) and "impervious" (119), like an "integer" within a pristine "vacuum" or a "supreme primal uterus" (114). She is even more pure than the earth and land around the Old Frenchman's place when still a "jungle" and an "unseparated chaos." Indeed, Labove, her hopeless admirer, describes her in terms of real estate: a "fine land rich and fecund and foul and eternal and impervious to him who claimed title to it" (119). She exists before "unnatural" profit-making trade.

As a polar abstraction, Eula retains a certain stability. Being "immobile" and "inert," "supine" and "immovable," "static, tranquil" and "motionless," she evokes the activity of men, even as her silence elicits their loquacity. Men move her – in a perambulator, of all things – and this inertia without any doubt codifies the woman's passive and servile role: all the Snopes women are paralyzed into "that immobile dreamy solidarity of statuary" (19). She learns to read, but only in order to give up her newly gained literacy – Eula's mother "did not read herself, though at the time of her marriage she had been able to read a little" (97). Marriage will force her, as it did her mother, to see "no need for literacy in women," since "the proper combining of food ingredients lay not on any printed page, but in the taste of the stirring spoon" (97). Will Varner, the hamlet's wealthy magnate, sends Eula to school as "the final odd cents of an interest calculation." Varner has the blacksmith "make miniatures of housekeeping implements – like brooms and mops, a small actual stove – hoping to make a sport, a game, of utility" (96): Eula must learn "the exigencies of sweeping and cleaning house and eating meals." Eula's "utility," in other words – both servile around the house and as mother of pure-bred whites – remains the driving force behind her massive mythification.

In the process of becoming useful, Eula (like Quentin) undergoes a Freudian *Spaltung*, this time, between body and mind: "mentality and body had somehow become either completely separated or hopelessly involved" (96); "There was one Eula Varner who supplied blood and nourishment to the buttocks and legs and breasts; there was the other Eula Varner who merely inhabited them" (100). Yet her "obliviousness" to her own sensuality is neither "obliviousness" nor lack of intelligence. It merely attests to the severity of the separating figures that surround her. She interprets her body differently from the men of her hamlet, who would reduce her to basic drives: "She simply did not move at all of her own volition, save to and from the table and to and from bed" (95), a bed-to-table circuit that has characterized male views of women's mobility since at least the character of Penelope in Homer's *Odyssey*.

Yet Eula transcends opposition, much like the category of the "natural" which Aristotle allowed to denote opposite actions. At the same time, her apotheosis makes it logically implausible that she could be solely "white" and solely "woman." The narrator describes Eula by "stylistic antithesis" and "rhetorical contradictions."[38] Her descriptions ("teeming vacuum") become oxymoronic. She becomes the parody of the absolute ideal of white womanhood. Eula, like the concept of the "Southern belle" itself, needs both white and black males to carry her – she exists by virtue of the white male's defense of her virtue, and by repeatedly resisting the concocted threat of rape by the black male: "she would be carried by their Negro manservant . . . the Negro man staggering slightly beneath his long, dangling, already indisputably female burden like a bizarre and chaperoned Sabine rape" (96). Eula promises primal wholeness but also primal dismemberment, as we shall see. Her combined male and female nature makes her merely an unsexed "foetus" (95, 114), even something of a "tomboy" (96). She portrays from her first appearance in the novel the ambivalence of "old Dionysic times," both benign – "honey in sunlight and bursting grapes" – and violent – "the writhen bleeding of the crushed fecundated vine beneath the hard rapacious trampling goat-hoof" (95).

In their transcendent mode, women can be contradictory: "at once virgins and the mothers of warriors" (113). Centrality characterizes Eula "for the reason that she would never be at either end of anything. . . . It would have to be but one point, that center . . . at once supremely unchaste and inviolable: the queen, the matrix" (115): the narrative voice makes her into an emblem of centrality, purity, origins, power, even as it consigns her to social subordination and separation.

Yet the illusion of Eula's purity will fade. The hamlet's transcendent version of Eula's inviolability meets dual obstacles: Labove, a "pure" and polar entity; and the marriage to Flem Snopes. As the fates of Ike's cow, Houston, Mink, and Labove demonstrate, the search for absolutes – purity or justice – beyond social norms or conventions results in dismemberment or separation: Ike-H-Mope's division from the hamlet grows absolute once his idealized cow is dismembered and slaughtered for meat; Houston, looking for justice, has his limbs pulled from his torso; Mink, looking for revenge, is sent to the state penitentiary, broken and exiled.

Division and exile also end Labove's search for purity. Labove, Eula's grade-school teacher, is Eula's polar opposite, but does not share her transcendence. Labove's monkishness recalls the monasticism of St Anthony:[39]

> It was a forensic face, the face of invincible conviction in the power of words as a principle worth dying for if necessary. A thousand years ago it would have been a monk's, a militant fanatic who would have turned his uncompromising back upon the world with actual joy and gone to a desert and passed the rest of his days and nights calmly and without an instant's self-doubt battling . . . he was the monk . . . he was the virile anchorite of old time. The heatless lean-to room was his desert cell, the thin pallet bed on the puncheon floor the couch of stones. (105, 118)

He reads just as he plays football, in a compulsive, yet sober and skeptical way, "sitting over the books which he did not love so much as he believed that he must read" (111), reading, in both cases, not the black, but the spaces between, "the white lines," "the white magic of Latin degrees, which was an actual counterpart of the old monk's faith in his wooden cross" (117). He understands, untypically, the absence that all absolutes cover up, the spaces that black lines separate. He sees that his eventual fate will involve a doomed merging with the polar Eula, who "stood between him and the final white line which he hated and must reach" (121). His transcendence, his "wholeness," can only mean mutilation, "the axe-stroke which will leave him comparatively whole again" (118).[40] Gaining Eula will represent a loss; he indeed becomes a "headless horseman": his encounter with an absolute opposite must castrate his reason. Labove at once extricates the school from "chaos," but falls into chaos of another sort. Just before his tussle with Eula, Labove fantasizes an exchange of position with her, revealing her to have been his projected fiction all along: "their positions would reverse. . . . He would be like a young girl, a maiden. . . . He was mad. he knew it. . . . And he knew too that . . . he would be the vanquished" (119).

Perhaps the overarching question of *The Hamlet* – whether exchange inevitably flattens the ideals it would construct – finds its answer in the marriage of Eula to Flem Snopes. The narration maintains that women exist in a pure, inviolate realm before marriage. For example, Labove sees a "quality in [Eula] which absolutely abrogated the exchange value of any single life's promise or capacity for devotion, the puny asking-price of any one man's reserve of so-called love" (118). Yet "unnaturalness" slowly infects even this pristine and most "natural" thing. *En route* to her honeymoon with Flem, Eula's "lost calm face vanished," no longer "centric," but now "concentric." Later, in book 4, she seems "not even doomed: just damned" (306), and finally her face seems "unseeing and expressionless" (362). Soon one might expect her to be "washing the dishes now, washing them like a man would, like they were made out of iron" (314). She has been "made equal" to men now. As we saw in *As I Lay Dying*, marriage seems to be an institution wherein women exchange relative freedom for the words "love," "devotion," "family." Once married, a woman no longer resembles "a kaleidoscopic convolution of mammalian ellipses" (100), but is just "like a man." Mrs Littlejohn seems quite masculine in this description, but the narrator still ignores the fact that a man would not wash dishes, so Mrs Littlejohn cannot but wash them "like a woman." Women, even being made to seem like men, may not equal them.

First men idolize women, but later they exchange them like written contracts. The hamlet's need for stability opens up gaps in the hamlet's myth of equality. Writing cracks under the strain of the proposals it would rigidify. The IOU that Ratliff receives is unceremoniously burned. Ike-H-Mope's "X" mark that presumably endorses the IOU reminds us of the marks that designate for blacks illiteracy and social absence in *Absalom, Absalom!* An "X" signifies exactly "nothing" ("X-out" means to "erase"), even as it is the conventional signature that "stands for" an analphabetic person. In narrative, Faulkner allows the written "X" to signify a much wider social insight, which is that whole orders of people excluded from writing are also erased from the ledgers of the commonwealth and its power, despite the false signifier of their presence, the "X." Mink (and, one might guess, the illiterate black as well) would revenge his separation from writing's power through acts of violence. In shooting Houston, the analphabetic Mink "would have liked . . . to leave a printed placard on the breast itself: *This is what happens to the men who impound Mink Snopes' cattle*, with his name signed to it" (218). The frustration of writing leads to violence in the hamlet, as the case of Mink demonstrates. Taken at its word, writing promotes absence under the guise of presence – for instance, a "Bend" is not always a bend. To the extent that Faulkner does not himself admit the failure of writing to bring about purity and priority, his own langauge becomes turgid and subject to signs of decay.[41]

Gleichsetzen – treating unequal things as equal – is facilitated by means of paper currency. Mrs Armstid insists that her money is as unique as what it claims to represent – "I would know them five dollars . . . I would know it when I saw it" (326) – but everyone else accepts the gap between "them five dollars" and their symbolic value. Similarly, Mrs Tull has seen "Buck Hipps" give Eck Snopes the horse, but she has also seen him not giving out a deed of sale. She sees the act, the deed, but thereby attests to the lack of a written deed, hence losing her suit, since she cannot prove ownership without writing. In diverging from and supplanting reality, written conventions expound upon the relationship between the hamlet's reality and its conventional truths about itself.

If "equality" is an illusionary forgetting caused by continuous exchanges, can one ever mitigate the effects of social variegation and classification? The case of "The Peasants," particularly of

Armstid, raises the vital question whether such inequalities of role and status simply result from the inevitable effects of differentiation and postponement that any signifying system must produce. *Différance* is *"the* economical concept," as Derrida calls it. But it is also *the* economic *question*, particularly where women, blacks, and poor whites have an uncanny way of forcing the issues of social justice by taking with deadly seriousness all the metaphorical exchanges and written artifacts – the Bible, the law, the courts – that define the dominance of white male society.

Equality and systematic division

I have argued that the myths of initiation, equal exchange, and purity protect an inequitable system in the present by bracketing it with stories of a pristine past and a segregated future. Such a cloaking ideology refers present inequality backward to a founding legend in which all hold equal shares. *Gleichsetzen* carries forward the guilt/debt of systematic difference into an all-white, "equalized" future. The question remains whether all notions of equality represent an illusory equivalence. If false systems of equality use unequal exchanges to support their illusions, then is it at all possible to create real equality by means of fair exchanges?

The novel addresses the question with great directness in the shape of the Armstids, who are the subjects of many such speculations, among which the most compelling must be: what has made them so poor? Henry Armstid takes his chances like everyone else at the horse auction, but has less room for error than most. Perhaps characteristically, the Armstids arrive at the horse auction as poor people: in a "battered and paintless" wagon drawn by "two underfed mules" wearing "a battered harness patched with bits of cotton rope," dressed in "faded" clothes (289). Mrs Armstid comments briefly on their economic state: "we got chaps in the house that never had shoes last winter. We aint got corn to feed the stock. We got five dollars I earned by weaving by firelight after dark" (291–2).

Three possible reasons for the Armstids' poverty emerge: insanity (people say Henry Armstid has "something about his eyes"); laziness; bad luck. The first two reasons, being "natural," exculpate the hamlet. The last reason also exculpates the hamlet, being a question more of accident than of social organization. The men of the hamlet wrestle with the explanation:

> "They're unlucky," the third said. "When you are unlucky, it dont matter much what you do."
> "Sholy," Ratliff said. "I've heard laziness called bad luck so much that maybe it is."
> "He aint lazy," the third said. "When their mule died three or four years ago, him and her broke their land working time about in the traces with the other mule. They aint lazy." (313)

Mrs Armstid, whose routine Ratliff and the others know, is not lazy:

> all she's got to do after she finishes washing Mrs Littlejohn's dishes and sweeping out the house to pay hers and Henry's board, is to go out home and milk and cook up enough vittles to last the children until tomorrow and feed them and get the littlest ones to sleep . . . and then come back and wash up the supper dishes . . . until it's light enough to chop the wood to cook breakfast and then help Mrs Littlejohn wash the dishes and make the beds and sweep while watching the road. (314)

It does not matter whether nature, human nature, or bad luck create the demise of the Armstids. More important than any of these factors is the system that mediates them. What is most striking about Frenchman's Bend is its citizens' passivity in the light of their own oppression. The townspeople are spectators looking idly at the drama of the Armstids' sufferings as if it belonged to a different class of experience – as if, that is, they were not exactly as poor and desperate as the Armstids:

> Then the wagons would begin to come into sight, drawn up in line at the roadside . . . the men and the larger children standing quietly along the ruined and honeysuckle-choked iron fence, watching Armstid as he spaded the earth steadily down the slope of the old garden. They had been watching him for two weeks. After the first day, after the first ones had seen him and gone home with the news of it, they began to

come in by wagon and on horse- and mule-back from as far away as ten and fifteen miles, men, women and children, octogenarian and suckling, four generations in one battered and weathered wagon bed still littered with dried manure or hay and grain chaff, to sit in the wagons and stand along the fence with the decorum of a formal reception, the rapt interest of a crowd watching a magician at a fair. (364)

The audience here comprises all ages and regions. It is a representative body, watching – like the ancient Greek audience at the Dionysian tragic festivals – the destruction of a victim who resembles them, yet whom they treat as anonymous. There are "two half-grown boys ... distancing him" (366), but they are, young and old, watching a man trying to climb the economic ladder by digging himself into a hole. In short, they are watching themselves through Armstid, who portrays their state no less well than Ratliff's "cynical" dog-kennel/household. They are watching their own higher aspirations being undermined with seeming inevitability.

Armstid comes to grief because he still believes he can buy into the system by a lucky windfall. He thinks his number will come up – Flem's last words, "Come up," give this hope a sardonic rebuff: Flem is on his way "up," but Armstid goes further and further "down." He despairs because he must repeat his role at the bottom of the economy regardless of the system in power. At least under Varnerism, things had appeared to be more benign. Others stole from Varner's store; he even stole from it himself – but he made up for it in the end by stealing from everyone. Under Snopes's more precise form of exchange, however, there is not even an illusory mitigation. Varner's brand of equality carried forward the promise that gain might eventually come from the peasants' multiple loss. Yet by the end it has become clear to Armstid that some people lose every time; the loss that Armstid must, in his own life, carry forward is no longer metaphorical.

Let us re-examine the idea that every signifying sytem requires a kind of imbalance in order to function at all, an idea best articulated in Derrida's notion of *différance*:

> *Différance* is the systematic play of differences, of the traces of differences, of the *spacing* by means of which elements are related to each other. . . . Therefore, one has to admit, before

any dissociation of language and speech, code and message, etc. (and everything that goes along with such a dissociation), a systematic production of differences, the *production* of a system of differences – a *différance*.[42]

Given the effects of spacing and difference upon any organizing structure, might it not be tempting to translate cognitive and philosophical spacing into social division and separation and thereby propose that social oppression is fated?

Much Faulkner criticism from Freudian or Derridean perspectives relies upon such a "new fatalism." Matthews speaks of Faulkner's world as "unalterably established on the discourse of society."[43] The "unalterably" is worrisome here. Matthews argues that "the economies of the hamlet are floating systems of signification" whose "exchange inscribes meaning in the community." Their meaning is "the exposure of absent centers in [the] community."[44] But were this the case, and the community were merely suffering under what Matthews calls "the différance of this irreducible difference," then it would be likely that "irreducible" inequality in the system would be equally distributed. Yet, in fact, the "exchange" only "inscribes meaning" in the form of Varner's consistent *profit*, and as the Armstids' constant *loss* and repeated suffering, a process that *Gleichsetzen* later makes "natural." In other words, there must be a covert principle of "fixity" in the exchanges of Frenchman's Bend. If (in another example of this interpretive tendency) Matthews claims that Eula is "somehow always already lost," then it might be wise to see whose interests her loss serves, rather than merely assuming the "loss" as an ontological or linguistic given. Are there reasons why Eula, in Faulkner's (and the hamlet's) overexerted prose, must be seen as a lack or loss that no one can recapture, no matter how hard they try? Indeed there are: the more extreme the "lostness," the more "inert," "immobile," and dependent the lost object or person would become.

The frozen gazes which the hamlet's men level at Armstid show how, through a fixed and self-imposed ideology, they blind themselves to their own self-interest. *The Hamlet* tests and rejects the idea that resignation is the solution to *différance*. Derrida concedes that the fixation of binary hierarchies can be overturned:

we must traverse a phase of *overturning*. To do justice to this necessity is to recognize that in a classical philosophical opposition we are not dealing with the peaceful coexistence of a *vis-à-vis*, but rather with a violent hierarchy. One of the two terms governs the other (axiologically, logically, etc.), or has the upper hand. To deconstruct the opposition, first of all, is to overturn the hierarchy at a given moment.[45]

What Faulkner elsewhere calls "interchangeability" must allow hierarchy to be questioned; the unveiling of systematic oppression must instigate the "phase of overturning." Thought must loose itself from the *Gleichsetzen* of bogus genealogies and false economies that rigidify social figures. If Freud identifies civilization as a compulsion to repeat hierarchies, Derrida at least points to the possibility and even the necessity of their "overturn." Rather than exchanging goods, words, or women at a profit, one must overturn the system that always apportions good and bad luck to the same people.

The Hamlet deconstructs the presumably pure and full initiatory commonplaces of Frenchman's Bend best in the final deception and self-deception of Armstid and his watchers. Our own "distancing" from the dramatic scene bestows upon us, as viewers, the privilege of action, forcing us to take a position *vis-à-vis* the deception in which we ourselves have half believed. One may conclude that, if signifying pairs may be false, then their owners may be swapped; if all opposites are conveniences of grammar and semantics, then switches of content will occur. Flem Snopes's fortunes illustrate that positions of dominance, even if unchanged, must be exchanged. Understood from this viewpoint, the novel requires us not to cover up present inequality by carrying it forward, projecting loss onto a tragic scapegoat on the basis of his or her natural deficiencies. There may be nothing underneath the earth – not pure gold, not minted coins, not even "lost dust." Yet this absence does not make inequality "unalterable," even if it is endemic. Hence the irony of a townsman's final statement about Armstid: "He's going to kill himself. Well, I dont know as it will be any loss." The loss of Armstid will be a general loss, but the townsman does not yet see the potential for a general gain.

Notes

1 Cleanth Brooks refers, apparently without irony, to Mink Snopes, "a man who has been brought up to believe in the clan and who possesses the clan virtues": *William Faulkner: The Yoknapatawpha Country* (New Haven: Yale University Press, 1963), p. 223.

2 William Faulkner, *The Hamlet* (New York: Vintage, 1964), p. 10. All subsequent quotations from this edition will be cited by page numbers in parentheses in the text.

3 Olga Vickery, *The Novels of William Faulkner* (Baton Rouge: Louisiana State University Press, 1959; rev. edn 1964), p. 197; Brooks, op. cit., p. 170.

4 Alone among commentators, Vickery understands "the complex tonal quality of *The Hamlet*," in which the pastoral "becomes itself the object of satire": op. cit., p. 198.

5 William Faulkner *Faulkner at Nagano*, ed. Robert A. Jelliffe (Tokyo: Kenkyusha, 1956), pp. 5, 77. See also pp. 48, 86–7, 99, 129, 166–8, 170, for almost exact repetitions of the "economic" thesis.

6 See, for example, Irving Howe, *William Faulkner* (1951), 3rd edn (Chicago: University of Chicago Press, 1975), p. 252, "a superb comic . . . a product of the American folk imagination," or Brooks, op. cit., p. 175, "spectacular yarns and anecdotes . . . among the finest that Faulkner has ever written."

7 Michael Millgate, *The Achievement of William Faulkner* (London: Constable, 1966), p. 191; David Minter, *William Faulkner: His Life and Work* (Baltimore: Johns Hopkins University Press, 1980), pp. 182–3.

8 Minter, op. cit., p. 180.

9 W. J. Cash, *The Mind of the South* (New York: Vintage, 1960), pp. 206–7.

10 See Charles H. Long's "Introduction," in *Alpha: The Myths of Creation* (Toronto: Collier, 1963), pp. 1–35, for how society justifies its existence after the fact by its initiation and emergence myths.

11 Sample statements on the theme might include Arthur F. Kinney, "*The Hamlet* is an anatomy of human possessiveness . . . a study of various forms of human greed," *Faulkner's Narrative Poetics* (Amherst: University of Massachusetts Press, 1978), p. 73; Joseph W. Reed, "Power, in a sense, is the unwritten theme of the trilogy," *Faulkner's Narrative* (New Haven: Yale University Press, 1973), p. 219; Brooks, "Flem is naked aggression, undiluted acquisitiveness," op. cit., p. 190; Howe, "the corruption of Snopesism, a corruption that stains everything in its path," op.

cit., p. 250; Vickery, "*The Hamlet* [presents] the acquisitive drive for money," op. cit., p. 192; Minter, "In earlier Snopes stories, swapping is an entertainment as well as a business activity. Part ritual and part game, a swap depends upon certain conventions," op. cit., p. 181; Millgate, "parallel and often inter-reflecting investigations of love and greed . . . are pursued in terms of various episodes of love and marriage, on the one hand, and of trading and barter on the other," op. cit., p. 186.

12 William Faulkner, *Collected Stories* (New York: Vintage, 1977), p. 90.

13 Max Horkheimer and Theodor W. Adorno, *Dialectic of Enlightenment*, trans. John Cumming (1944; New York: Continuum, 1972), p. 22; German title: *Dialektik der Aufklärung* (Frankfurt a.M.: Fischer, 1969).

14 Howe, op. cit., pp. 243–4; Brooks, op. cit., p. 175; John Bassett (ed.), *William Faulkner: The Critical Heritage* (Boston: Routledge & Kegan Paul, 1975), pp. 258, 261.

15 Fredric Jameson, *The Political Unconscious* (Ithaca: Cornell University Press, 1981), p. 26.

16 As long as one has possessions, Aristotle suggests (*Politics*, Bk 1, 1257a), one can either use them or exchange them for other possessions. The use of food, shelter, and clothing is "natural" or "proper," since "property, in the sense of a bare livelihood, seems to be given by nature herself to all" (Bk 1, 1256b). The "unnatural" intrudes where use ends. Exchange in the service of need is fine. But soon this "barter" becomes "unnatural" retail trade that redistributes wealth for the sake of individual accumulation. Aristotle considers profit a deviation from pure "use value" transactions. Aristotle sees "use" criteria as crucial for determining what is "natural" in political economy, although the term "natural" varies whenever his discussion requires it. Faulkner shows the atrophy of "use" criteria in Frenchman's Bend with the example of the peasants' horses, which, once purchased, cannot even be caught, much less ridden, or in the case of Mrs Snopes, who through a series of unequal transactions actually regains her cream separator from Pat Stamper by giving up the cow, the source of the cream that she would have used the machine to separate. In the end, she runs the same gallon of milk repeatedly through the machine, ostensibly "separating" it, making it "purer" white. No apter image of the enclave of Frenchman's Bend would be possible. In the hamlet, to be sure, a tautological "separation" of the same hides the knowledge of fraud under the illusion of an even more purified "whiteness."

17 Millgate, op. cit., p. 186.

18 "Jeder Begriff entsteht durch Gleichsetzen des Nichtgleichen." in "Über Wahrheit und Lüge im Außermoralischen Sinn," Friedrich Nietzsche, *Werke*, vol. III, ed. Karl Schlechta (Frankfurt a.M.: Ullstein, 1969), p. 1021, my translation. Gayatri Spivak's introduction to Jacques Derrida, *On Grammatology* (Baltimore: Johns Hopkins University Press, 1974), p. xxii, helped put me on the track of Nietzsche's "making equal" passage, although I have followed it to different ends.

19 Friedrich Nietzsche, *The Will to Power*, trans. Walter Kaufmann (New York: Vintage, 1968), p. 277.

20 "White emblemizes purity, but purity implies a purification, a removing of impurities ... it is upon this symbol of whiteness that the psychohistory of our racism rests," in Joel Kovel, *White Racism: A Psychohistory* (New York: Vintage, 1970), p. 107.

21 Fredric Jameson, *Marxism and Form* (Princeton: Princeton University Press, 1971), p. 243.

22 See, for example, Richard Lewis and Ian Gillespie, *Foundation in Accounting I* (Englewood Cliffs: Prentice-Hall, 1976).

23 Millgate, for example, notes that, "throughout the novel, Flem's silence is scarcely broken: his longest speech consists of 25 words, and he speaks only 244 words in all, with a further 33 in the Hell scene created in Ratliff's imagination. For long portions of the novel he is out of sight": op. cit., p. 194.

24 In this respect, I differ with Matthews's notion that "Flem's power in the hamlet ... depends ... on his strict conformance to the conventions of the society as it exists": John T. Matthews, *The Play of Faulkner's Language* (Ithaca: Cornell University Press, 1982), p. 167. These "conventions" are latent, unspoken, and invisible – hence, Flem has already exploited them well before the members of that society have even recognized them as "conventions."

25 Richard P. Adams, *Faulkner: Myth and Motion* (Princeton: Princeton University Press, 1968), p. 14; Warren Beck, *Faulkner: Essays* (Madison: University of Wisconsin Press, 1976), p. 645; Howe, op. cit., p. 251. Minter is probably closest to the mark: "Ratliff balances involvement and detachment. ... Ratliff moves to and fro, in and out ... ascetic ... monastic ... celibate": op. cit., p. 182.

26 Brooks, op. cit., pp. 171, 218. "Ratliff stitches the counties together by both his words and his commerce": Matthews, op. cit., p. 167.

27 Selected examples of *The Hamlet*'s "animalization" of humans follow: Houston elides with his dog (the second section of "The Long Summer" was originally titled "The Hound"); Ab and family

remain in the Varner shack, even though "it aint fitten for hawgs" (13, 20); the Snopes women are like "heifers" (14, 47); Ike has a "mowing and bobbing head" like a cow (85); Ratliff guesses one of the Snopeses' names "thinking *Fox? cat? oh yes, mink*" (89); later, Ratliff says that Mink "seems to be a different kind of Snopes like a cotton-mouth is a different kind of snake" (91) – and, indeed, Mink's name in "the Hound" was "Cotton"; Jody Varner says that Eula is "just like a dog" (99) and hauls her around in a perambulator "almost as large as a dog-cart" (95); Labove's legs are "haired-over like those of a faun" (118), and when he attacks Eula she cries, "Stop pawing me" (122); Flem is "heeled as by a dog by a man a little smaller than himself but shaped exactly like him," Lump Snopes (144); perhaps most comically, the Texas horse-trader is a "horse" himself by the likely name of "Buck Hipps" (272).

28 For Waggoner, Flem "is a Horatio Alger hero, rising by shrewd attention from rags to riches. He parodies the American dream, caricatures the American success myth": Hyatt H. Waggoner, *William Faulkner* (Kentucky: University of Kentucky Press, 1959), p. 185. Soon after the novel appeared, F. W. Dupee similarly characterized Flem's rise as "a sort of parable of the workings of monopoly capitalism": review dated April 2, 1940, in the *New York Sun*, quoted in Bassett (ed.), op. cit., p. 252.

29 Howe, op. cit., p. 246.

30 Ibid.; Vickery, op. cit., p. 169; Brooks, op. cit., p. 182.

31 William Faulkner, *The Town* (New York: Random House, 1957), p. 317. Like Sutpen, Flem and Ratliff share in the apparently endemic restlessness of the free-enterprise entrepreneur, and it will not have escaped our notice that Flem's "northwest crawl" retraces the physical progress of Western culture.

32 See Brooks, op. cit., p. 182, and Vickery, op. cit., p. 171, for the "honor" hypothesis.

33 Kinney, op. cit., p. 73.

34 Infernal wealth is a commonplace temptation in Western literature, best verbalized by Mephistopheles in Goethe's *Faust II*: "Doch Weisheit weiß das Tiefste herzuschaffen. / In Bergesadern, Mauergründen / Ist Gold gemünzt und ungemünzt zu finden" (ll. 4892–4) ("Yet wisdom delves in treasure's deepest place. / In mountain-veins, old walls, or underground, / Is gold, uncoined or minted, to be found": trans. Philip Wayne (Harmondsworth: Penguin, 1959), p. 32.

35 Matthews, op. cit., pp. 168–9, 198.

36 Eula's significance remains a critical obsession. One critic notes that in the novel "Eula is associated with fertility and the forces of nature and evoked in terms of repeated allusions to the pagan

deities, to Helen and Venus and Persephone"; she is an "earth-mother," and, continuing this equation, the "earth . . . as Other, is feminine": Millgate, op. cit., p. 191; Adams, op. cit., p. 46; Gail L. Mortimer, *Faulkner's Rhetoric of Loss* (Austin: University of Texas Press, 1983), p. 100.

37 David Williams, *Faulkner's Women* (Montreal: McGill/Queen's University Press, 1977), p. 197.

38 Walter J. Slatoff's chapter, "The Polar Imagination," in *Quest for Failure* (1960; Westport, Conn.: Greenwood Press, 1972), pp. 79–132, gives a wide-ranging analysis of Faulknerian antithesis and oxymoron. The study remains inconsequential, however, by consistently taking the notion of polarity as an idiosyncrasy of Faulkner's "imagination" or "mind." See also Adams, op. cit., p. 110.

39 Faulkner frequently mentioned the influence upon his writings of Flaubert's *La Tentation de Saint Antoine*. See William Faulkner, *Lion in the Garden: Interviews with William Faulkner 1926–1962*, ed. James B. Meriwether and Michael Millgate (New York: Random House, 1968), interview with Cynthia Grenier (1955), p. 225, and interview with Jean Stein vanden Heuvel (1955), p. 243. See also *Faulkner in the University*, ed. Frederick L. Gwynn and Joseph Blotner (Charlottesville: University of Virginia Press, 1959), p. 56. There are many possible sources for this passage, but St Anthony's opening monologue, and Flaubert's first section in general, approximates the tone. See Gustave Flaubert, *The Temptation of Saint Antony*, trans. and intro. by Kitty Mrosovsky (1874; London: Secker & Warburg, 1980), pp. 61–72.

40 Here, as elsewhere in Faulkner, bodily dismemberment or loss seems to bring about wholeness and recovery. Addie Bundren, for instance, speaks of how her "aloneness had been violated and then made whole again by the violation" in *As I Lay Dying*.

41 Many critics have argued that *The Hamlet* marks the inception of "Faulkner's late style, with its prolixity and irritating mannerism" and "reliance upon a high-powered rhetoric . . . wanton excess": see Adams, op. cit., p. 158, and Howe, op. cit., p. 283. The "outrageous metaphors" and "verbal overrichness" of the Ike episode may be a "parody of romantic prose" that "defeats its own end, the parody by its very excess parodying itself": Adams, op. cit., p. 115; Slatoff, op. cit., p. 95; Brooks, op. cit., p. 247.

42 Jacques Derrida, *Positions*, trans. Alan Bass (Chicago: University of Chicago Press, 1981), pp. 27–8; French title: *Positions* (Paris: Minuit, 1972).

43 Matthews, op. cit., p. 164. John T. Irwin's otherwise admirable study, *Doubling and Incest/Repetition and Revenge*, (Baltimore:

Johns Hopkins University Press, 1975), also cannot avoid this totalizing and even fatalistic tone, as in this excerpt: "Viewing Quentin's suicide in the context of Christ's willing sacrifice of his own life, we find in the very concept of sacrifice a link that joins those two triadic structures whose interplay shapes *The Sound and the Fury* and *Absalom, Absalom!* – the Oedipal triangle (father, mother, son) and the three generations of patrilinearity (grandfather, father, son, or father, son, grandson)": op. cit., p. 125. For other instances of this tendency in Irwin, see op. cit., pp. 69, 81, 93, 97, 119.

44 Matthews, op. cit., p. 168.
45 Derrida, *Positions*, p. 41.

7

Go Down, Moses (1942)

Go Down, Moses continues and concludes *The Hamlet*'s meditation on the vitiating nature of exchange. It explores Ike McCaslin's desire for a pre-exchange state of things, an origin before the need for articulation, division, difference, and domination. In *Go Down, Moses*, "first-ness" is the narrative's fervent goal; since "now-ness" is spoiled, the wilderness must represent for us the past. The core stories of *Go Down, Moses* take place in the woods, not out of any pastoral or environmental obsession, but because natural terrains exert a powerful counterclaim to society's figures of division. The Big Woods invariably make the hunter the potential quarry. *Go Down, Moses*'s overriding metaphors of the bear-hunt, the slave-hunt, and the treasure-hunt all signify potential failures for the dominant hunter because he no longer sets the rules. Hunting, as a reciprocal act, often unpleasurably upends accustomed hierarchies of subject and object.[1] In the Big Woods we find "men, not white nor black nor red, but men, hunters."[2] In such a realm, the Southern youth, Ike, seeks figures of merging and unity rather than figures of segregation and division.

The lineage of wholeness

The Hamlet describes an enclave – spatially distant from Jefferson – in which several citizens are searching for racial purity, economic equality, or psychological wholeness. In *Go Down, Moses* the search for ideal states takes both spatial and temporal forms: the hunters seek not only a distant resort but a primeval one as well, a pure and intact preserve of pastness. The titles or opening lines of individual stories in *Go Down, Moses* display a fascination with temporal recovery. The first story is called "Was." "The Fire and the Hearth" begins with the word "First." "Pantaloon in Black" compares the somber present with a happier past: "He stood in the worn, faded clean overalls which Mannie herself had washed only a week ago, and heard the first clod stri[k]e the pine box"; "The Old People" emerges from vacant origins into temporality: "At first there was nothing. . . . Then. . . . Then." "The Bear" places us in the middle of a temporal series whose beginning we must research: "There was a man and a dog too this time"; "Delta Autumn" sets the present between the future and the remembered past: "Soon now they would enter the Delta. The sensation . . . had been renewed . . . each last week in November for more than fifty years." Moreover, the quest for an original "time," in *Go Down, Moses* as in *The Hamlet*, presumes that the voice antedates and hence surpasses the written word. Writing's late arrival itself foretokens a certain kind of doom to come.

Faulkner's Snopes trilogy goes from the myth of buried treasure at the Old Frenchman's place in *The Hamlet* to the final scene in *The Mansion* in which Mink Snopes, a penniless and homicidal ex-con, feels that his return to the soil will make him "inextricable from, anonymous with all of them: the beautiful, the splendid, the proud and the brave, right on up to the very top itself" (435–6). The quest for wholeness there begins and ends with the "earth"; Mink's vision of interment as a final merging that eliminates social classifications seems ironic. The search signaled in the second paragraph of *Go Down, Moses* seems more hopeful. Here the quest for an original and communal "earth" seems to have reached its goal: "the earth was no man's but all men's, as light and air and weather were" (3). Not just earth but all of nature ("light and air and weather") binds human beings. To the young Ike, nature seems a lesser Garden, the primal site of human equality. The Big Woods and "the earth" play havoc with man-made hierarchies, mixing the unmixable. Nature nullifies the social significations that Faulkner's novels trace; in the woods – opposed to Jefferson – stereotypes do not pass as knowledge, classifications do not feign comprehension, and naming is not enough. In the Book of Genesis, creation of nature from nothing predates both the human species and human names. Faulkner engages the related problem of returning, through creations, to the origin when "there was nothing." What route might one take to the past?

The written route seems already spoiled. Tradition means speaking and writing, routes that Ike will traverse to the past in *Go Down, Moses*. Ike seeks out truth in its immediate form (the wilderness itself), testing whether the Big Woods might not recapture nature's chaos. The Bible, far from a direct measure of truth, is an indirect transcription, written by those "who wrote his Book for Him . . . who were that near to Him as to have been elected from among all those who breathed and spoke language to transcribe and relay His words" (260). Violations of wholeness resulted in the current state of things, so any retracing of the past to the origins must re-encounter the violation.³ Once the threat of chaos at the beginning is encountered, violence and division – the tragic defenses against merging – return and repeat a prior violation and fall. Ike's plot continues a long series of failed rebellions against division in Faulkner's works. Ike finally rejects the mergings that his search recovers, and finds himself compelled (as his grandfather was) to employ discriminatory figures of division to calm his anxieties about impending racial confusions. Ike's quests for Old Ben, the bear, the pure-blooded Indian or black ancestor, and the "taintless" hunting dog all attempt to reverse history's itinerary of defilement. The sought-after origin would be chaotic, "dimensionless" like the bear itself, and beyond extremes of measure – seeming pure and mixed, containing all polarities. *Go Down, Moses* makes clear at the outset that the quarry of the novel's various hunts is in fact the past itself.⁴ "Was" sets the rhythm for the entire novel: the memory of a storyteller (Cass) forges the past for an absent party (Ike; the reader).

In the primal wilderness, rational thought and its dictates

become nothing. The hunt has little to do with logic or thinking: Old Ben is "the bear which they did not even intend to kill." The *arche* is anarchic, says Anaxagoras: "thinking by division" is a late development. The customs played out in the woods are like those "myths, rites, and beliefs" that "have the aim of reminding men that the ultimate reality, the sacred, the divine, defy all possibilities of rational comprehension."[5] Faulkner's often mystifying plot sequences attempt to assert a non-logical, non-temporal voice within the traditionally all too "linear" story line. Ike sees that temporal sequence in the form of history has contributed to the decay of the present. Sequence is the analogy in literature for history, but Lucas Beauchamp and Ike sense that no-time (watchless time; 37, 208) is best.

Faulkner's prose mimics the subjective loosening of the causal principle; in *Go Down, Moses* the linear story diverges from the narrative told out of order – the *histoire* diverges radically from the *récit*. Many have found Faulkner's non-sequential narratives a strange kind of literary "mannerism."[6] But more is at stake here than literary caprice. Indeed, the a-sequential narration of *Go Down, Moses* tends to confuse and reassemble chronology because of the prior repression of events that break racial and sexual taboos. Lucas Beauchamp, for instance, confronts Zack about having "borrowed" his wife only *after* she has already been returned, but senses that he has already confronted him well *before*:

> it seemed to him he had already entered and that only an instant before, standing with the open razor above the breathing, the undefended and defenseless throat, facing again the act which it seemed to him he had already performed. (52)

In narratology as in the human mind, the present may appear almost like a flashback, even as it is happening, and in this way anticipation and retrospection become subjective equivalents. Freud underscores this point in his notion of the *Nachtrag* and the *déjà raconté*.[7]

Ike's quest for wholeness also has a religious and a sexual aspect. Jung speaks in his autobiography of "a feeling of great fullness," "floating in space, as though I were safe in the womb of the universe," "the ecstasy of a non-temporal state in which present, past, and future are one," "a wedding, a *mysterium coniunctionis*. The soul attains, as it were, its missing half, it achieves wholeness."[8] Enticing as these states sound, it is curiously difficult to distinguish in the above quotations which ones refer to a feeling of "unconscious prenatal wholeness" and which ones describe the visions he experienced when he "hung on the edge of death" after a heart attack in 1944.[9] The drive for wholeness in penetrating and uniting with the earth is explicitly sexual in Lucas's case – the Indian "mound" he digs has a virtual orgasm:

> the earth working easily under the invisible pick, whispering easily and steadily to the invisible shovel until the orifice was deep enough for the worm and kettle to fit into it . . . it was probably only a sigh, but it sounded to him louder than an avalanche . . . the entire overhang sloughed. (38)

The violence that orders chaos is the violence that penetrates the womb, disfigures nature, and brands the slave. Attempting to undo this series of outrages recalls the fearful violence of "men with plows and axes who feared it because it was wilderness" (193).

"It" refers to the Big Woods, but also to Indians, women, blacks – any otherness which white male settlers have despised yet desired as projections of an originality from which they are now forever separated.[10] "It" hoards "impenetrable" secrets. "It" seems unassailable – "he could not even discern yet how, at what point they could possibly hope to enter it" – but somehow the men "enter" it through a "very tiny" "orifice" (195, 208). The woods repeatedly present "impenetrable walls of cane and brier," "the walls of the wilderness . . . seemingly impenetrable in the gray and fading light" (176–7). Blacks' faces seem like the woods, especially Lucas's face, in being "impenetrable" to whites, "absolutely expressionless, impenetrable . . . absolutely blank, impenetrable . . . again the young white man saw a face absolutely impenetrable, a face absolutely impenetrable, even a little cold" (69, 71, 82; also 70, 121–2). "It" is outside of time, as when Ike penetrates "the chaste woman, the wife" – "Yes, it was like nothing he had ever dreamed, let alone heard in mere man-talking until after a no-time he returned and lay spent" (315). "No-time" is the realm behind the face and the orifice; it is the forest that, along with Ike's wife, will soon suffer the insistent and improper advances of progress.

The Big Woods are consecrated through certain rituals such as the regularity of the hunt itself (a "yearly rendezvous . . . yearly pageant-rite"; 194), the poker games, the whiskey ("there was always a bottle present"; 192), the breakfasts cooked by Ash, smearing the apprentice hunter's face with the blood of his first deer-kill, storytelling by the campfire. In *Go Down, Moses, Absalom, Absalom!*, and *The Hamlet*, "talking" is itself a kind of ritual, one that invents an imagined history, a legend of the Big Woods. The human voice, in this context, tries to conjure up a sense of primal origin and power:

> It is not by chance that the thought of being, as the thought of this transcendental signified, is manifested above all in the voice: in a language of words [*mots*]. The voice is *heard* (understood) . . . closest to the self as the absolute effacement of the signifier: pure auto-affection that necessarily has the form of time and does not borrow from outside of itself, in the world or in "reality," any accessory signifier, any substance of expression foreign to its own spontaneity.[11]

The woods are "primal," in other words, at least partly because they can serve as a locus of "time" itself, in the form of a "voice" telling a story, creating its own version of (narrative) time, re-enacting the very creation of the world from the voice of God. A proximate voice attempts to feign the proximity and authority of nature: "the best of all talking. It was of the wilderness, the big woods, bigger and older than any recorded document" (191). The antecedent of "bigger and older than any recorded document" is left unclear here; the sentence's syntax literally merges "woods" and "it" (talking). "It" intertwines with the wilderness; one cannot tell whether the genitive "of" is subjective (the talking is about the wilderness) or objective (the wilderness encompasses the talking).

For Ike, the "talking" is not exclusionary: "The best of all talking" mixes without bias with "the best of all listening," in a ritual of merged recall. The spoken tale retraces a historical line, starting at the most recent era of Europeans, and going backwards to the times of the Indians and blacks, people better connected with origin through "blood" that "was pure ten thousand years when my own anonymous beginnings became

mixed enough to produce me" (71; italics removed). In relation
to this black and red "blood," white blood is still green.

Naming, writing, and division

Such a vision of originary time decays as naming begins. All
voices seem to date back to before the first "recorded
document": the talking, Sam Fathers's "old tongue," the
woods, the bear, the earth's voice itself. Only Sam Fathers and
Jobaker can speak in the "old tongue" (172, 184, 242) about the
"old people" and the "old times" and the "old days" (171).
Paper money, IOUs, the ledger, Lucas's fictitious "map" ("a
letter or something that tells where *it* was buried"; 91; my
italics) – writing, in short – is man's chief tool in *Go Down,
Moses* for violating nature. The nomenclatures of society have
denatured reality by naming it: "The white people called it an
Indian mound" (37), but its Indian name remains pure, silent.
"Delta Autumn" explicitly claims that man degrades the
wilderness by a "signature": "The woods and fields he ravages
and the game he devastates will be the consequence and
signature of his crime and guilt, and his punishment" (349).
Only in the final story, "Go Down, Moses," does a victim of
writing turn it to her advantage. Here, the illiterate black
woman, Molly Beauchamp, demands of the white men: "I
wants hit all in de paper. All of hit . . . Miss Belle will show me
whar to look and I can look at hit. You put hit in de paper. All
of hit" (383). The "all of hit" certainly reflects the novel itself,
whose evolutionary history of the black and white Beauchamps
might well be "all of hit," now preserved "in de paper." For all
that the article/novel freezes in time the triumphs and the pain
of the history that "curves from civil war to social decay," one
cannot but regret this final voluntary translation of black
reality to white writing.[12]
   Adorno cautions that the "picture of a temporal or extra-
temporal original state of happy identity between subject and
object is . . . a wishful projection at times, but today no more
than a lie."[13] Yet, to Ike, Sam's tales of original time have a
stature that reduces the inferior present to insignificance:

> The boy would just wait and then listen and Sam would
> begin, talking about the old days and the People whom he

had not had time ever to know and so could not remember
... and in place of whom the other race into which his blood
had run supplied him with no substitute.

And as he talked about those old times and those dead and
vanished men of another race from either that the boy knew,
gradually to the boy those old times would cease to be old
times and would become a part of the boy's present, not only
as if they had happened yesteday but as if they were still
happening, the men who walked through them actually
walking in breath and air and casting an actual shadow on
the earth they had not quitted. (171)

The stories of original ancestors have an effect on Ike similar to
the apparition of the buck that Ike knows he has seen ("But I
saw it! ... I saw him!") despite Cass's suggestion that "they
dont have substance, cant cast a shadow –." They throw an
oxymoronic "actual shadow," both real and insubstantial. The
generality of such outlining abstracts away particular differences;
just as the general category "black" negates specific traits,
the higher category of "men" suspends the societally limiting
category "black." These stories occur prior to trivial distinctions, effortlessly recovering "the old time when men black
and white were men" (37), as we see in the opening paragraph
of "The Bear," which, tracing the path of historical decline,
goes from general, unifying terms such as "man," "dog," and
"bear" to specific names that already divide: "Sam Fathers,"
"Boon Hogganbeck," "Old Ben." The past is ghostly, because it
approaches a nirvana-like emptying-out of restrictive social
markings. Recovering the past inevitably restores it in a
spectral manner. Even as Cass speaks, "the boy saw his hand in
silhouette for a moment against the window" (186).

Originally, the bear had been most intact exactly where it
left no print, for the earth and nature tend rather to erase than
to preserve inscriptions:

On the third day, he even found the gutted log where he had
first seen the print. It was almost completely crumbled now,
healing with unbelievable speed . . . back into the earth from
which the tree had grown . . . the crooked print, the warped
indentation in the wet ground which while he looked at it
continued to fill with water until it was level full and the

water began to overflow and the sides of the print began to
dissolve away. (205–9)

Nature's "healing" dissolves away prints and markings. But
soon after men gain names, Old Ben does also: "the big old
bear . . . had earned for himself a name, a definite designation
like a living man" (193). The bear's transmutation from
"dimensionless" to "definite" repeats the process whereby
whites turn "impenetrable" physiognomies into "niggers."
Lucas has escaped his white designation by changing his
name "Lucius" to "Lucas," but even he cannot evade the
defilement of naming itself. Similarly, in taking on the name
"Old Ben," the "old bear itelf, so long unwifed and childless as
to have become its own ungendered progenitor" (210), and
once privileged by such a self-creating priority, now becomes a
title whose origins trace back to a dubbing by men. The bear,
once it is no longer "an anachronism indomitable and
invincible out of an old dead time, a phantom" (193), has
already lapsed from nothingness into meaning. Where the bear
appears, it already signifies loss and warped mutilation; Ike
sees "the print of the enormous warped two-toed foot" (200).
     Naming implies reduction and falsification. The marshal
in the earlier short story "The Tall Men" describes this
phenomenon: "We done invented ourselves so many alphabets
and rules and recipies that we can't see anything else; if what
we see can't be fitted to an alphabet or a rule, we are lost."[14]
The hunters translate the ephemeral bear into a man called
"Old Ben," or even into a Trojan king, "Old Priam." The
hunters take an animal they had formerly called "dog" and
optimistically dub him "lion." As we have seen, the mind
reacts to chaos with naming, and even with violence: "Where
boundary-lines are injured, the defensive fear of mixing is
easily aroused."[15] The reigning belief is that titles and
signifiers of "original" power would remedy perceived power-
lessness and loss of identity. Miss Sophonsiba's "Warwick"
compulsions – including the name itself, the dinner horn, and
possibly even the toddy ritual – repeat humorously other large-
scale acts in the novel whereby white society orders the
"other." The name may desecrate the named, but it also brings
a certain unhappy "entitlement." Hence, the unnamed wife
(and it is striking how few of the key women in the novel have

any other title than "wife"), in falling outside the lines
of power and inheritance, paradoxically attains a special
privilege.

Even in an "anachronistic" realm, tenses merge in an
unwelcome sense: far from recovering an intact past, the
backward look finds it already corrupted by what is to come.
Genesis, even by the most sympathetic account, seems already
adulterated. Tropes of double negation, or litotes, give us both
the violation and the optative suspension of that violation. For
instance, the term "untitled" at least temporarily refutes
man's "titling" urge. The bear is "indomitable" and the woods
"impenetrable" as if to renounce the reality of their domination
and penetration by men. Man's paths mark up the forest's
flank even as Sam walks "unpathed through the markless
afternoon" (179–80). Against the inevitability of "plows and
axes," we hopefully scan "unaxed woods" (193, 154). Such
negations of negative states hope to cancel what already has
become intolerable.

The primal forest region contains the traces, the mutilated
footprints, of its own future despoilment. The inevitable
capitulation of the woods to technology was there to be seen in
the first pages of "The Bear," where pastness merges with the
debasements of the present: Old Ben progresses with "the
ruthless and irresistible deliberation of a locomotive" (193),
and at the end of "The Bear" the locomotive conveying Ike to
the Big Woods (now much reduced) resembles "a small dingy
harmless snake vanishing into weeds" (318). It is the Edenic
serpent, in the form of man's technology pushing back the
wilderness. But in this late, ruined Garden, Ike confronts an
actual snake in the woods and salutes it, as Sam had saluted
the ghost of the aboriginal buck: "Chief . . . Grandfather" (184,
330). The most recent snake in nature, the locomotive,
actually resembles the oldest evil. The fatedness of the woods'
destruction through technology and greed was already there at
the beginning in disguised form. Ike travels within an iron
snake to the Big Woods (now no longer "big"), and salutes a
real snake as if both were aboriginal.

Sam Fathers – in the young Ike's view, a paragon of integrity
– comes from a family whose history is marred by several
instances of sordid victimization, poisoning, and usurpation.
The feud between the cousins Ikkemotubbe and Moketubbe is

not without pertinence to Ike's relationship with his second cousin Cass, a fight in both cases for material and psychic hegemony over the next generation. Ike wishes, by not having children, to make sure there is no next generation. So the Indians, despite their antiquity, have failed to see that the land has become "nothing" because

> it was never Ikkemotubbe's fathers' fathers' to bequeath Ikkemotubbe to sell to Grandfather or any man because on the instant when Ikkemotubbe discovered, realised, that he could sell it for money, on that instant it ceased ever to have been his forever, father to father to father, and the man who bought it bought nothing. (256–7)

The "ultimate doom" (354) of the purity notion is that the woods, the bear, the Indian ("Doom") and his son (Sam Fathers) surrender to history. Any attempt to reverse time and loss, even by Ike's renunciation of a jaded inheritance, necessarily reintroduces the terms of decadence.

The crimes against aboriginal beings all seem to derive from the needs of thinking: imprinting and classifying the other, hoping to defend against the chaos it represents; strengthening through inheritance a line of authority "known father to son to son" (105) and passed "father to son to son" (299). Ordering reduces variety to stereotype, and flattens physical surfaces to emblems of moral or intellectual qualities. Whenever unequals are made falsely convertible, a certain despoilment takes place. As a result, classes – of thinking, of society – come into being. Such separating habits are a primary source of racism, particularly in marking any black as interchangeable with any other black. The mythology of "negro behavior" (83) seems to many, such as the deputy in "Pantaloon in Black," a set of unexceptionable rules about all blacks:

> he had forgotten when [*sic*: "what"?] even a little child should have known: not ever to stand right in front of or right behind a nigger when you scare him. (19)

> "Them damn niggers," he said . . . "they aint human. They look like a man and they walk on their hind legs like a man, and they can talk and you can understand them and you think they are understanding you, as least now and then. But when it comes to normal human feelings and sentiments of

human beings, they might just as well be a damn herd of
wild buffaloes." (154)

The very usage of the word "man" here to signify "white man"
already shows how rhetoric hides a wider social and ideological
division of black from white. The notion of "negro behavior"
bridges differences, not to merge but to divide.

Blacks seem without past, property, or male lines of
inheritance, giving them a certain timeless nobility to roman-
tics such as Ike – "a people who had learned humility through
suffering and learned pride through the endurance which
survived the suffering" (295); "it will be all right because they
will endure" (299) – but in a more negative sense making them
perfect "goods" of a system that tries to overlook its past
crimes. One might suggest that white men suffer from the
opposite problem: they are unique in the present, but interchangeable with respect to their ancestors (as the recurrence of
male names every other generation – "Carothers," "Lucius,"
"Quentin" – indicates). As we have seen, they are caught in a
vicious "grandfather clause," since for them the question
"What should I do?" inevitably becomes the question *"What
would father done"* (265). Ike hates the seemingly fated return
in his own life of his ancestors' crimes against blacks which
now shame him, a white man. He has in fact been made the
slave of slavery.

The false signification of human beings as commodities
requires, as we have seen, mechanisms of separation. But
throughout the early sections of *Go Down, Moses* we see
nothing but mixing. Perhaps in a novel dedicated "To Mammy
/ CAROLINE BARR / Mississippi", the writing is already on
the wall. The replacement of the real white mother by a surrogate black "mammy," frequent as it was in the South, brings
up the threat of more illicit mixings not at all in tune with the
popular ideologies of racial separation. Lucas Beauchamp fears
(rightly, given the family history) that Zack Edmonds, after
"borrowing" his wife Molly, might have become sexually
intimate with her.[16] Whether or not he has, the more startling
aspect of this subplot in "The Fire and the Hearth" is that Zack
Edmonds can feel free to exchange his white wife without
much hesitation for Lucas's black one, as if the racial
difference were insignificant. The wives' structural equivalence

(in the story as well as in society) is seen in the shoes they share, and "the white woman who had not died, who had not even ever existed" (52) seems only an abstract transfer item. The white wife's reduction has revolutionary (or scandalous) import: "It was as though the white woman had not only never quitted the house, she had never existed—the object which they buried . . . a thing of no moment, unsanctified, nothing" (46). Here, as in the case of the original land grant of the Big Woods, objects (and humans) of substance become "nothing," through their exchange. Mr Hubert, "telling how many more head of niggers and acres of land he would add" as Miss Sophonsiba's marriage dowry (6), does nothing less than equate his sister with "niggers and land." Economic exchange equates unequal values. Sophonsiba will always be "equal" to "niggers and acres of land," just as "niggers and acres of land" themselves have been equated to the money that "bought" them.

Even as figures of division distinguish, exchange effaces these distinctions. Ike and Cass surmise that blacks are larcenous: they suffer from an "inability to distinguish between mine and thine" (294). Yet, even as they accuse blacks of being unable to distinguish, they seem unable themselves to distinguish which of the various terms of filial position should govern their own relationship: Cass is "more his brother than his cousin and more his father than either" (164), "his kinsman, his father almost" (297), "second cousins" (311), "his cousin (his older brother; his father too)" (350). Blacks' so-called "inability to distinguish" is simply the realization that possession is not the same as hoarding. In this respect, blacks are closer to market logic, which works by exchanging "mine" for "thine" and "thine" for "mine" in a controlled setting. Ultimately, such possessive (no less than personal) pronouns lose significance within a system of non-exclusive relations.

In *Go Down, Moses*, the patriarch, Lucius Quintius Carothers McCaslin, illustrates through various deeds and misdeeds how the mentality of possession confronts and contradicts the mentality of classification. He is largely responsible for making actual, through an act of incest, the normally theoretical ambiguity of kinship terms. As Freud suggests, *eros* is the instinct to combine or merge with rather than withdraw from other entities. Through erotic relations with his "possessions,"

Old Carothers has paradoxically erased his society's chief figures of division: economic (between "property" and "owner"); racial (between "black" and "white"); and genealogical, through incest with his mulatto daughter Tomasina (between "daughter" and "wife–lover", "father" and "husband–lover"). Such a need for attachment begins well before the formulation of the ego, and, indeed, might be termed "original," beginning in the womb and at the breast – in Freud's words: "An infant at the breast does not as yet distinguish his ego from the external world as the source of the sensations flowing in upon him. He gradually learns to do so, in response to various promptings."[17] The sort of human brotherhood that Ike would like to experience in the woods has an equivalent in a less remote time of original erotic connection with another race, beginning at the black mammy's breast – an "infant" experience, both as *infans* (an infant is one who is "speechless") and *infandum* (socially "unspeakable"); what the white infant could not speak of, the white adult does not wish to admit:

> Still in infancy, he had already accepted the black man as an adjunct to the woman who was the only mother he would remember, as simply as he accepted his black foster-brother. . . . Even before he was out of infancy, the two houses had become interchangeable: himself and his foster-brother sleeping on the same pallet in the white man's house or in the same bed in the negro's and eating of the same food at the same table in either, actually preferring the negro house. . . . It did not even need to come to him as part of his family's chronicle that his white father and his foster-brother's black one had done the same; it never even occurred to him that they in turn and simultaneously had not had the first of remembering projected upon a single woman whose skin was likewise dark. (110)

Because of the institution of the "mammy" to which Faulkner's dedication pays homage, the "interchangeable" black and white mother, as an impression arising in "infancy," would probably have existed whether or not Roth's mother had died. Traditionally, black and white children would have shared the same wet-nurse, a black woman. The proximity of the black and white worlds, and the equanimity with which the young Roth accepts it, takes precedence over the exchanges which demote blacks to barter objects. In this regard, Faulkner makes an implicit analogy between the joint sharing of the fertile black breast and of the fertile black soil: "the land which they had all held and used in common and fed from and on and would continue to use in common without regard to color or titular ownership" (268) – both are provinces that, for a time, suspend division. As in *Absalom, Absalom!*, the earth is equated with black skin, indistinguishable from the "croaching and pervading mud" (37), into which Sutpen put his "seed" and "tore violently" plantations or offspring. Once it is no longer "used in common," but "owned" as property for its commodity and exchange value, the earth (like blacks, women, and the land) is lost. Roth must learn to treat his black "foster-brother" Henry with the same impersonality that Mr Hubert Beauchamp applies to his sister Sophonsiba: they must be treated not as members of a nuclear or human family, but merely as indicators of the white male's market position.

The white child's erotic tie through the shared breast with his black brother ends when "the old curse of the fathers, the old haughty ancestral pride" mandates division (about the age of 7 in Roth's relationship with Henry).[18] Indeed, the decay of the McCaslin family tree begins when its black members are separated from their rightful inheritance. For Roth McCaslin, the erotic bond is "projected upon a single woman whose skin was likewise dark," although its primary value in the white male's life remains latent and unspoken in "his family's chronicle." Yet this erotic, unifying recall must be repressed and censored. A defiling fiction takes its place, and the brotherhood of the shared breast effaced, as if the mammy should all along have had "white" and "colored" signs on the appropriate breasts.[19]

The separation of brother from foster-brother, black from white, carries with it all the weighty trauma of the child's entry into what Lacan calls the "symbolic order," the chain of relations, including family, language, and sexual difference, which construct the subject socially and hence displace its claim to autonomy or self-sufficiency. *Go Down, Moses* rather explicitly connects the individual's entry into the "symbolic order" (particularly titles, names, and deeds) with the birth of division. Although the novel seems to valorize the power of the spoken word, spoken language is not less immune than written language to the taints of separation. Dialect and word choice are non-written signifiers of racial differences: "invisible, a bird, the big woodpecker called Lord-to-God by negroes, clattered at a dead trunk" (202); "a mongrel, of the sort called fyce by negroes" (211). Even the visual register encodes racial disparity. In "Pantaloon in Black," for instance, "black language" consists of the "shards of pottery and broken bottles and old brick and other objects insignificant to sight but actually of a profound meaning and fatal to touch, which no white man could have read" (135). Yet blacks and whites share a linguistic and psychic terrain: the word "fyce," which the narrator calls a "Negro" word, appears four times on the same page in the narrator's discourse, and whites later use it more or less indiscriminately to designate "any small dog."

Similarly, there is no racial scheme for thought. Lucas Beauchamp and his grandson Samuel Worsham Beauchamp speak and think in "white" language and not in black dialect. Sam speaks "in a voice which was anything under the sun but a southern voice or even a negro voice" (369). Interestingly, in early drafts of this story, Faulkner has Lucas using a heavily "Negro" dialect, but by the final drafts of *Go Down, Moses* Faulkner has made his language almost completely "white."[20] Mixing of tongues pervades this novel. White and black dialects impinge upon the "proper English" of the privileged. That unspoken tongue of Sam Fathers (of which we only have the word "Oleh") is close to the English of the novel, not a "pure" tongue at all, but really a "mixture of negroid English and flat hill dialect and now and then a phrase of that old tongue" (172). Sam Fathers dies speaking this oddly integrated language, mixing it with English: "He spoke again in the tongue of the old fathers; then he said clearly: 'Let me out. Let me out'" (245).

Ledgers and free papers

Writing and hunting are central, linked images of *Go Down, Moses*. The written word represents that place where the hunter/slaveholder falls into his own trap. Writing, the snare in which the chronicler wishes to trap the fluid unknown, reveals – and by its nature preserves – the brutality of his designs. A commissary ledger, for instance, aims to record successful "one-way" exchanges of goods (or human beings) for money. Paper tries to enforce a greater stability, exactness, and authority than the spoken word. Yet, even though the written message characteristically preserves and repeats censorships and omissions, these gaps become the seams in the text's ideological meaning. Particularly in covering up threatened or actual racial mixing, writing falls short of its repressive aims. Writing is at once mnemotechnique and the power of forgetting.[21]

To take the most blatant example, the ledger in *Go Down, Moses* attempts to use the authority of writing to cover up the McCaslins' successive crimes and frauds. Yet what Ike might have missed when told once or twice can now be cross-checked, given the fixity of the written ledger: "what the old books contained would be after all the years fixed immutably, finished, unalterable, harmless" (268). One might both agree and disagree with this sentiment. Writing, which aims to be permanent, is exactly for this reason vulnerable to acts of interpretation, reinterpretation, and verification. It may be "fixed immutably," but precisely this "fixedness" of the written text permits meaning to be "alterable." Buck, Buddy, and Ike can correct and compare distortions by spotting discrepancies that writing makes all too clear.

Writing always asserts its freedom, often without the author knowing it; written texts themselves become "Free paper," despite the "*Fathers will*" (269). The commissary ledger comes to us in a dialogic style, and its spelling indicates that it is more a transcription of speech than a fixed record of social norms. The "freedom" of the ledger might seem unexpected from a record of slave transactions, and even more unusual coming from "twins who were identical even in their hand-writing." Since they were "long since past any oral intercourse" (263), their written intercourse might be expected to be the very image of consensus and identity. Yet discrepancy and difference emerge in their handwriting, significantly, only when Ike is able to *compare* them on the same piece of paper: "this time it was the other, the hand which he now recognised as his uncle's when he could see them both on the same page" (264). The transference of language to written signifiers whose differential functions a reader may compare immediately prevents any one voice or claim from being taken as "the last word." Writing reveals the comparative nature of truth. Only through the discovery of difference in the written account (the discovery, that is, that paper is "free") can Ike uncover his grandfather's crime, and trace back its various cover-ups.

One such cover-up appears in the example of the black heirs' names. In the McCaslin family tree, naming has distorted reality. The name "Beauchamp," used of Old Carothers's illicit black offspring, both perpetuates the myth of matrilineal inheritance among blacks (a form of determining lineage that was economically necessary to a slaveholding system that would sell males singly, but usually kept mothers and children together) and derails all claim that Old Carothers's black male heirs might have to the McCaslin name and property. Yet the renaming also defeats itself. It mocks the importance generally attached to "blood," specifically to "McCaslin blood," and shatters the claim that "blood" is an inner virtue signified by outer features and temperament (rather than by name or skin color). Lucas Beauchamp, actually a McCaslin, shows unmistakable signs of his "McCaslin blood," signs that not even his renaming by white relatives has been able to efface. His name, "Beauchamp," in supporting a false version of events, attests forever to the crime it tries to hide.

Here, as elsewhere, "common sense" turns nonsensical and paradoxical at its limit. Societal notions of patrilineal inheritance, white supremacy, and primogeniture clash and self-negate. An "Edmonds" (Cass) inherits the wealth of Old Carothers McCaslin, even though the black McCaslin heir, Lucas, "was descended not only by a male line but in only two generations, while Edmonds was descended by a female line and five generations back" (104). Hence either the inheritance of "blood traits" is a lie or Lucas's family name "Beauchamp" is false. Both cannot be true simultaneously. In a similar clash between reality and writing, Buck and Buddy, unable to get rid of the slave Percival Brownlee by setting him free, must literally "account" for his continued presence despite the ledger's confirmation that his "Free paper" has been bought for a sum of money. The brothers have tried to enforce written fictions upon an intransigent black reality. Unable or unwilling to alter the written declaration that Brownlee is "sold free,"

Buck asks *"What would father done."* Buddy's answer is telling: *"Renamed him."*

Even deeper revelations come in the story of Old Carothers's couplings, first with his slave Eunice and then with the daughter of that union, Tomasina. In the ledger entries concerning Eunice's suicide, the discrepancy between *Drownd in Crick* and *Drownd herself* gives the first hint of these events. Neither statement in itself tells the truth, but the dialogic interaction between Buck and Buddy halts the story in its tracks, snaring it, forcing the intrusion of truth. Buck's immediate reflex is to censor the unspeakable truth about the drownings by using an *ad hoc* generalization about Negro behavior: *"Who in hell ever heard of a niger drownding him self."* Throughout the ledger account, Ike's father Buck insists on obfuscating the truth while his brother challenges his facts at every juncture. Buck's concealing habits are the perfect inverse of his son Ike's desire to uncover the truth. Here Buck, the censor, wants to confirm truth as what people have or have not "heard of" and hide the gender of the female victim by using the male third-person pronoun "himself." Yet Buddy's contradiction salvages the truth precisely by a written correction: *"Drowned herself."* The difference between "him self" and "herself" defines the split between the censored text and its emendation. Hence, although Buck's and Buddy's "two identical entries might have been made with a rubber stamp save for the date" (267), they are mixed and not univocal, making apparent the self-critical potential of written language.

The censorship of Old Carothers's act and the act itself partake of general habits of behavior in the slaveholding and post-bellum South. They are part of the division of races and the corruption of nature that public language tries to make seem natural. The intent to censor racial injustice relies upon a false sense of *déjà raconté.* Looking at the ledger, Ike "knew what he was going to find before he found it" (268) and yet "did not need to look" (292). Old Carothers's misdeed has been silenced. We know about it only through the discrepancy between two written statements, each one seeming harmless by itself. For Old Carothers's self-indictment comes in a curious but telling bit of indirection:

old Carothers' bold cramped hand far less legible than his

sons' even and not much better in spelling, who while capitalising almost every noun and verb, made no effort to punctuate or construct whatever, just as he made no effort either to explain or obfuscate the thousand-dollar legacy . . . bearing the consequence of the act of which there was still no definite incontrovertible proof that he acknowledged. (269)

Old Carothers, who indeed has tried to "capitalise" almost everything in sight, tips his hand in what his hand omits. He allows a literal anomaly to be written: he bequeaths money to slaves whose kinship he can never acknowledge. He has exercised his *"Father's will"* without *"saying My son to a nigger"* (269). He would become a "father" whose "will" must be obeyed, and a "father" whose fatherhood may not be acknowledged. Yet at the same time his ledger is a "Free paper": the reader is "free" to read between the lines, but not encouraged to – a common characteristic wherever figures of division are treated as "natural" or "commonsensical." Many readers, of course, will not read in this way, especially when their status depends on keeping certain things unspoken and unspeakable. Our examination of Old Carothers's fraudulent ledger entries reveals a further, Sutpen-like irony. Old Carothers pretends that Eunice's slave husband Thucydus is the father of the black children he has begotten. Old Carothers has, by his own hand, "manumitted" Thucydus (literally "freed" him and placed him "by his hand" into the role of being Tomasina's father). He has decked his own paternity with the name of a slave. Old Carothers violates a female slave, then, but represses the violation by trading places himself with a male slave.

If Ike's "inheritance" were "fixed immutably, finished, unalterable, harmless" (268), then it might indeed be a "distance back to truth" (260). Yet Ike discovers that its meaning and value are subject to interpretation. The ledger transmits not "a Legacy, a Thing, possessing weight to the hand and bulk to the eye" (301), but instead a series of vague words and gaps, signifying "nothing." Indeed, like the owned and bequeathed land, the inherited ledger decays in the process of transmission, as indicated on the simplest level by its physical decrepitude, its "yellowed pages scrawled in fading ink" (261), and on another level by its moral and conceptual dubiousness. It passes on a paradoxical atonement for a crime: an expiation that repeats the form of the crime itself. The very act of passing property down gives rise to the idea of tradition. What is "traditional" "changes hands," but tradition is also "handing over" – livestock, slaves, and other "property" – for betrayal.

In the same manner as an oral tale, the written record of slave transactions passes "from father to son" just as the ownership of an actual slave family would. Yet Ike has inherited a written absence, one which Old Carothers wishes to replace but not redress with the thousand dollars bequeathed to his slaves' descendants, a bequest that only functions to prevent the truth from being told. The ledger does not even hand down "just two words" of remorse for Old Carothers's outrage. Since it perpetuates a censorship, the money cannot fill its gaps. In "Was," we see Buck and Buddy – dimly acknowledging the overdue need to expiate their ancestor's crimes – altering the *form* of master–slave relationships without altering by confession their *substance*. They triple the thousand-dollar reparation and pass it on to Ike. Postponing debt, then, becomes a way to avoid acknowledging guilt. In the end, IOUs, having only an exchange value, cannot supply the omitted truth, hence the money itself represents a censorship forever carried forward, the sum of deceit growing larger in each generation that refuses to admit the truth.

Ike ultimately relinquishes his inherited land. To atone further, he tries to carry out his grandfather's "will," hoping to pay off the descendants of the violated black women, Eunice and Tomasina. But the effort will be endless. The debt to the blacks that he carries cannot be paid in monetary terms, even if Ike were to find all the descendants concerned. Old Carothers's legacy to his white heirs is a conceptual debt/guilt (German *Schuld*) derived from a mentality that privileges money over people. Since the overvaluation of money is itself the crime, one cannot "pay off" its victims. Buck and Buddy, facing such a quandary, carry forward their father's debt rather than attempting the impossible. From them, Ike inherits his grandfather's literal "debt" (money owed to others) and figurative "guilt" (his misdeed and its censorship). Paying off the former will only increase the latter, because the guilt precisely attaches to the false name ("Beauchamp") in which the check would be written as well as the fact that paying the check repeats the crime's repression, even as it postpones its confession.[22]

The "telling": the ways of chaos

If the written past is beyond salvage, and if the physical woods do not restore the past, then there seems only one pure route left. Let us review the crucial passage:

> The boy would just wait and then listen and Sam would begin, talking about the old days and the People whom he had not had time ever to know and so could not remember. . . . And as he talked about those old times and those dead and vanished men of another race from either that the boy knew, gradually to the boy those old times would cease to be old times and would become a part of the boy's present, not only as if they had happened yesterday but as if they were still happening, the men who walked through them actually walking in breath and air and casting an actual shadow on the earth they had not quitted. (171)

> the boy even at almost eighty would never be able to distinguish certainly between what he had seen and what had been told him. (291)

"Telling," "the story," seems to have completely replaced experience; the act of narration in the present attempts to conjure up the past as presence. Storytelling presupposes a triplicate absence: the event is no longer happening; the listener did not experience it; the storyteller, even if present, is carrying the news of the event, and not the event itself, to the hearers. Temporal separation of past from present is a prerequisite, not a liability, for narrative. The listener will not say (as Shreve does, in *Absalom, Absalom!*) "Wait" or "No, that's not it," if the alternative to inaccuracy is silence.

The "telling" fills present absences with narratives of the past "as if they were still happening." The men incant a ritual simulacrum that remains unassailed. As in *The Hamlet*, the town is an audience to its own shared "talking":

> They came up mounted and on foot and in wagons, to enter
> the yard and look at him and then go on to the front where
> Lion lay . . . talking quietly of hunting, of the game and the
> dogs which ran it, of hounds and bear and deer and men of
> yesterday vanished from the earth. (248)

While embellishing the old tale, the citizens of Jefferson
fabricate the new one into an artificial consensus that
resembles all too closely the ideology of division it wants to
annul. The "men of today" valorize the "men of yesterday,"
confident that they too will posthumously be valorized. This
"told" past is a sort of fairy tale that conveys important lessons
about how to behave in society, but never needs to meet the
test of accuracy. The "old time when men black and white
were men" exists in the present, not because it existed in the
past, but because it can as a fiction lay absolute claim to the
imperfect tense.[23] In the "telling," the listener wishes to fill
absences and contradiction. An audience will rarely refute a
plausible, entertaining narration, even if it is provably untrue.
"Telling" is the realm of the father's authoritative voice,
wherein oracular or evangelic tones suggest to the ear an echo
of priority and credibility. Yet, while *Go Down, Moses* shows
the awe of the young boy who hears the "telling," it does not
actually repeat the tales themselves. We only learn of – and
grow to suspect – the awe that the stories create.

"Was" is the prime example of a questionable "telling"
through which Ike receives the past. As with the hunters' stories
about Old Ben and the "old men," this story was "not
something participated in or even seen by himself, but by his
elder cousin, McCaslin Edmonds . . . not something he had
participated in or even remembered except from the hearing,
the listening . . . out of the old time, the old days" (3–4). "Was"
crystallizes the merits and demerits of the "telling" route to
the past. Conceived as a harmless story about chase and
pursuit in love and hunting, "Was" argues in a nostalgic, semi-
comic tone that the Golden Age of the South may be found in
that suspended quiet year of 1859 (just before the Civil War
erupted) when blacks and whites worked out *ad hoc* arrange-
ments for dealing with wider racial problems. Everything else
grows out of the story: Ike's parents first share a bed in it; the
black McCaslins (later called "Beauchamp") begin their line

with Teenie and Tomey's Turl – the story is truly etiological, designed to display and explain origins.[24]

But Cass tells this story, not "Faulkner." Cass's seniority and proximity to the events seem to give him a certain measure of authority, yet the account omits much, even as it reveals these omissions. "The moral problem of slavery is not so much ignored as denied by the perspective in which we see it here," writes one critic.[25] Neither its nostalgic gloss nor its "love plot" can hide the truth: this story tells of a slave escaping and being hunted down by his white owners/relatives. The tale's ideology implies (as do the stories of Percival Brownlee and of Lucas) that most blacks, given the chance, would rather remain slaves under whites' protection than be "free," however that term is understood. Yet the tale undercuts its own benign veneer. For instance, when Uncle Buck shouts "Stole away!" in referring to Tomey's Turl (8), he unwittingly uses the phrase typically applied to runaway slaves; indeed, in the spiritual "Stole Away to Jesus," blacks trope this usage into a hymn of heavenly freedom. The black who "stole away" (already regarded as only slightly more than an animal to be hunted) receives here the metaphorical figuration of animals. Uncle Buck says he wants to catch his runaway property and "bay him at the creek ford" (8), "before he can den" (18).

The arrangement between Uncle Buck, Uncle Buddy, and Tomey's Turl compares not to a "gentleman's agreement" (262) but to a slightly more onesided compact between man and animal in which the rules are set by the dominant party. As Major deSpain says of the bear, Old Ben: "I'm disappointed in him. He has broken the rules. I didn't think he would have done that" (214). Such predictability is the goal of ideology: just as Ike "did not need to look" (292), Buck and Buddy "knew exactly where Tomey's Turl had gone, he went there every time he could slip off, which was about twice a year" (5). Although he could "slip off" much more frequently, the story would have it that he does not want to "disappoint" the other players by doing so.

Buck and Buddy attempt to change the etiquette of slavery while leaving its antithetical poles intact.[26] They quite literally "act like niggers," without questioning the role of "nigger" itself:

there was in the land a sort of folk-tale . . . of the unspoken gentlemen's agreement between the two white men and the two dozen black ones that, after the white man had counted them and driven the home-made nail into the front door at sundown, neither of the white men would go around behind the house and look at the back door, provided that all the negroes were behind the front one when the brother who drove it drew out the nail again at daybreak. (263)

The brothers' "self-enslavement" ritual comments upon the reality of the South in microcosm. Their "gentlemen's agreement" temporarily alters social intercourse between blacks and whites, but only so long as the whites have the appearance of control. In Cass's telling of "Was," the horrible truth of kinship between slaves and enslavers remains unspoken, even as a minor detail gives the secret away: "Tomey's Turl's saddle-colored hands came into the light . . . Tomey's Turl's arms that were supposed to be black but were not quite white" (29). This crucial piece of description explodes the binary mentality of racial separation. Indeed, Faulkner's earlier drafts show him with a "face of a very dark Arab." Faulkner's "lightening" of Turl in the later drafts allows us to discern a first indication of the repressed and unspoken crimes whose visual traces are still evident. The difference between "very dark" and "saddle-colored" exactly defines the difference between a narration that cloaks Tomey's Turl's kinship with Buck and Buddy and one that, albeit indirectly, demonstrates it.[27] The detail seems minor, but it is actually a tonal prolepsis, anticipating the discovery of the truth underneath Cass's whitewashed storytelling. Only after the narrative sheds the (in every sense) lighter tone of "Was" does the pathos of this scene become apparent, because in retrospect we can see that Buck and Buddy are hunting down not just any anonymous "nigger," but their own first cousin.

The context of "telling" intensifies an inviolable yet illusory separateness. In *Go Down, Moses* and elsewhere in Faulkner's fiction, the "telling" is usually by males and about males. The stories concern "the old days, the old time, and better men than these" (44), and continue to circulate among "not women, not boys and children, but only hunters"(192). The hunters' community seems to create a multiracial community at the price of excluding women: "It was of the men, not white nor black nor red but men, hunters, with the will and hardihood to endure" (191). Gynophobia is rampant in "Was." Buck praises his domain, "where ladies were so damn seldom thank God that a man could ride for days in a straight line without having to dodge a single one" (7). The realm of women is strange and dangerous, a veritable "bear country" (22), which Buck and Buddy avoid by having Buddy assume the "wifely" duties of cooking and housekeeping. All whites are by definition "men" in this world, as when Lucas thinks: "a group of five or six white men, including two women" (37). Women are, of course, excluded, even from the man's bed: the white hunter Boon and his dog Lion sleep on the same pallet, and it seems "as if Lion were a woman – or perhaps Boon was the woman" (220); General Compson proposes to Ike "to take him into his own room, to sleep in half of his own bed" (309), in order to understand his actions better.

As we have seen, such an exclusion imagines an illusory aspect of the thing excluded. Here, the woman is the "distaff," the "other" genealogical line that none the less attains to its inheritance. In general, though, the otherness of the hunters' community is not women or blacks or the poor white, but the story itself, the "dark other" of fiction that covers over the "original" it wants to replace. An aesthetic surrogate for the absent past, the "telling" simulates tradition repeating itself. But its relations show gaps repeating. Those "dead and vanished men" might cast an "actual shadow," but such an oxymoron exposes the resurrected past as a mere "silhouette": the dead "dont have substance, cant cast a shadow" (186–7), least of all an "actual" one. As a narrator, Faulkner is aware of the definitional separation of the audience from the narrative events. But this deficit becomes a pretext, not for the exercise of narrative authority, but for play. The answer is not to replace a debased past with an invented one, but to accept nature's denaturement without erasing the loss with a narration that seems to be a remembrance.

Foremost among Faulkner's major novels, *Go Down, Moses* commits a sort of narrative miscegenation, a negative reversal of original division. Faulkner's "mongrel" prose takes down the "purity" idea, much as the mongrel dog, Lion, "takes down" and dies with the bear, Old Ben. *Go Down, Moses* violates literary conventions and segregations such as the difference between "short story" and "novel."[28] "Whatever does not keep to the discipline of established zones counts as unruly and decadent, although those zones themselves are not natural, but historical, in origin."[29] Undoing the history of "order" in narrative may serve to undo other collective orderings. The prose of *Go Down, Moses* is in the truest sense a "dialogue," not an authoritarian "telling."

Formal miscegenation removes "stops" and "barriers." The novel's myriad grammatical suspensions and parentheses (as in the first section of "Was" or the fourth section of "The Bear") extend mixed syntax. As in the ledger, the writing is "identical," seeming to be "in the same hand," but the writing also self-corrects, benefiting from its own meta-perspective. Here, the text effectively "interrupts itself" by upsetting the expectation of repetition. That is to say, the text interrupts what readers expect should come next, supplying a style that disappoints by breaking the rules. If this were not the case, Cass's narrative of "Was," sections 2–4, would be the dominant tone of the novel, equal to the dominant all-male telling that completely neglects its own destructiveness, a telling that fixates on its objects, the woods and the bear, without calling the tellers' position into question: "Once radically parted from the object, the subject reduces it to its own measure; the subject swallows the object, forgetting how much it is an object itself."[30]

Faulkner's "difficult" prose really is a kind of preventive inoculation against the fear of chaos and merging with a threatening tide of blackness. The prose becomes formless as if to camouflage itself against a perception of societal formlessness; it mixes modes to counter the widespread mergings that reality brings. The case of "Delta Autumn" exemplifies this point. "Delta Autumn" questions how we defend ourselves against chaos, in no uncertain language. Here, Ike struggles against his fear of mixing. The woman who comes into his tent embodies and thereby violates several zones: she is "queerly colorless" and white, even though what society would call "Negro"; she wears "a man's hat and a man's slicker and rubber boots"; she wears the garments "of a country woman," but has noble eyes. In short, she confuses all expected figures of social division. Ike's "amazement, pity, and outrage" come when he realizes that she is his blood relative, and perhaps even more from the vision this realization sets off in him of America's future, a time when the already frequent but hidden mixings of his and the South's heritage take place unashamedly, without apology, no longer *sub rosa*. His advice to the mulatto woman is pathetic, even shocking: "Wait. . . . Go back North. Marry: a man in your own race. That's the only salvation for you. . . . We will have to wait. Marry a black man." Ike here only repeats the ideology of division upon which racism thrives. He shatters our faith in the egalitarian, harmonizing vision of the Big Woods with which his tale begins. "The fear that motivates Isaac is, like his society's, a racial fear, a fear that springs from the threat of sexual freedom between the races. This erupts in 'Delta Autumn,' and that story might well be called 'The Return of the Repressed.' Miscegenation remains the unshakable taboo."[31]

Taking that vision further leads Ike to a literal contradiction:

This land ... where white men rent farms and live like niggers and niggers crop on shares and live like animals, where cotton is planted and grows man-tall in the very cracks of the sidewalks, and usury and mortgage and bankruptcy and measureless wealth, Chinese and African and Aryan and Jew, all breed and spawn together until no man has time to say which one is which nor cares. . . . No wonder the ruined woods I used to know dont cry for retribution! (364)

As in Shreve's glib synopsis of the world's interracial future at the end of *Absalom, Absalom!*, this version of a mixed future evokes horror with its chaotic identities and promiscuous mergings. But the protest is too late. Typography admits the miscegenation that Ike repudiates; his horrified reaction mixes italics with roman type. The written characters, amazingly, are more sympathetic to mixing than the character they represent.

The story leaves Ike in the position of a corpse, "the blanket once more drawn to his chin, his crossed hands once more weightless on his breast" (365), dreaming still of purity in the beginning. He calls upon "the ruined woods" to avenge themelves, as if hybridization had been their ruin. Yet he represses the truth of repetition: if the present is impure and mixed, then the past probably was too. Reality has always been "chaos" and "ruined." The text cannot but underline Ike's fears about an interracial future. It does so by typographical mixing. Truth undermines Ike's self-deception at a most unexpected place – the place where writing figures the past and prefigures the future, not as "nothing," or as "was," but as "now." The story "Was" seems to show a happier, purer origin before the Civil War, but Faulkner's own words expose the fallacy of such an ideological nostalgia: "There is no such thing as *was* – only is."[32]

Notes

1 Many readers note the overarching hunting metaphor – "Structurally, the framework of each story is a ritual hunt": Olga Vickery, *The Novels of William Faulkner* (Baton Rouge: Louisiana State University Press, 1959; rev. edn 1964), p. 124 "In the hunting episodes the love is mainly that of the man for the beast he hunts and kills": Michael Millgate, *The Achievement of William Faulkner* (London: Constable, 1966), p. 204 – yet few have remarked on its intrinsic and dangerous reversibility.

2 William Faulkner, *Go Down, Moses* (New York: Vintage, 1973), p. 191. All subsequent quotations from this edition will be cited by page numbers in parentheses in the text.

3 Robert Penn Warren calls this violation "a contamination implicit in the human condition," in John Bassett (ed.), *William Faulkner: The Critical Heritage* (Boston: Routledge & Kegan Paul, 1975), p. 318.

4 Hence Lionel Trilling's basic misreading of *Go Down, Moses* in finding "tiresome Mr Faulkner's reliance on the method of memory to tell his stories": in Bassett (ed.) op. cit., p. 297.

5 Nicholas of Cusa's *coincidentia oppositorum*, Plato's vision in the *Symposium* of the "first" human, a *unio mystica* of man and woman (later taken over in the alchemical notion of the *rebis*, which sparked Jakob Boehme's notion of the mystical androgyne), or C. G. Jung's *mysterium conjunctionis*, all exemplify the long-standing belief that in the origins of things the orderings of things may be found. Such "beliefs implying the *coincidentia oppositorum* reveal a nostalgia for a lost Paradise, a nostalgia for a paradoxical state in which the contraries exist side by side without conflict and the multiplications form aspects of a mysterious Unity." Mircea Eliade, *The Two and the One* (New York: Harper & Row, 1965), pp. 82, 102–3, 107, 122–3. French title: *Méphistophélès et l'Androgyne* (Paris: Gallimard, 1962).

6 See Trilling, in Bassett (ed.), op. cit., p. 296.

7 The *nachträgliche* describes "a particular sort of extremely important experience occurring at an early stage of childhood, lived at that time without being understood, and only comprehended and interpreted *retroactively*" (my translation): "Erinnern, Wiederholen und Durcharbeiten," *Studienausgabe, Ergänzungsband*, p. 209 ("Recollecting, Repeating, and Working Through" (1914), in *Standard Edition*, vol. 12, p. 149). The *Nachtrag* is a kind of "flashback" of the psyche that is actually a "carrying forward," or recovering of repressed material. Freud mentions, however, another related action of consciousness – perhaps more closely related to the Lucas/Zack confrontation – which presents a previously repressed *intention* to speak or act, not a repressed or obscure *experience*. Such a *fausse reconnaissance*, as Freud calls it, is "completely analogous to other instances wherein one spontaneously has the feeling 'I have been in this situation before,' 'I have experienced this before (the "*déjà vu*")' without being able to confirm this conviction by calling back to memory that earlier instance" (my translation): "Über *fausse reconnaissance*", *Studienausgabe, Ergänzungsband*, p. 234 ("On *Fausse rconnaissance*" (1914), in *Standard Edition*, vol. 13, p. 202). For this reason, Genette reserves a general term, "*anachrony* to designate all forms of discordance between the two temporal orders of story and narrative," a term encompassing prolepsis ("any narrative maneuver that consists of narrating or evoking in advance an event that will take place later") and analepsis ("any evocation after the fact of an event that took place earlier than the point in the story where we are at any given moment"): Gérard Genette, *Narrative Discourse*, trans. Jane E. Lewin (Ithaca: Cornell University Press, 1980), p. 40.

8 C. G. Jung, *Memories, Dreams, Reflections*, trans. Richard and Clare Winston (New York: Vintage, 1961); German title: *Erinnerungen, Träume, Gedanken*.

9 Ibid., pp. 324, 289.

10 As Eliade points out, "This is why the ideas of a *coincidentia oppositorum* always arouse ambivalent feelings; on the one side, man is haunted by the desire to escape from his particular situation and regain a transpersonal mode of life; on the other, he is paralysed by the fear of losing his 'identity' and 'forgetting' himself": op. cit., p. 123.

11 Jacques Derrida, "The End of the Book and the Beginning of Writing," in *On Grammatology*, trans. Gayatri Spivak (Baltimore: Johns Hopkins University Press, 1974), p. 20.

12 Irving Howe, *William Faulkner* (1951), 3rd edn (Chicago: University of Chicago Press, 1975), p. 88.

13 Theodor Adorno, "Subject and Object," in Andrew Arato and Eike Gebhardt (eds), *The Essential Frankfurt School Reader* (New York: Continuum, 1982), p. 499.

14 William Faulkner, *Collected Stories*, (New York: Vintage, 1977), p. 59.

15 Theodor Adorno, "Die Kunst und die Künste," in *Ohne Leitbild/ Parva Aesthetica* (Frankfurt a.M.: Suhrkamp, 1967), p. 170 (my translation).

16 His anger, given what he knows about the McCaslin family tree, does not at all seem to have come "suddenly and almost unaccountably," as Cleanth Brooks suggests: *William Faulkner: The Yoknapatawpha Country* (New Haven: Yale University Press, 1963), p. 250.

17 Sigmund Freud, *Civilization and its Discontents* (1930), *Standard Edition*, vol. 21, p. 14.

18 Robert Coles's analyses of Southern children indicate that "Each of these children has learned to identify himself, somewhat, by his or her own skin color – learned so during the first two or three years of life": *Children of Crisis* (Boston: Little, Brown, 1964), p. 71.

19 Mark Twain, in *Pudd'nhead Wilson*, makes the same point in a rather more biting way. The black mammy, Roxy, exchanges her child, Chambers, for the white child Tom Driscoll. Not only do the boys share the same breast, but both appear white: their widely divergent fates illustrate the dividing effects of certain figures upon an earlier unity.

20 See the precursor stories of "The Fire and the Hearth" – "Gold is not Always" and "A Point of Law" – in Faulkner, *Uncollected Stories*, ed. Joseph Blotner (New York: Random House, 1979), pp. 213–37.

21 Derrida, "The End of the Book and the Beginning of Writing," p. 24.

22 Ike describes a similarly paradoxical moment in the transition from Ikkemotubbe's evil to Old Carothers's. "He used the blood which had brought in the evil to destroy the evil as doctors use fever to burn up fever, poison to slay poison" (259).

23 Thomas Mann calls the epic, narrating voice the spirit of the "it was so" and the narrator "dieser raunende Beschwörer des Imperfekts," or "this whispering conjuror of the imperfect tense," in "Kunst des Romans," *Essays*, vol. I (Frankfurt a.M.: Fischer, 1977), p. 344.

24 In "Was" the theme is also the method. Reed notes that "Every story grows out of 'Was' in two ways: every cause that has an effect in the book and every pattern that develops through the other stories can be found there": Joseph W. Reed, *Faulkner's Narrative* (New Haven: Yale University Press, 1973), pp. 186–7.

25 Hyatt H. Waggoner, *William Faulkner* (Kentucky: University of Kentucky Press, 1959), p. 200. See also Warren Beck, *Faulkner: Essays* (Madison: University of Wisconsin Press, 1976), p. 434.

26 Brooks's felicitous term for the brothers is "singularly undoctrinaire abolitionists": op. cit., p. 248.

27 See James Early, *The Making of* Go Down, Moses (Dallas: Southern Methodist University Press, 1972), pp. 9–10, for the sequence of these revisions.

28 As in other works of Faulkner, the "genre" issue looms large here. Once more, critical opinion runs the spectrum from Richard P. Adams's description of *Go Down, Moses* as "loosely related stories," *Faulkner: Myth and Motion* (Princeton: Princeton University Press, 1968), p. 8, to Brooks's "more overall unity than a superficial glance might suggest," op. cit., p. 244, to Beck's idea that the novel "is not an adventitious roundup of discrete narratives but an aggregation into a basically unitary composition," op. cit., p. 334. Most critics have taken their cue from Faulkner's rejection of the original title *Go Down, Moses and Other Stories*, and Reed was the first to suggest that Faulkner has a somewhat radical purpose: "The whole is as close as Faulkner ever comes to combining his two chosen genres into a distinct and almost independent third ... remarkable in the self-sufficiency of the stories and their simultaneous connection into a rather complexly unified whole," op. cit., p. 200.

29 Adorno, *Ohne Leitbild*, p. 170 (my translation).

30 Adorno, "Subject and Object," p. 499.

31 Stuart James, "The Ironic Voices of Faulkner's *Go Down, Moses,*" *South Dakota Review*, 16, 3 (1978), p. 84.

32 William Faulkner, *Lion in the Garden: Interviews with William Faulkner 1926–1962* (New York: Random House, 1968), p. 255.

8

Conclusion: The late novels

> *In all his movements Simon was a caricature of himself.*
> (Flags in the Dust, 274)

Faulkner's best novels analyze the often man-made separations between ideal and reality, need and satisfaction, hope and encounter. Faulkner depicts life as an uneasy striving towards ever-receding goals, an oscillation between reach and attainment whose endless conflict, not any a priori essence, creates man's "endurance" and will to live on. Characters such as Dilsey or Sam Fathers who grapple with losses also understand that their treasured ideal will return . . . and vanish again. Loss participates in a larger cycle of loss–recovery–loss; the Grecian urn may have flaws, but it may also turn. Cycles of loss and redemption – notably in *As I Lay Dying, Light in August*, or *The Hamlet* – constitute Faulkner's thematic terrain, his heroes emerging from their sufferings with, at best, a greater quantity of truth. "Man errs as long as he strives," the Lord says in Goethe's *Faust*, but errancy, while seeking wholeness and perfection, finds as its apparent goal not wholeness but further "error." The Aeschylian *pathei mathos*, "learning through suffering," finds a modern vehicle here. The further lesson is precisely that a lesson, and not just a futile suffering, has taken place. Characters such as Quentin or Ike, who wish against all evidence to perpetuate absolute ideals, only end up perpetrating further error, making themselves and their environment miserable along the way.

Notoriously erratic, Faulkner's early search for new hypotheses and arguments had seemed to some erroneous from the start. Yet it gains power and credibility exactly through the risks that it takes. Faulkner, for his part, criticized Hemingway because "he did not have the courage to get out on a limb as the others did, to risk bad taste, overwriting, dullness, etc."[1] Yet Faulkner's early stylistic "failures" differ in important ways from his later ones. In the novels written before 1945, Faulkner's literary excesses represent absence, whereas the post-1945 novels represent excess. He takes pains in the early novels to illustrate that paradoxical aspect of writing wherein rhetorical surfeit exactly uncovers the virtual paucity it wants to cover up. In contrast to his later prose, Faulkner's earlier style quests obsessively to conjure up presence, but always uncovers absent centers, as in his description of John Sartoris's apparition in *Flags in the Dust*:

> Freed as he was of time, he was a far more definite presence in the room than the two of them cemented by deafness to a dead time and drawn thin by the slow attenuation of days. He seemed to stand above them, all around them, with his bearded, hawklike face and the bold glamor of his dream.
>
> Old Bayard sat with his feet braced against the side of the fireplace, holding the pipe in his hand . . . on the bit were the prints of his father's teeth.[2]

The prose here has "density," "complexity," even rhetorical vigor, but it finally conveys no more than a feeling of "attenuation." The surplus of negative terms in this passage, for instance, is striking: the "definite presence in the room" is really an absence; the "presence" or apparition does not even "appear." The "glamor" of the ideal "dream" remains distanced, inaccessible; present are "the prints of . . . father's teeth." A thematic and stylistic concern with the absent "father" as white male – the signifying center against which all other reality is measured and defined – infuses Faulkner's early work. Required here are not the ever-distanced "teeth," but "prints": writing, anything that can acknowledge the absence and thereby supplement it – even "printed words" and rhetoric as a surrogate in the present, filling up the gaps of the lost past. From *The Sound and the Fury* through *Go Down, Moses*, Faulkner's remarkable prose experiments counter this constitutional absence by encountering and representing it, echoing with their own near-misses their protagonists' heroic failures to recapture a lost or vanishing sufficiency.

The shadow-obsessed and asyntactic language of Quentin and Benjy or Darl and Vardaman, insisting on actual and grammatical "emptying," Addie's emptied "I," finding space in vaginal non-inscription; Joe Christmas's shadowy and self-effacing presence; the multiple absences, concealments, negations, and gaps of *Absalom, Absalom!*, whose males have vanished, leaving only an "impress" (like Homer Baron in "A Rose for Emily"); Labove, Armstid, and Ratliff, each experiencing in turn the destruction of their respective ideals; Ike, whose search for wholeness beyond social classifications only leads him to witness the destruction of the woods and of his earlier love of equality: literary style in all these plots conditions and continues characters' errors. The often paratactic, often elaborately structured prose in the major novels vacillates together with the main characters between vision and loss, synthesis and dissolution, merging and division. The fluctuations of this "erring" pose constitutive dilemmas: even as the characters rail against the losses in their lives, the style surrounds them with absence.

The play of absence and presence takes several forms. On the historical level, the effects of the Civil War have destroyed what seems a purer, more powerful past. More generally, temporality and progress remove every past time, an absence that reactive and retroactive conservation – storytelling, myth-making, ritual actions – attempts to recover. Yet these expedients, inadequate to their task, only lead to new absences. On the social level, any real encounter on the part of the dominant white male with blacks, Indians, women, or poorer whites evokes the simultaneous allure and fear of their radical difference. The lack of "normality" in such relations requires the creation of binary masks and stereotypes ("forms of behavior") by which the unknown other can be manipulated and segregated. These remedies, however, lead to further awareness of lack, since they divide one group from another. In any case, miscegenation – almost exclusively initiated by white males and not black ones – already undermines the attempt to divide perfectly. The absence of pure divisions leads to violent enforcement of various segregations, but this expedient merely increases the desire to encounter the other. On an economic level, "equality" of society is missing, because of profit motivation and the exchange principle that brings class structures into being. Yet systems of economic partition are themselves no solution. In reducing each citizen's individuality to the "lingua franca" of capital, they increase insecurity and deception in every economic stratum. Most importantly, psychological and epistemological integrity are lacking, on account of the separating and postponing attributes of language itself. Uncertain designations and slippery definitions involve figures whose temporary orderings inevitably trope into paradox, creating at best awkward misrecognitions and at worst mental chaos.

The late novels no longer gloss this plot of absence and presence. Their style betrays deeper changes of emphasis. Faulkner's late style condenses; his early style sprawls. Where the early style had atomized and broken down the pretense of representational wholeness, sufficiency, and purity, the late Faulkner concentrates and monumentalizes. In a letter written to Malcolm Cowley in 1944, Faulkner admits the interminability of his enterprise of "trying to say it all": "This I think accounts for what people call the obscurity, the involved formless 'style,' endless sentences. I'm trying to say it all in one sentence between one Cap and one period." Faulkner's concession about his stylistic difficulty is ambivalent. Faulkner's infinite, "endless sentences" aim to compress the world into a single, finite sentence. It is questionable whether Faulkner recognizes the paradox. At best, we may take his self-assessment (written less than a year before an "Appendix" that condenses and rewrites *The Sound and the Fury*) as a fruitful way of distinguishing Faulkner's early and late periods.

In *The Town*, Eula Varner Snopes, former paragon of white female beauty, dies and gets a Sartoris-like funeral monument. Faulkner contrasts this monument to Flem Snopes's monument – a water tank: "At first we thought that the water tank was only Flem Snopes's monument" (3) – "Except that it was not a monument: it was a footprint. A monument only says *At least*

I got this far while a footprint says *This is where I was when I moved again"* (29). Perhaps Faulkner's own metaphors aptly describe his late work: monumental and static, it does not compare to the "footprint"-like and richly suggestive absences of the early prose, which had been the "print" of someone looking forwards and not backwards to better things.

Instead of representing through rhetorical tropes the endless oscillation between presence and absence, merging and division, Faulkner's later novels reify rhetorical tropes and concepts that had once configured his struggle. He recalls the trappings of important cognitive and rhetorical moments, without, however, recovering the moments themselves as renderings of loss and absence. Formerly, he had portrayed an *inquest* into truth, not a one-sentence digest of it. Previously, he had shocked and even outraged his readership with defamiliarizing experiments in prose form. In his later work, however, Faulkner domesticates even his bravest literary ventures. Instead of continuing the impossible challenge of uttering a socially ineffable "it" and accepting that "failure," the later Faulkner – like the pretentious figure I. O. Snopes – reduces prickly reality to glib, self-referential "saws and proverbs."

The "Appendix" to *The Sound and the Fury* (1946) marks the beginning of Faulkner's late period – represented in the main by *Intruder in the Dust* (1948), *A Fable* (1954), and the continuations of the Snopes saga, *The Town* (1957) and *The Mansion* (1959). Faulkner's "Appendix" to *The Sound and the Fury* underlines the general manner in which his later style reduces earlier complexity. Its prolix and often hermetic references resuscitate "Faulknerian" words such as "dispossessed," "imperishable," "avatar," and "doomed" as if they were talismans of a more glorious past. What the "Appendix" lacks is mystery; it is explanatory, didactic, in the truest sense a *Nachtrag*, or "appendix," hence particularly *nachträglich*, Freud's term for reactions to and explanations of the past which try (not always successfully) to resolve and conclude earlier events. Faulkner's *nachträgliche* texts, which attempt to close off questions that earlier plots leave open, already seem doomed to an unexpected failure.

Gavin Stevens, whose bombast Faulkner manages to restrain in *Light in August* and *Knight's Gambit*, comes back with a vengeance to plague *Intruder in the Dust, The Town,* and *The*

Mansion. Whether he is Faulkner's "mouthpiece" or not, Stevens's excesses constitute one of Faulkner's least convincing tonalities and verge on the ridiculous. As one reader says of Stevens, "In verbal style, he comes near to being Faulkner's self-parody."[3] This self-caricature, no doubt unintended, represents a kind of unconscious literary kitsch. If wit may be defined as an unexpected recognition, and parody as a device that forces the audience to recognize its expectations, then kitsch may be the art form that forces us to recognize the great disparity between our failed moral and aesthetic expectations and the grandiose icons of familiarity with which we hide that failure. Hence follows the peculiarity of reading Faulkner's late novels: the more Faulkner one already has read, the more kitsch-like, in the context of Faulkner's entire opus, these late derivations seem.

The element of surprise or discrepancy that Freud discovered in "the comic" – an "unintended discovery . . . the *difference* between the two cathectic expenditures" – can also provide an indirect explanation for the effects of Faulkner's later style.[4] By this explanation, the *difference* between the claim made by style for an idea's *magnitude* and the *condensed* nature of the idea's expression creates an unintentional discrepancy leading to laughter. In the wrong context, the large is deflated, the small dilated – both with comic results.

Faulkner's late style enacts a kind of false metonymy in which those more vibrant earlier forays into doubt, abstract, and absence can now only be recalled by the signifiers that accompanied them, without a context that is at all adequate to the claims the style pretends to make. A couple of examples from *A Fable* – among the shortest available – will illustrate the point:

Man pouring steadily into the tabernacle, the shrine itself, of his last tribal mysteries, entering it without temerity or challenge, because why not? it was his, he had decreed it, built it, sweated it up: not out of any particular need nor any long agony of hope, because he was not aware of any lack or long history of agony or that he participated in any long chronicle of frustrated yearning, but because he wanted it . . . to be no symbol nor cradle nor any mammalian apex, harbor where the incredible cockleshell of his invincible dream made soundings at last from the chartless latitude of his lost beginnings and where, like that of the enduring sea, the voice of his affirmation roared murmuring home to the atoll-dais of his unanimity where no mere petty right, but blind justice itself, reigned ruthless and inattentive amid the deathless shells of his victories: his stale tobacco spit and his sweat.

Because they endured, as only endurance can, firmer than rock, more impervious than folly, longer than grief, the darkling and silent city rising out of the darkling and empty twilight to lower like a thunderclap, since it was the effigy and the power, rising tier on inviolate tier out of that mazed chiaroscuro like a tremendous beehive whose crown challenged by day the sun and stemmed aside by night the myriad smore of stars.[5]

Although the by now standard figures of Faulknerian rhetoric are here – "not . . . nor . . . because . . . but because" – as well as its key words ("mammalian," "invincible," "endured," "impervious," "inviolate," "myriad"), along with suggestively negative prefixes, their appropriateness is limited to a kind of evocative resonance.

Faulkner's self-translation is as quixotic as Gavin Stevens's project "of translating the Old Testament back into the classic Greek of its first translating; after which he would teach himself Hebrew and really attain the purity" (*The Mansion*, 392). As in the fate of the erstwhile "avatar" of purity, Eula Varner, Gavin's and Faulkner's search for "purity" ends up in a misconceived and inappropriate "monument," a representation as phallic presence of a prior representation of emptiness. Late in his career, Faulkner, like Stevens, "told, repeated, the gist" (390), not realizing that "the gist" of his earlier masterpieces was not any particular phrase or statement or series of them but rather what his writing left unsaid.

The quest for "purity" that ultimately victimizes Ike's ideals also plagues Gavin Stevens in the notoriously didactic chapter 7 of *Intruder in the Dust*:

Only a few of us know that only from homogeneity comes anything of a people or for a people of durable and lasting value – the literature, the art, the science, that minimum of government and police which is the meaning of freedom and liberty, and perhaps most valuable of all a national character worth anything in a crisis – that crisis we shall face someday when we meet an enemy with as many men as we have and as much material as we have and – who knows? – who can even brag and boast as we brag and boast.

And as for Lucas Beauchamp, Sambo, he's a homogeneous man too, except that part of him which is trying to escape not even into the best of the white race, but into the second best.[6]

Such a yearning for an unmixed or uncomplicated racial, cultural, or even linguistic essence not only contradicts all the premises of Faulkner's plots here and elsewhere – Lucas is not only not "homogeneous" but he is also not "Sambo" in any sense, being about as mixed as anyone and as "white" as Stevens himself – but also exemplifies the desire for closure and immanent explanation that characterizes Faulkner's late aesthetics. One might say that in the end the fear of chaos conquered Faulkner as much as it did his hero Ike. Realizing the tenuousness of arbitrary social division, and having entertained his reader with this theme for almost twenty years, Faulkner now returns to versions of discreteness, Apollonian clarity, and "homogeneity" in his own works. In effect, the "gist" should not have been what it becomes – a futile retranslation of a translation to get an earlier "purity" – but rather a consultation of the "original," leading to a further exploration of its challenging deficiencies and "footprints."

In designating literary kitsch as a necessary concomitant of Romantic aesthetics, Hermann Broch exactly states how it prematurely terminates an inquiry in order to reconcile a finite representation with an infinite claim:

For just as knowledge and particularly scientific knowledge as logical systems will continue to develop infinitely, so too does art constitute such a system. In the former, truth is the systematic goal that looms in the infinite distance; in the latter, it is beauty; in both, the goal is a Platonic Idea. . . . Wherever there is no question about the unattainable nature of this goal – as in those structures that, in the nature of science and art, proceed step-by-step by an inner logic from discovery to discovery, and where therefore the goal remains beyond the system – the system may and ought to be called "open." Yet romanticism demands the opposite: it wants to transform the Platonic Ideas of art or beauty into the direct and tangible goal of every art object. In a sense, the systematic character of art is suspended here, yet insofar as it remains, it is given the stamp of closure; the infinite system becomes finite.[7]

The kitsch-object closes off the possibility that its promised comprehensiveness and expansiveness will ever be carried out. The "gist" is simply repeated, such that, in subsequent repetitions, the barest trappings of an event, and not the event itself, become the sought-after instance.

Such a process is – like a retranslation back to the original – doubly metaphorical, in the Lacanian sense of a process whereby a new signifier displaces the original one, which then falls to the rank of signified.[8] Yet, if an earlier signifier becomes the new signified, then this procedure only reproduces *differential* terms, getting further and further from the "first" signified/signifier pair, without there ever being a reference to that instance. All figurative language, of course, works this way, but the pretense of "perfect" reproduction and displacement in each transmission of differences gives parody and kitsch their particularly comic attributes. For the replacement of the signifier is never "the same," if only because in every case a context or linkage has been entirely disposed of. To translate an English text of the Old Testament back into Latin, then Greek, then Hebrew, would really be an exercise in error masking as a quest for authenticity. The result of this philological game would hardly be an "original text," but, even were it a word-for-word duplication of the "original," it would not be pure, but merely a modern replica whose fallaciously imitative "authenticity" would make it, no less than a plaster-of-Paris *pietà*, a prime candidate for the designation kitsch: "Kitsch is also a system of imitation," Broch writes; "it can copy art down to the smallest detail."[9] Faulkner's later works – all, except *A Fable*, retranslations of earlier novels – turn his greatest writings into what one is tempted to call stereotyped "gists," without the beneficial compulsions of his early themes. For example, *The Mansion* summarizes the plot of *The Sound and the Fury* as follows:

The tale was that they [the Compsons] had sold a good part of [their land] off back in 1909 for the municipal golf course in order to send the oldest son, Quentin, to Harvard, where he committed suicide at the end of his freshman year.[10]

This perhaps intentionally humorous reduction does capture the "gist," but has little in common with the novel written in 1929 except the name of the main protagonist. Elsewhere in the same novel, Ratliff gives the following definition of Greenwich Village: "A little place without physical boundaries located . . . in New York City, where young people of all ages below ninety go in search of dreams" (151). Again, the intended humorous exaggeration is clear, but becomes less clear in the absence of any countervailing or complicating judgments. Greenwich Village, like so much else here, reduces to a stereotype, "Grinnich Village" (151).

Surmise, so often criticized in *Light in August* or *Absalom, Absalom!* as malicious, fallacious, or discriminatory, here poses as fact. In both *The Town* and *The Mansion*, the narration is less a discovery – as in *Absalom, Absalom!* or *Go Down, Moses* – than a commentary on what is *already finished*. It assumes the perspective of the formerly suspect and over-generalizing "town" or "consensus" mind – rather artificially in Charles Mallison's case at the opening of *The Town*: "So when I say 'we' and 'we thought' what I mean is Jefferson and what Jefferson thought" (3). There is no realm of "otherness" here; even Ratliff, formerly both an insider and an outsider, both peripatetic and implicated at the center, fully shares here in communal mores. The narrative complicity in such a restrictive optic would be far less striking were it not for instances such as in chapter 7 of *Intruder in the Dust*, where Stevens's sententious speech on the American racial problem (quoted above) issues directly into third-person narration without closing the quote:

"... and as for Lucas Beauchamp, Sambo . . . a basic fear of a failure of national character which they hide from one another behind a loud lipservice to a flag.
   Now they were there and not too long behind the sheriff. (156)

Even if a misprint is to blame here, the example shows the

troubling consonance of Stevens's restrictive and stereotyping tone with the general tendency of Faulkner's late prose.

Earlier in his career, Faulkner had dealt with the problem of social and personal freedom on the level of language, following in an interesting way the various levels of combinational and integrative freedom that Jakobson finds in language:

> Thus, in the combination of linguistic units there is an ascending scale of freedom. In the combination of distinctive features into phonemes, the freedom of the individual speaker is zero: the code has already established all the possibilities which may be utilized in the given language. Freedom to combine phonemes into words is circumscribed; it is limited to the marginal situation of word coinage. In forming sentences with words the speaker is less constrained. And finally, in the combination of sentences into utterances, the action of compulsory syntactical rules ceases, and the freedom of any individual speaker to create novel contexts increases substantially, although again the numerous stereotyped utterances are not to be overlooked.[11]

One can see that Faulkner exploits this "freedom" on the level of words in the novels from *Soldier's Pay* through *Light in August*, with their myriad compound words, neologisms, onomatopoeiae, paronomasiae, and tropological innovations. In subsequent texts, Faulkner moves on to even larger-scale rearrangements – even those whereby his literary narratives can, as in *Absalom, Absalom!* or *Go Down, Moses*, dare to manipulate the constraining narratives of society. Quite possibly, no force can completely eliminate the dividing polarities "black/white," "female/male," and so on, but their attributes may be recombined and thereby altered.

Yet there seems some truth in the contrary linguistic insight that, although recombinative freedom increases as units of combination grow larger, so does the need for large-scale figures of social division. Barthes sums up this notion as developed by Emile Benveniste:

> A sentence can be described, linguistically, on several levels (phonetic, phonological, grammatical, contextual) and these levels are in a hierarchical relationship with one another, for, while all have their own units and correlations (whence the

necessity for a separate description of each of them), no level on its own can produce meaning. A unit belonging to a particular level only takes on meaning if it can be integrated in a higher level; a phoneme, though perfectly describable, means nothing in itself: it participates in meaning only when integrated in a word, and the word itself must in turn be integrated in a sentence.[12]

As re-creative freedom increases, so too does the requirement of structural coherence. It is not an accident that the epic and novel as genres of large-scale combination have always seemed quintessentially by, for, and of *society*, whereas lyric has always been contrasted as a genre of *private* or *semi-private* utterance. Readability puts constraints on the freedom of rhetorical and narratological combination. Whereas *The Sound and the Fury*, like all of Faulkner's best narratives, applied to its macro-discourse (paragraph, scene, chapter, subplot) the same experimentalism that had deformed and reconstructed its micro-discourse (words, phrases, sentences), the later novels of Faulkner are pre-eminently "sane," displacing a prior "vertical" openness onto a "horizontal" determinism that serves the interests of "stereotyped utterances" rather than "novel contexts," "word coinage," or deformation of the given.

In short, after 1945, Faulkner rarely uses a familiar device or style in a new context so that it takes on a new or unexpected meaning (as in the Brechtian *Verfremdungseffekt* or Shklovsky's *ostranenie*).[13] Rather, he repeats a familiar device outside of the context which had lent it meaning, expecting as if by a kind of "sympathetic magic" to recover that meaning. The figure of the deaf Linda Snopes in *The Mansion* is a touching internal image of this problem. Linda Snopes symbolizes (as her mother Eula Varner Snopes had done earlier) a male's desire for an "other" unmarred by the defilements of language and voice. For Gavin Stevens, Linda and Eula Snopes embody abstract words such as "reputation" and "good name," about which he believes that "Merely to say them, speak them aloud, give their existence vocal recognition, would irrevocably soil and besmirch them, would destroy the very things they represented, leaving them not just vulnerable but already doomed" (202). The silence that keeps the silent woman pure is like the black's color that insures his redemptive distance and otherness from the white, as *The Mansion* claims: "no white man understood Negroes and never would so long as the white man compelled the black man to be first a Negro and only then a man, since this, the impenetrable dividing wall, was the black man's only defense and protection for survival" (308).

The quasi-epistolary relationship, full of missed encounters, between Gavin and Linda in *The Town*, in which Stevens communicates with her by sending books of Donne's poetry or writing to her "in pencil, in my hand" (213), becomes one in *The Mansion* where the now deaf Linda lives in a cocoon of silence:

> That was it: silence. If there were no such thing as sound. If it only took place in silence, no evil man has invented could really harm him: explosion, treachery, the human voice. . . . But she [Linda] had beat him . . . herself no mere moment's child but the inviolate bride of silence, inviolable in maidenhead, fixed, forever safe from change and alteration. (203)

The Keatsian echo here, repeated later (230), indicates that Linda is but a new object of a Romantic ideal of beauty and purity. As Gavin says of Eula in *The Town*: "That's what you thought at first, of course: that she must of necessity repeat herself, duplicate herself if she reproduced at all. Because immediately afterward you realised that obviously she must not, must not duplicate".[14] Linda, like a kitsch offprint, duplicates her mother Eula with a difference. Linda is pure not by virginity, but by a kind of linguistic and auditory "chastity," and yet she speaks "in that dry quacking that deaf people learn to use" (*The Mansion*, 199), saying words that even the text must omit: " 'But you can   me,' she said. That's right. She used the explicit word, speaking the hard brutal guttural in the quacking duck's voice" (238). The omitted word (which rhymes with "duck") is the brutal opposite of the space of autonomy that Addie Bundren found in a similar textual chasm in *As I Lay Dying*. Linda is the final distillation of a linguistic paradox: both "immaculate" and "lost" (216, 219), she both conceals the sound of violation and asks to be violated.

The clash between Linda's ideal silence and her real speech materializes only in the mind of Gavin and those others who alone can hear the difference. They try to penetrate her silent realm with phallic writing, but she can erase it all at will with her "magic-pad":[15]

> She – Linda: a present from Guess Who – had a little pad of thin ivory leaves just about big enough to hold three words at a time, with gold corners, on little gold rings to turn the pages, with a little gold stylus thing to match, that you could write on and then efface it with a handkerchief or a piece of tissue or, in a mere masculine emergency, a little spit on your thumb and then use it again. (216)

As an exemplar of potential openness and linguistic invention, Linda indeed resembles more a "footprint" than a "monument," despite such narrative idealizations as the Keats allusion. In general, *The Mansion* is more satisfactory than any other novel written by Faulkner after 1945 (except, for different reasons, *The Reivers*) precisely because of its willingness to portray such underdefined characters as Linda Snopes (Kohl) and, perhaps even more so, Mink Snopes, whose plot literally encircles the novel in a suspended waiting – the prolongation and deferment of his ultimate revenge, first on Houston and then on Flem: "That was it. Prolongation. Not only the anguish of hope deferred, not even the outrage of simple justice deferred" (12).

Yet it may itself be a kind of false contextualization to expect Faulkner's early experiments in language to continue later in his life, especially given his external circumstances. Increasingly, from the publication of *The Portable Faulkner* in 1946 until his death in 1962, Faulkner time and time again was called upon to make conclusive, definitive, unambiguous comments on his writing and to propose solutions to the American racial dilemma. These ranged from the reasonable (the letter of 1950 to the Memphis *Commercial Appeal* criticizing the light sentence given to three white Mississippians convicted of murdering three black children) to the grotesque (for instance, "A Word to Virginians" in 1958, which argued that "[the Negro] is competent for equality only in ratio of his white blood"). Faulkner found his fictional insights often impossible to translate into a practical agenda for social change. Racial division might be irrational and often criminal, but solutions, utopian or otherwise, were hard to surmise. Racial

mixing, either in legal or in physical terms, never seemed as
inevitable to Faulkner the Mississippian as it often seemed to
Faulkner the novelist. His early literary discovery of emptiness,
arbitrariness, and abnormality in divisions that others liked to
call "the normal and natural (natural? God Himself had
ordained and decreed them) barriers between the white
man and the black one" (*The Mansion*, 312) made excellent
fiction, but poor exposition; his later expository decrees made
terrible fiction and also frequently poor exposition. The realm
of the "unknown," the "shadowy," the "absent," which had
complicated the standard relationships of life in Faulkner's
earlier works, gives way, if only for convenience, to the
category of the fixed, the rational, the defined in the late
works.

Faulkner in his later years had to strike a difficult balance
between experimentation and declamation. In the end, he
packaged a self-referential principle of rhetorical complexity to
signify value rather than using that complexity to unmask
society's betrayal of its self-professed values. The Faulknerian
stylistic recipe seems, in *The Mansion*'s definition of life, "not
so much motion as an inventless repetition of motion" (197).
The "reproduction" parallels the very kitsch-like stereotyping
process whose malignant effects we have seen. Yet Faulkner
seems, to his credit, to have been aware that this sequence of
expansion and constriction was the very essence and paradox
of writing. Of the major stages of Faulkner's writing one might
paraphrase Gavin's comment about Eula Varner Snopes.
Faulkner's themes and allegories had to of necessity duplicate –
it is in the nature of tales to be repeated – but immediately it
becomes clear that they should not have duplicated. Faulkner's
late progeny, his necessary yet failed self-repetition, is akin to
Linda Snopes Kohl – pure yet impure, native yet foreign,
wrapped in silence yet grotesquely verbal, a flawed yet
magnificent urn that is both the take and the return of an
entire literary career.

Notes

1 William Faulkner, Letters to Brig.-Gen. C. T. Lanham, June 28,
  1947, *Selected Letters*, ed. Joseph Blotner (New York: Random

House, 1977), p. 251. Wolfe and Dos Passos, he continues, took more chances and failed more often than Hemingway, but were better writers. Faulkner considered *The Sound and the Fury* his favorite novel, "to me the finest failure," and surely includes himself among those chance-taking writers who were better than Hemingway.

2 William Faulkner, *Flags in the Dust* (New York: Vintage, 1973), p. 5.

3 David Williams, *Faulkner's Women* (Montreal: McGill/Queen's University Press, 1977), p. 219. Howe calls Stevens "the greatest windbag in American literature" and asserts that he is Faulkner's "mouthpiece" (Irving Howe, *William Faulkner* (1951), 3rd edn (Chicago: University of Chicago Press, 1975), pp. 286, 243), an assessment that Brooks rejects (Cleanth Brooks, *William Faulkner: The Yoknapatawpha Country* (New Haven: Yale University Press, 1963), p. 194). Yet, on some level, we are meant to take his lengthy assertions seriously, and, indeed, "Faulkner's special power and his occasional special weakness spring in part from his ability – sometimes his compulsion – wholly to adopt the point of view, even the errors and confusions, of his characters": Hyatt H. Waggoner, *William Faulkner* (Kentucky: University of Kentucky Press, 1959), p. 189.

4 Sigmund Freud, *Jokes and their Relation to the Unconscious*, *The Standard Edition*, ed. James Strachey (London: Hogarth Press, 1953–74), vol. 8, pp. 189, 196; *Studienausgabe*, vol. IV, pp. 176, 182.

5 William Faulkner, *A Fable* (New York: Vintage, 1978), pp. 145, 202.

6 William Faulkner, *Intruder in the Dust* (New York: Vintage, 1972), pp. 154, 155. All subsequent quotations from this edition will be cited by page numbers in parentheses.

7 "Einige Bemerkungen zum Problem des Kitsches: Ein Vortrag" (1950), in Hermann Broch, *Schriften zur Literatur*, vol. 2: *Theorie* (Frankfurt a.M.: Suhrkamp, 1975), p. 168 (my translation).

8 Martin Thom, "The Unconscious Structured Like a Language," *Economics and Society*, 5, 4 (1976), p. 453.

9 Broch, op. cit., p. 170.

10 William Faulkner, *The Mansion* (New York: Vintage, 1965), p. 322. All subsequent quotations from this edition will be cited by page numbers in parentheses.

11 Roman Jakobson, "Two Aspects of Language and Two Types of Aphasic Disturbances," in *Selected Writings*, vol. II: Word and Language (The Hague: Mouton, 1971), pp. 242–3.

12 Roland Barthes, "Introduction to the Structural Analysis of

Narratives," in *Image/Music/Text*, trans. Stephen Heath (London: Fontana, 1977), pp. 85–6.

13 Terence Hawkes, *Structuralism and Semiotics* (London: Methuen, 1977), p. 62.

14 William Faulkner, *The Town* (New York: Vintage, 1961), p. 133. All subsequent quotations from this edition will be cited by page numbers in parentheses.

15 Freud uses a similar mechanism as an analogy for repression: the imprint of the event is slippery and can be "effaced," but leaves a recoverable trace none the less. See "A Note on the Mystic Writing Pad" (1925), *Standard Edition*, vol. 19, p. 225; *Studienausgabe*, vol. III, p. 363.

INDEX